Can Deliberation Cure the Ills of Democracy?

Can Deliberation Cure the Ills of Democracy?

James S. Fishkin

OXFORD
UNIVERSITY PRESS

Great Clarendon Street, Oxford, OX2 6DP,
United Kingdom

Oxford University Press is a department of the University of Oxford.
It furthers the University's objective of excellence in research, scholarship,
and education by publishing worldwide. Oxford is a registered trade mark of
Oxford University Press in the UK and in certain other countries

© James S. Fishkin 2025

The moral rights of the author have been asserted.

All rights reserved. No part of this publication may be reproduced, stored in a retrieval system, transmitted, used for text and data mining, or used for training artificial intelligence, in any form or by any means, without the prior permission in writing of Oxford University Press, or as expressly permitted by law, by licence or under terms agreed with the appropriate reprographics rights organization. Enquiries concerning reproduction outside the scope of the above should be sent to the Rights Department, Oxford University Press, at the address above.

You must not circulate this work in any other form
and you must impose this same condition on any acquirer.

Published in the United States of America by Oxford University Press
198 Madison Avenue, New York, NY 10016, United States of America

British Library Cataloguing in Publication Data
Data available

Library of Congress Control Number: 2024946952

ISBN 9780198944416

DOI: 10.1093/9780198944447.001.0001

Printed and bound by
CPI Group (UK) Ltd, Croydon, CR0 4YY

Links to third party websites are provided by Oxford in good faith and
for information only. Oxford disclaims any responsibility for the materials
contained in any third party website referenced in this work.

The manufacturer's authorised representative in the EU for product safety is
Oxford University Press España S.A. of El Parque Empresarial San Fernando de Henares, Avenida
de Castilla, 2 – 28830 Madrid (www.oup.es/en or
product.safety@oup.com). OUP España S.A. also acts as importer into Spain
of products made by the manufacturer.

For Shelley—nearing yet

Acknowledgments

This book is my synthesis of a long journey of discovery. I have been thinking about deliberative democracy and methods for implementing it ever since I was a fellow at the Center for Advanced Study in the Behavioral Sciences at Stanford in 1987–1988. I am particularly grateful to Bob and Nan Keohane, the first people I discussed the idea with, who were fellows at the Center that year. Instead of dismissing what I called "my crazy idea," they encouraged it.

My time at Yale, particularly the influence of Robert Dahl, Ed Lindblom, and Doug Rae, had a big impact on my thinking about democracy. My time at Cambridge, particularly my dialogues with Bernard Williams and Peter Laslett, was equally influential. My forays into empirical work were greatly aided by collaborations with Robert C. Luskin and Norman Bradburn. My work on the series of national US Deliberative Polls, which we entitled *America in One Room*, has been greatly enriched by Alice Siu, Larry Diamond, Norman Bradburn, Joshua Lerner, and Valentin Bolotnyy. My long-standing dialogue with Larry Diamond in our joint course "The Spirit of Democracy" has been an immense learning experience for me in considering challenges facing democracy around the world. The collaboration with Henry Elkus, Sam Feinburg, and more recently Jeff Brooks and Erika Yorio, at the Helena Group Foundation has made the America in One Room series possible and much more impactful. The collaboration with NORC at the University of Chicago, particularly Mike Dennis and Jennifer Carter, has been instrumental to our success.

Jenny Mansbridge has been a source of advice—indeed wisdom—since the start of this research program. An example of the range of our discussions can be found in the *Daedalus* volume we edited together on the prospects and limits of deliberative democracy.

The growth and global reach of the Stanford Deliberative Democracy Lab is really attributable to the energy and judgment of Alice Siu. To take just one example, our new collaboration with Close Up and Generation Lab for *America in One Room: The Youth Vote* is just coming to fruition as this book goes to press. It signals an important direction for our attempts to spread deliberation amongst the next generation.

I am also indebted to Dan Werner, former President of MacNeil/Lehrer Productions who helped us from the start to envision and realize broadcast possibilities for the Deliberative Poll. I am similarly indebted to Roger Jowell from what was then the SCPR (now the National Centre for Social Research) in London and David Lloyd of Channel 4 in the UK who helped launch Deliberative Polling on a national basis.

My work with Gombojavyn Zandanshatar, Speaker of the Parliament in Mongolia, has institutionalized Deliberative Polling for constitutional change in that country. He is a visionary leader and I was fortunate to be able to work with him.

I received invaluable comments on this manuscript from Gaurav Sood, Samuel Chang, Joseph Fishkin, and Robert and Shelley Fishkin.

My decades-long dialogue with Bruce Ackerman has helped me reconceptualize the implications of deliberation for political and constitutional theory. I think his influence is well reflected in the direction my work has taken, especially in the last decade.

I have learned so much from those I disagree with, and from those who advocate different models or applications of deliberation, or none at all. Mentioning them all would take another book, but I want to especially note Larry Lessig, Cristina Lafont, Helene Landemore, Jane Suiter, John Gastil, David Farrell, Mark Warren, Baogang He, and Lynn Sanders. Kimmo Grönlund has opened up new areas of collaboration in our joint experimental work for applications in Finland with the Finnish Parliament. He has become an important advisor to all our work.

Ashish Goel and Lodewijk Gelauff from Stanford's Crowdsourced Democracy Team have provided invaluable collaboration and insight into new technologies to assist deliberation. The Stanford Online Deliberation Platform has the potential to scale dialogue and create a more deliberative society.

I want to thank them all—collaborators, advisors, and critics. Deliberation requires a certain kind of dialogue, and that dialogue, about the merits and limitations of deliberation itself, has guided my work over nearly four decades.

James Fishkin
Stanford, CA, August 2024

Contents

List of Figures — xi
List of Tables — xii

1. **Overview** — 1
   - Autocratic Challenges — 2
   - Toward a More Advanced Democratic Country — 3
   - Madison's Vision — 5
   - Deliberation and Democracy — 6
   - Phantom Opinions — 8
   - The Allure of Technocracy — 10
   - Citizen Deliberation — 11
   - Supplementing or Replacing? — 13
   - What is Scalable? — 14

2. **When the People Rule: Criteria for Popular Control** — 16
   - Popular Control of What and by Whom? — 16
   - Inclusion — 17
   - Popular Control and Equality — 19
   - Meaningful Choices — 21
   - When the People are Thinking — 23
   - "Democracy Inverted?" — 25
   - To What Effect? — 25
   - The Challenge for Competitive Democracy — 26
   - "The Spirit of Party" — 29
   - Four Forms of Democratic Practice — 31
   - Apathy in Competitive Models — 32
   - Participation as a Value — 33
   - "Tyranny of the Majority" (and Minority) — 37
   - Revising the Scheme — 42

3. **Deliberative Democracy: A Dialogue between Theory and Practice** — 46
   - Athenian Democracy: An Early Deliberative System — 46
   - The Deliberations of a Random Sample: "Usurpation" or the "Will of the People"? — 49
   - Deliberation versus Populism — 60
   - Institutionalizing Deliberation: The Case of Mongolia — 64
   - Deliberative Distortions? — 67
   - No "Shortcuts"? — 74
   - Facilitating Deliberative Cues — 77

4. Toward a Deliberative–Competitive System — 79
- Moderating "the Spirit of Party" — 79
- Depolarizing Extreme Partisan Divisions: Results from "America in One Room" — 81
- "Accuracy-Based" Motivated Reasoning — 87
- Creating More Deliberative Voters — 90
- Using Technology: Adding the AI-Assisted Moderator — 93
- Strengthening the Norms of Electoral Democracy — 97
- Persistence Following Deliberation — 101
- Design Criteria for Deliberative Microcosms — 104
- A Contrasting Model — 107
- Is it Scalable? — 110

5. Institutions for a More Deliberative Society — 112
- Proliferate Deliberative Minipublics — 114
- Institutionalize Deliberative Minipublics — 121
- Does Deliberation Serve Social Justice? — 127
- Deliberation and Future Generations — 130
- If Deliberation with Random Samples Works So Well, Why Not Just Eliminate Elections? — 131

Appendices — *136*

Endnotes — *142*
References — *164*
Index — *173*

List of Figures

4.1	How Republicans softened their views on immigration	82
4.2	The limits of liberalism?	84
4.3	Delegates versus control group	92
4.4	Depolarizing changes with deliberation on climate change	95
4.5	Depolarizing changes with deliberation on the conduct of our elections	99
A.1	Republican candidates showed increased support among Democrats	141
A.2	Democratic candidates showed increased support among Republicans	141

List of Tables

2.1	Three kinds of competitive democracy	27
2.2	Four forms of democratic practice	31
A.1	Deliberative Polls analyzed for deliberative distortions	136
A.2	Domination	137
A.3	Polarization	139

1
Overview

The question I pose in the title of this book may seem fanciful. The problems confronting democracy are so profound, our disagreements so intense, that it might at first seem naïve to think there is a talking cure.[1] After all, deliberation is ultimately a certain kind of talk.[2] How could it even begin to solve our problems? Nevertheless, my answer to the question will be a qualified "yes." Provided we could muster enough political will, there is promising evidence that the talking cure would work. But it would need to be applied systematically and in some novel ways.

I urge those who are skeptical to join me in engaging their political imaginations. Political theory is ultimately about imagined communities,[3] but such visions are more convincing when they are supported by empirical evidence. This book brings empirical findings to bear on how our modern democracies can be redesigned to seriously incorporate deliberations that represent the people and ultimately create a more deliberative society. The results are not armchair theorizing but based on a research program that has already spread across the world.

We begin by re-examining some central and recurring questions of democratic theory through the lens of deliberative democracy—in both theory and practice. In my view deliberation provides a new angle on classic questions: What do we mean by the "will of the people"? How can we avoid "tyranny of the majority" (or of the minority)? What is the appropriate mix of direct democracy, elected representative institutions, and possible new institutions built around random sampling (or "sortition")? How can our democratic practices best be organized to facilitate thoughtful popular control? What kinds of reforms should we be aiming to realize in the short term? In the long term?

This book distills my reflections on some classic examples that have long preoccupied me: the Athenian case (and the debate about it); Madison and the debate over the American founding; modern writings such as those by Joseph Schumpeter and Robert Dahl (and their different visions of what democracy is, or could be). Most importantly, it draws on contemporary empirical work on deliberative democracy that I have engaged in with various

Can Deliberation Cure the Ills of Democracy?. James S. Fishkin, Oxford University Press. © James S. Fishkin (2025).
DOI: 10.1093/9780198944447.003.0001

collaborators (and that many others have engaged in as well) over several decades. It is not a history of political thought nor is it a new empirical analysis. Rather, I draw on a range of work, much of it already published or publicly reported, whenever it is appropriate for the argument. This book is my attempt at an analytical synthesis.

Democracy is under siege, both in the great global conflict of ideas and in the lived experience of people around the world. We have been grappling with a "democratic recession," a pull-back in the number of countries that fulfill accepted standards for party competition-based democracy.[4] And there is the disquieting rise of "competitive authoritarianism": regimes that keep many of the formal trappings of democracy but actually practice grossly uncompetitive or rigged elections. Meanwhile, many countries confront populism, with parties that stir up popular anger and raise questions about whether, if they gain power, they will ever give it up.[5] Hence the basic point of party-based democracy—that "the competitive struggle for the people's vote"[6] should determine who is in power—is at risk. It is at risk if parties that do not like the results scheme to stay in office if they lose. We need a democracy not just for winners, but also for losers, so that those who lose will stay in the game with hopes of winning sometime in the future.

Even when the ideal of vigorous party competition is realized, it may produce only deadlock and intensified divisions, fueling perceptions that polarized parties are not solving the people's problems but just looking to win the next election. The more evenly tuned the balance of power, the more intense the competition and the fewer the incentives for productive cooperation.[7] In this situation the impartial guardrails that help protect the terms of competition are at risk.[8] Parties may try to do almost anything to win if they think that losing puts the whole system at risk.

Autocratic Challenges

There is also the threat of non-democratic models. Representative government has long faced the challenge of whether some benign form of autocracy might produce better results for the people. After all, an enlightened autocrat might have the policy levers to do what is needed without all the complexity of checks and balances and competing arenas of decision. By comparison to such an energetic autocrat, democracy might seem to yield mostly deadlock, division and, indecision.

J. S. Mill argued that even if such a "good despot"[9] could be installed and relied upon, the fundamental question to ask is: what kinds of citizens would inhabit such a system? They would have a shrunken sense of public responsibility because they were asked to do so little for the public good.

If the practical challenges to setting up the rule of such a benign autocrat were to disappear, Mill asks: "What should we then have? One man of superhuman mental activity managing the entire affairs of a mentally passive people. Their passivity is implied by the very idea of absolute power."[10] Without a meaningful role in popular control, "the nation as a whole, and every individual composing it, are without any potential voice in their own destiny. They exercise no will in respect to their collective interests."[11]

However, in the modern large-scale nation-state, how meaningful a role do individual citizens actually have now, at least on a regular basis? Most are involved very little in public affairs and their minuscule (individual) effect on policy leads to the common calculation that it would be "rational" for them to be uninvolved and uninformed ("rational ignorance" in Anthony Downs' famous phrase).[12] If I have only one vote in millions, why should I pay a lot of attention to complex public issues? In the modern era, we seem to have mostly "audience democracy" where we are all largely spectators.[13] Hence for most of us, most of the time, we are not much more involved in democratic processes than we would be in the policy-making of a benign autocracy or despotism (if such a thing were actually possible).

Of course, there would be great challenges in ensuring that any "good despot" stays benign. But in principle, if a group of "mandarins" or policy elites (think of the so-called China model)[14] or a cadre of professional policy experts (think of Singapore) actually acted to the consistent benefit of the people, what would be the advantage of democracy as compared to such a system? The answer to that question, building on Mill's answer, is part of the central thesis of this book. Ultimately, it depends on renovating our institutions to achieve a more meaningful form of democracy with the active and thoughtful participation of the people. The one we have now has precious elements that must be defended against threats of autocracy, even benign ones, but it is far from realizing our democratic ideals. Trying to sketch what such a system would look like is the eventual task of this book.

Toward a More Advanced Democratic Country

The problem is not that our democratic systems, with their current designs, are malfunctioning. Even when our currently dominant model of party competition-based democracy functions well, we will question whether it is enough to live up to our core democratic aspirations. One of the most influential democratic theorists of recent times, the late Robert Dahl, hesitated even to call party competition-based systems "democracies." He felt compelled to make up a new term for these systems, "polyarchy," so that we would not be fooled by the use of the normatively charged word "democracy" into thinking we had achieved something that really lived up to our ideals. At the end of *Democracy and Its Critics*, he offered what he called "sketches for an advanced democratic country"[15] and it is in that spirit that I put forward the argument of this book. His "sketches" were just that—brief suggestions at the end of an otherwise systematic account of actually existing "polyarchies." I hope to carry that work farther, based on the fruits of a research program, both normative and empirical, on "deliberative democracy."

While party competition is the dominant model by which some form of democracy has been achieved in countries around the world, it is not the only model that has nurtured democratic practices. As I explore the problem of how to make deliberation part of governance in a modern democracy with robust party competition, I will return periodically to two cases—ancient Athens and Madisonian theory—that lacked any organized political parties at all. Later, I will consider the problem of how—even in a democracy with party competition—we might be able to use deliberation to keep the "spirit of party" in check.

Under the dust of many ages past, we can glimpse some arguably democratic practices without organized party competition. Particularly in ancient Athens, where these practices are best documented,[16] key decisions were made by randomly selected groups of 500 or more citizens.[17] While Athenian democracy was also distinctive for the direct democracy of the Assembly open to the participation of all male citizens, that direct democracy was decisively influenced by the institutions of random selection. The Council of 500 was randomly selected and set the agenda for what could be discussed in the Assembly. If someone raised an "illegal" or clearly unwise proposal in the Assembly, he could be prosecuted in a special court, the *graphe paranomon*, whose jury was once again constituted by a random sample of 500 or more. Lastly, in the fourth century BC the Athenians added another randomly selected institution, called the *nomothetai*, which made the final decision on whether a "proposal" passed by the Assembly could become law.[18] After the vote in the Assembly, the cases for and against the proposal were prepared and a new random sample would hear the arguments on either side and vote on whether or not it would become law. The deliberations in these randomly selected bodies were clearly designed to foster a reasoned decision, weighing competing arguments and perhaps taming the passions that the orators could stir up in the Assembly. As with the *graphe paranomon*, this new jury-like institution of 500 was designed to engage the citizens thoughtfully on whether a proposed law was a good idea.[19] In this case, it was empowered to make the final decision.

One might argue that this ancient history holds little in the way of lessons for the modern large-scale nation-state. After all, the entire population of Athens ranged between the fifth and fourth centuries BC only from 30,000 to 60,000 adult male citizens.[20] The rest of the population—women, slaves, and "metics" (non-citizen residents such as Aristotle)—had no rights to participate in the democracy. Yet it was a successful decision-making system[21] and there may be elements of its practices that are scalable.

Madison's Vision

When the American Founders considered options for the design of a Republic, or some other system that might not require a monarch, they were unaware of these distinctive details about Athenian practices, particularly about the widespread use of random samples that made key decisions after deliberation (or at least after the presentation of competing arguments). They knew about the direct democracy in the Assembly and they seemed to assume that most of the key offices in Athens were elected.

The distinctive character of the institutions constituted by random sampling was not widely known until the discovery of Aristotle's *Constitution of Athens*, about a century later. While it is not clear what the American Founders would have done with this information, if they had had it before their deliberations in the Constitutional Convention, they had hopes of implementing some of the values served by the Athenian institutions, especially deliberation, but with more familiar designs, mostly building on their extensive experience with self-government in the colonies (and then states) during the colonial period and the Articles of Confederation.[22]

Madison aspired to achieve a Republic that had a prime place for deliberation by representatives. He did not place deliberation so much with the people themselves but with representatives who would, in the famous phrase of *Federalist* 10, "refine and enlarge the public's views" with the ultimate aim, as Hamilton put it, that the "deliberative sense of the community should govern."[23] The "refining" of the public's views would happen in the deliberations of the Senate, the Constitutional Convention, the ratifying conventions (and the public debate that accompanied them), and even in the Electoral College on a state-by-state basis. All of these institutions were to operate without organized political parties, at least so far as he could envision their operations at the time the new republic was being conceived.

Madison was reluctant to use the term "democracy" for what he and the Federalists were proposing because "democracy" was identified with mob rule, conjuring images of Shays's rebellion or the conviction of Socrates in ancient Athens.[24]

Madison's novel institutional design, with its talk of "refining" the public's views, may have been inspired by David Hume's proposal for "A perfect commonwealth" in which the public elected representatives who elected higher-level representatives who then elected others in turn, with each level successively refining both public opinion and the character of representatives.[25] In Madison's scheme (included in the original US Constitution before the 17th Amendment for the direct election of senators), the people elected the state legislatures and the state legislatures selected the members of the US Senate. Similarly, the people (or the legislatures) selected the Electoral College, and the Electoral College was charged with selecting the most qualified person to be president. All of these decisions were imagined to take place without the involvement of political parties.

Madison gave a primacy to deliberation, but he proposed a different method for achieving it and a different institutional location than could have been found in the Athenian institutions, of which he was, in any case, largely unaware. In both cases—Athenian practice and Madisonian theory—there was, as we will see, no place for organized political parties. Yet both systems aspired to implement arguably democratic values, including deliberation, at least within the confines of the citizenry they regarded as relevant.

Deliberation and Democracy

What does deliberation add to democratic practices? This is a topic to which we will return throughout the book. But the short answer is that democracy, as we have come to collectively understand and embrace it, has to make some connection between the "will of the people" and what is actually done. That is a key desideratum that distinguishes democracies from autocracies, even benign ones (if such can be found).

Whenever an election is won, the victors will claim that the "people have spoken" and they have a mandate from the public.[26] But how plausible is that mandate when the issues are murky, when they are the subject of competing propaganda efforts and perhaps blatant misinformation, when focus group-tested messages are designed to distract and mislead—or outrage—the public in order to mobilize (or demobilize[27]) voters? Are elections a mandate producing a judgment of the people or are they more often a trial of strength between competing tribes, mobilizing their respective loyalties and resources? Of course, the answer is that they are almost inevitably some mixture of the two, but can we reform the system to make it more like the former and less like the latter? Or should we conclude, as some have, that the system of competitive elections is not reformable[28]—that it should just be junked for a new one aspiring to realize democratic values in a different way? Or, alternatively, that we should give up on democratic aspirations altogether and focus on technocratic solutions to public policy?[29] My approach will be none of these. Instead, it will be to supplement representative democracy with deliberative institutions to clarify and amplify the will of the people. This aim, by giving a major but not exclusive role to citizen deliberation, will help us fill out our picture of a more advanced democratic country.

In our current system, how are we to gauge "the will of the people?" When Gallup discussed his pioneering efforts to develop the public opinion poll for political issues, he justified it as especially needed in the *periods in between* elections, presuming that elections would be the ultimate measure of public opinion on a periodic basis.[30] Gallup was responding to Lord Bryce's call for such a measure between elections. James Bryce, a distinguished British visitor and observer of American politics, viewed this "mechanical difficulty" of evaluating opinion between elections as the principal impediment to the US becoming the first country in the world to achieve "government by public opinion."[31] Now we are in a world of near-continuous public polling. If our government's actions were even more poll-directed than they are now, would that give us adequate assurance that we are achieving the "will of the people"?

There is an extensive literature showing that the public is not well-informed about the details of public issues.[32] On some issues they may use heuristics or short cuts to approximate what they would think about an issue, or an election, if they were to spend the time and effort to become better informed. But these heuristics (party labels, endorsements of prominent figures, likeability or attractiveness of politicians) are very rough proxies and may easily mislead or become the subject of manipulation themselves.

Acquiring information is only one aspect of what happens with deliberation. The root of deliberation is "weighing." When people deliberate, they weigh the merits of competing arguments for and against some proposal for action. One key element of the quality of that deliberation is whether there is a plausible factual basis for the arguments considered. But the key point is that people do not just acquire information, they gain access to arguments that weigh in favor or against the proposed action and they come to considered judgments about the merits of those arguments about what should be done.

Does this necessarily require discussion? I would say not necessarily, but instrumentally. In theory one could imagine deliberation happening entirely within the thinking of an isolated person. Robert Goodin has called this "deliberation within."[33] However, we have found that by far the most effective input to deliberation is moderated discussion with diverse others. Perhaps one could do this in isolation, or perhaps future technology will sufficiently dramatize the issues that people will approximate their deliberative views in a simulation of deliberation. But so far, mere exposure to competing arguments and background information seems to have little effect. In controlled experiments we have found that most of the movement in deliberation comes from discussion.[34]

Phantom Opinions

On many issues the public may not actually have a view. Some responses to polls are "non-attitudes" or phantom opinions, responses people offer with near-randomness because they prefer not to admit that they "don't know." This phenomenon was discovered in pioneering work by the late Philip Converse of the University of Michigan.[35] Later, it was perhaps most famously dramatized by George Bishop of the University of Cincinnati with surveys about attitudes toward "the Public Affairs Act of 1975," a law which was fictional so people could not have had real opinions about it.[36] The public answered, nevertheless, and when asked by *The Washington Post*, some twenty years later, whether or not the "Public Affairs Act of 1975" should be repealed, Republicans and Democrats responded in significantly different ways. Half the sample was told that the Republicans in Congress wanted it repealed and half that the Democratic President wanted it repealed. Partisanship provided the cue that allowed people to respond with an apparent opinion, even though the law never existed.[37]

On other issues the public may have a wisp of an opinion, a vague impression, perhaps easily manipulated by messages in TV ads or social media. Given that the two parties have developed "issue ownership" of certain topics, one common method of manipulation is to "prime" the issue that your party "owns." Democrats have traditionally liked to emphasize social security and Republicans have liked to emphasize crime. If a dramatic example gets people to emphasize that dimension in their thinking about the election ("priming" that issue) then that issue can become a key basis for voting.

The classic case was the so-called Willie Horton ads focusing the public's attention on an obscure furlough program in Massachusetts to discredit Governor Dukakis.[38] While that is a well-known case, the playbook is ongoing.[39] Immigration and crime continue to serve that purpose for Republicans and abortion rights and social security tend to serve that purpose for Democrats.

On some questions, the public may have a view, even a strongly held one. But it is open to debate whether those views are based largely on partisan loyalties or whether they reflect judgments about the issues. What would it even mean for the public to make substantive judgments on the issues? That is part of what our explorations into deliberative democracy are about.

Some versions of party competition-based democracy view it as simply a myth or a "folk theory" that the people could competently arrive at their own views on the issues and then assert some collective control over what should be done in order to realize their preferred policies. Joseph Schumpeter dismissed such an aspiration as part of the outdated "classical theory" of democracy, to be replaced by a more modern competitive model that had no role for the public will. Democracy was reduced to the "competitive struggle for the people's vote." Winners take office and then other winners take their place in turn via further elections. Parties can be expected to manipulate the public will to their political advantage just as firms attempt to create desires for their products through advertising. Parties and candidates create a "synthetic" public will as a by-product of the competitive process. To a great extent "the will of the people is the product and not the motive power of the political process. The ways in which issues and the popular will on any issue are being manufactured is exactly analogous to the ways of commercial advertising."[40] On this view, the appearance of popular mandates should not be mistaken for the real thing.

Since Schumpeter's influential picture of democracy, variations of the theory of "liberal democracy," especially Dahl's polyarchy, have provided some further criteria that might address public will formation in a party-competition democracy. Liberal democracy is not just the competitive struggle for the people's vote. It requires, as Dahl argued, at least three other key conditions—freedom of expression, alternative sources of information, and associational autonomy (freedom of association). These conditions also assume a backdrop of rights and the rule of law. Dahl connects these conditions to polyarchies achieving what he calls "enlightened understanding."[41] This is his proxy for the kind of public will formation that should be achieved in a democracy. However, it seems questionable that these conditions of liberal democracy (or "polyarchy") are enough to tame the partisan pressures Schumpeter identified that give us only a "synthetic" public will largely created by parties and interests that would benefit from their acceptance. The rise of social media and the transformation of our system of political communication have probably only increased the problem. So the challenge is to develop further conditions and institutions that will give voice to a more credible public will. That is the role we hope to assign to deliberative institutions.

This argument does not question the centrality of core values of liberal democracy such as freedom of expression and association and the availability of alternative sources of information. Far from it. But the issue is the extent to which these value-laden practices are sufficient to overcome the competitive pressures for distortion and manipulation in our current system of political communication.

To the extent that the pure Schumpeterian theory is correct (or to the extent that liberal democracy does not adequately address the problem either), democracy loses a major advantage in the global competition of ideas. If there is not really a "will of the people" to be realized via our current version of modern democratic processes, then why bother with all the complicated and often messy mechanisms of voting and party competition? They often lead to deadlock, delay, and/or confusion. Why not just leave our policy-making to experts? Singapore is a showcase example of this approach. It is remarkably successful at offering its residents evidence-based policy-making. It is largely governed by technocrats, many of them schooled in cost–benefit analysis and other techniques of expert judgment.

I believe it would be a mistake to dismiss the Singapore model because of the country's small size, just as it would be a mistake to dismiss the relevance of Athens because of its even smaller size (and much greater remoteness in time). Both cases have some characteristics that are scalable. One offered democracy without party competition, while the other offers technocracy without much in the way of democracy.

The Allure of Technocracy

Can technocratic decisions supplant the need for public deliberation? In Singapore the expert judgments are heavily informed by cost–benefit analysis, a seemingly neutral process for weighing the benefits and costs of any policy. However, like all policy decisions, it depends ultimately on value judgments informing a claim about what is to be done. In this case, it is a utilitarian calculation with dollars (or other currency) as placeholders for utility, often with distributional weights (because an incremental dollar to a poor person likely means more than one to a rich person) and with some discount rate for effects in the further future. Utilitarianism is not value neutral but a potential, but contested, first principle.[42] It is a fundamental value, one that is widely shared but also one that has serious competition: Rawlsian distributive justice, rights-based notions, equality . . . the list goes on. Any of these could also be reduced to decision algorithms to be applied by experts. Which of the competing fundamental values should be implemented in policy? Or, one might ask, *whose* fundamental values should be implemented? The technocrats arguably have their own values, and the public may not have thought much about the implications of utilitarianism as an ultimate guide to decision, nor about its conflicts with other fundamental values. But that is what the technocrats, at least those acting in the spirit of Bentham, are offering in place of the public's values and concerns. Jeremy Bentham did not need to be embodied as the "auto-icon" (his mummy, which is a statue of himself still sitting in University College, London). His spirit is more effectively spread by cost–benefit analysis practiced by policy-makers around the world.

Perhaps there is great wisdom in the decisions that experts make *for* the people, sometimes in obvious conflict with what the people would decide for themselves. For example, in Singapore there are extraordinarily high taxes on private automobiles to encourage public transportation.[43] Only the very well-off can afford private automobiles given the tax. The result is indeed much more use of public transportation and probably some beneficial effects on the environment. But this result is a strongly paternalistic judgment in the technical sense that the coercion of the state should be imposed on a population for its benefit and regardless of its own views. Virtually all states do this on some issues (e.g. the imposition of seat belts justified in terms of the benefits to the user). However, in a state unhinged from democratic processes, this imposition can become routine, leading to a very different relation between the state and the people who have to live with its decisions, based on the state's view of their welfare rather than their own. An alternative is to consult the people directly, but thoughtfully, so that they have a voice in determining the laws they must live with.

Citizen Deliberation

We do not expect the public to play the role of philosophers (or economists), but perhaps they can weigh the arguments in favor or against particular policies (especially those they will have to live with) and come to their own informed conclusions. That is a finding confirmed in a great many deliberative democracy projects around the world with random and representative samples of the mass public. It is not just the extraordinarily competent or the most educated who can do this. It seems most people, on most issues, can do so, provided the issues are communicated to them in an environment conducive to deliberation.

In such projects we will see that it is not academics or philosophers who are weighing the merits of competing policies. It is the mass public in microcosm. However, one of the key limitations of these efforts is that normally most people, most of the time, do not have much occasion to deliberate or participate in such efforts. Hence the deliberating microcosm should be considered an alternative form of representation and not a substitute for mass participation. The merit of the deliberating microcosm is that it can be explicitly designed to give voice to the will of the people (via the deliberations of a random and representative sample). In this way it can aspire to perform the role that Madison assigned to elected representatives (originally indirectly elected ones). But it does not, on its own, achieve *mass* deliberation by the people themselves. The number that deliberate *on behalf of the people* is obviously small.

However, there may be occasions when there is, in fact, mass deliberation by the people themselves. What Jane Mansbridge calls "everyday talk"[44] has deliberative qualities.[45] But the effects of deliberation can surely be heightened in an organized design. Depending on the issue and the social context, everyday talk can sometimes begin to approximate mass deliberation. The constitutional theorist Bruce Ackerman has developed a "dualist" theory according to which most people, most of the time, are not deliberating in any depth. After all, most people most of the time are too busy just surviving and supporting their families and maybe their communities. But every once in a while, there are great debates and big issues to be confronted and the public is roused to come to grips with the collective problem of what is to be done. Ackerman offers a compelling picture of occasional periods of mass deliberation, which he calls "constitutional moments." The rest of the time, he argues, we practice "normal politics" where all the deficiencies we have listed, and more, are present. The public is disengaged, inattentive; elections do not seem to matter. But when there is a great national debate, the public and its representatives consider the competing arguments on their merits, and sometimes there is a new shared view that emerges. In the United States, given the near-impossibility of formal constitutional amendments (satisfying the conditions of Article V of the US Constitution), the Constitution changes informally with new shared understandings resulting from the mass deliberations in that period.[46]

The theory encompasses at least four "moments" in US history: the Founding, Reconstruction, the New Deal, and the Civil Rights movement.[47]

In between we live with the shared understandings, including revised understandings, of our Constitution, forged in the previous periods. Whether or not this reconstruction of American constitutional history is accurate in every detail is not our concern here. Rather, our focus is on the vision whereby the mass deliberations of the people could, in theory, enter into a system that accounts for both the usual tendencies toward mass inattention and disengagement and the capacity for mass public deliberation under certain conditions of heightened but thoughtful mobilization.

Supplementing or Replacing?

On Ackerman's picture, such "moments" arise organically in the life of the political system. They are not social science experiments or academic undertakings. Rather, they are political happenings for the system when the people and their representatives come to satisfy certain conditions. But could a system incorporate *organized* deliberation to give voice to the "public will," at least at crucial moments outside of those rare historical occasions? Could such deliberations give focus and attention to critical issues and help improve the public dialogue and decision process when deliberation about grand issues is most needed? Can such arrangements be part of an organized system rather than depending on happenstance or the occurrence of some great crisis? Outside of great crises, could organized deliberation be part of a continuing system of popular control? We will turn to such questions in Chapter 5, when we focus on our own sketches for an advanced democratic country.

But why focus on supplementing, rather than replacing, our current institutions of representative democracy? In the US, institutions that were intended to exemplify deliberation have come to serve other purposes. When was the last time you heard the United States Senate sincerely characterized as the "world's greatest deliberative body"? If an elector to the Electoral College changes his or her vote based on sincere convictions, he or she is subject to prosecution in many states as a "faithless elector." The whole idea that the Electoral College was originally intended as a deliberative institution to select the most qualified candidate to be president, rather than a simplified state-by-state voting mechanism, strikes many observers as a fantasy. Yet it was the original design and arguably worked only as intended in the case of our first president. As George Washington predicted in his famous "Farewell Address," these institutions (and others) have been transformed by partisanship.

Even setting aside partisanship, a topic to which we will return, there is the issue of time and generational change. We can wait generations for a "constitutional moment" and in the meantime we are constrained by decisions of the distant past. No matter how thoughtful and deliberative those decisions might have been, the people who made them lived in an utterly different world and may have had only some partial overlap with us in their key values and concerns. Their deliberations are not ours. Why can't we bring the will of the people to life among the living, rather than, in effect, giving extra votes to the dead?

Setting aside for the moment the possibility that a system of representative government could give rise to mass deliberation even on rare occasions, the voters and representatives in such a system would be relegated for years, perhaps generations, to the "normal politics" of non-deliberative, manipulative campaigning and policy-making. Would significant modifications in our current design provide a more enduring and practical input for deliberation? If so, there would be a continuing basis for a more credible "voice of the people" to be incorporated into our public decision processes.

What is Scalable?

We will return to that question in Chapter 5, but in the meantime, I noted earlier that some key elements of the Athenian system could be scalable. If the goal of random sampling is to create a representative microcosm of the citizenry and then to have it engage in a process whereby its members weigh competing arguments about what should be done, then such a process can be scaled to samples drawn from much larger populations. Some people are surprised that you do not need a larger sample to represent a larger population. We now understand that the statistical precision with which a sample can represent a population depends almost entirely on the size of the sample and not the size of the population. So a larger sample is not needed to represent the population of a modern nation-state as compared to that of a small Athenian city-state. Of course, if we are interested in sub-populations (and their changes of opinion) we may need a larger sample (but not for representing the population as a whole, even if it is very large). So random sampling is scalable, and of course many techniques have been developed in modern times to implement stratified random sampling (stratified to ensure that subgroups are represented and chosen randomly when they are assigned to those strata).

Going back to ancient Athens, there is some controversy as to precisely why the Athenians engaged in random sampling (or "sortition"). Some have argued it was representativeness. The Council of 500 was praised by ancient commentators as "the polis in miniature."[48] Sortition or random selection was also regarded as an expression of equality.[49] But it was also a method of avoiding corruption by providing for rotation among decision-makers.[50] Perhaps this was also one of the motivations. In light of current knowledge, we know that samples of 500 plus were more than adequate to provide representation of the relevant population (adult male citizens). The same process, or a version with modern improvements, could be applied to represent the US, or France, or modern Athens.

So random sampling—sortition—is scalable. However, the Athenians, by having many occasions for political participation, provided multiple opportunities to "rule and be ruled in turn."[51] They combined random sampling with rotation. Setting aside the direct democracy of the Assembly, and the self-selected participation in the ostracism, there were frequent opportunities to be drawn randomly to serve in the courts as well as the other institutions we have sketched (the *graphe paranomon*; *nomothetai*; and, once each year, to the Council of 500). In other words, there was a social infrastructure of rotation in which people could expect to participate frequently. The process added up to a kind of deliberative participatory model in a small society. Could those aspects be scaled up to a large, modern one? At the large sale, if one's name were drawn against all odds for a national sample, it would be a bit like winning a lottery ticket. While people might get excited by the opportunity, it would not really be a continuing component of ordinary life for most people in a large-scale society. So a key question might be: while the civic lottery of random selection is certainly scalable, is the rotation method that gave it social context and meaning also scalable? We will return to this question as we return to the question of whether deliberation (via random samples) should, ideally, supplement or replace our current representative institutions (see Chapter 5).

Our current representative institutions are designed to combine participation (via voting and elections) with the selection of representatives and other government officials who will govern in between elections. Does this mass participation embody a distinctive value? Voting for elected representatives can be interpreted as a form of consent.[52] It also provides opportunities for holding representatives accountable. Even if most of the time the public does not feel a need to hold the elected accountable, the possibility is ever-present (except for those office-holders not running for re-election). Voting gives each citizen a tangible role in the process, making the citizen more than a mere observer or someone who theoretically could be chosen in a lottery or random sample. Even if voting is not central to the lives of most citizens most of the time, it becomes salient when big issues are at stake, or in times of crisis, in which leaders can be held accountable.

2
When the People Rule

Criteria for Popular Control

Popular Control of What and by Whom?

The ultimate aspiration for democratic systems is that the people rule. Through elections, or in whatever other way the public has influence, the "public will" should affect who is in charge and what decisions are made. Even to state this claim raises a host of questions. Which people? Just those who feel intensely or who make their voices heard? Or the electorate as a whole (with equal representation)? On what issues? Just the most salient? Or perhaps broad packages of issues that competing parties can, in effect, run on? What is the "public will" that has influence? How is it formed? Is it primarily the subject of manipulation by politicians and interest groups? If that were the case, then who would really be in charge? Are the expressions of the public will that have influence just episodic events, like a one-off referendum or mobilization, or are we discussing an organized system of popular control?

On packages of issues, some complexities immediately come to mind. As Dahl famously showed, packages of issues can be constructed from items that are each intensely supported by a subgroup but that, overall, are immensely unpopular. Suppose one group supports X as its voting issue, another group supports Y, and another group supports Z. The votes of X, Y, and Z can add up to a large majority for a package or platform even if each part of the package is very unpopular.[1] This is the pattern Dahl identified as "minorities rule," which he thought would prove to be the rule rather than the exception in US politics.[2] However, it is also a kind of majority rule (because the overall package has majority support). For our purposes here, we will say that if an overall package of policies is popular then the public would be asserting popular control via the adoption of that package (what used to be called a "platform," or in some countries a "party manifesto," when party platforms were taken more seriously). This applies even if elements of the package are unpopular when considered in isolation.

Even with this caveat in mind, Schumpeter's modern successors say that popular control via the "will of the people" is an unrealistic fantasy. It is just a "pipe dream hardly worthy of the attention of a serious person."[3] Achen and Bartels, in their systematic defense of the "realist theory" of democracy, call it a "fairy tale." It is part of the "folk theory of democracy."[4] On their view, "voting behavior primarily reflects and reinforces voters' social loyalties," hence "it is a mistake to suppose that elections result in popular control."[5]

Suppose for purposes of argument that the "realist" theory is largely accurate about the way our institutions operate now. Would that mean that we must give up on reforming democracy so that it might better live up to democratic ideals? Achen and Bartels imply at various points that the unavoidable limitation is citizen competence. However, they come to this conclusion without addressing civic education or how voter competence could be improved.[6] Furthermore, they accept the design of our current institutions without any serious considerations of reform. On my view, the problem might be the design of our institutions rather than the competence of our citizens.

Before we get to questions about long-term redesign, the first step is to more clearly specify the relevant democratic ideals we are trying to realize. Begin with the question of popular control, a central concern for distinguishing democracy from autocracy. What does it mean?

We can specify four criteria for popular control.[7] I believe each of them is a part of our shared public culture of democracy as it has come to be developed. None of them are surprising. Yet the challenge for institutional design will be to devise a system that will reliably satisfy all four.

Inclusion

Our first criterion is:

1. Inclusion on an equal basis: All adult citizens should be provided with an equal opportunity to participate equally in the democratic process.

If we are talking about voting in elections as a mechanism of popular control, then all adult citizens should have the same right to vote, the same right to register to vote (if that is a separate step that individuals need to undertake), and the same right to have their votes counted in the same way regardless of the identity of the person casting the vote. If there is a different decision process, such as a process of random sampling for members of a deliberative minipublic charged with making some decision (or recommendations about some decision), then each citizen should, in theory, have an equal chance of being selected. And then, once selected, each citizen should be able to participate on an equal basis.

Why do I distinguish "equal opportunity to participate" and then also specify that the participation is equal? There have been prominent democratic theorists who specify *unequal* participation in the sense that some citizens have, in effect, more than one vote. J. S. Mill notoriously advocated "plural voting," which gave extra voting power to the more educated.[8] In a crude sense, the UK actually followed this approach for decades by giving extra votes to the graduates of Oxford and Cambridge. They could not only vote for Members of Parliament in their constituencies but also vote for members who would represent their respective universities in the House of Commons. This arrangement lasted until soon after the Second World War.

Extra votes for the more educated violates inclusion on an equal basis, as did the many unrepresentative districts with unequal population in the US before the Warren Court decisions requiring redistricting on the basis of "one person one vote" (beginning with *Baker v Carr* (1962)).[9] In the US, this principle of equal populations per representative is still grossly violated by the very design of the US Senate (with two Senators each for California and Wyoming) as well as the Electoral College (over-representing the small states). More broadly the history of voting rights in the US can be viewed as the progressive realization of greater, but still very imperfect, inclusion: the addition of voting rights for those without property, those of different races, women, those who are younger (the 18-year-old vote). Serious impediments to voting rights continue but at least the ideal has been articulated, and partially achieved despite setbacks. Further, the great limitation of our "first past the post" method of conducting elections is that it requires geographical districts whose boundaries can be manipulated (gerrymandered) to partisan advantage. We will return to these issues later.

Voting power indices calculate the probability that the vote of any individual could be decisive based on the size of the electorate and some assumptions about the election system.[10] The probability of being the decisive voter is obviously very low in modern large-scale societies. But, theoretically, it is equal for districts of similar population with a voting system such as first past the post.

The tiny probability is what fuels calculations about "rational ignorance," if one assumes that the reason to try and become informed about a vote is that your vote, individually, might matter to the outcome.[11] But theoretical voting power, based on the size of the electorate, does not necessarily correspond to effective voting power in the social context of other factors such as the partisan balance of power in a district and how the district lines are drawn.

Equal voting power is a minimum criterion. The more ambitious criterion of what might be called *effective voting power* might be facilitated by the adoption of other voting systems. Suppose we call "effective voting power" your actual probability of providing the decisive vote, in the context of the system you are actually participating in. Of course this will also be very low, but the question is whether or not it can be something approaching equality with other citizens.

Consider ranked choice voting, sometimes called "instant runoff voting." It gives everyone multiple choices and if your first (or second or third, etc.) choice is not in the running, your next choice comes into play in an "instant run-off" calculation. Your preference from among the choices that are effectively on offer might well be decisive even if it is for a choice far down your preferred list. My point is that gerrymandering obviously demonstrates the limitation of theoretically equal voting power as a criterion for inclusion on an equal basis. If you are gerrymandered into permanent minority status in an equal population district, your theoretically equal voting power is an illusion because with "first past the post" elections you can be denied any realistic possibility of ever being on the winning side despite the fact that your voting power is theoretically equal to the others in that district. Hence, a more robust and defensible criterion would seem to be *equal effective voting power*, requiring that in social context, my vote has a realistically equal chance (compared to that of other voters) of being the decisive vote. Even if the probability is small, it can be the same (or close to the same) as that of other voters. Ranked choice voting can bring everyone closer to effective equal voting power because it opens up the possibility of your actual choices coming into play in the instant run-offs. By contrast, if you were gerrymandered to be a permanent minority in a single-member district your vote could be effectively eliminated at the outset.

Popular Control and Equality

But why the emphasis on equality? Isn't it possible to have popular control where everyone's voice or vote counts, but in a system where some people's views routinely count much more than others? Such a system is indeed possible. Some believe many democracies are actually in that category. But then we would be looking at decision processes, even in the ideal case, that are inherently oligarchic, not democratic.

Some have argued that instead of inclusion on an equal basis, people should be included on other grounds. The principle of "all affected interests" would have us include all those who are affected by a decision. If taken seriously this becomes complex very quickly and it begins to include massive numbers beyond our borders in our increasingly global political-economic system where our decisions affect people all around the world.[12] Even within the borders of a country it quickly becomes unworkable, as the criterion of "all affected interests" will quickly cross all the boundaries of any geographic divisions (such as between states) and the people affected are also quite varied in how much they are affected.[13] While the principle of allocating voting power or influence according to the interests affected is not only likely unworkable, it also is an affront to equal membership. Inclusion on an equal basis gives everyone the same sense of membership in the polity and the same entitlement to participate. It has become a component of what we mean by democracy.

Another alternative might be to include people on the basis of competence. Dahl argues that people should be presumed to know their own interests best and so everyone should have a rebuttable presumption of being equally included on that basis. However, democratic processes are not just about one's own interests but also about the public interest. And, as Dahl notes, this is an empirical and rebuttable claim. If we start considering degrees of competence, either about one's own interests or about the interests of others (or that of the public overall), we will quickly introduce inequalities into the basis for inclusion.

A core democratic ideal, so often invoked in theory and violated in practice, has been inclusion of all adult citizens on an equal basis. Some version of the commitment to equality is at the center of democratic practice going all the way back to ancient Athens (although they had the stark limitations already noted, on who was considered a citizen worthy of inclusion).

In this chapter I am examining the implications of core assumptions within democratic theory without purporting to justify all of them further. Hence, in what follows I will assume the applicability of "inclusion on an equal basis" as a core component of democratic theory fully granting that people will come to this claim via different routes (some religious or metaphysical; some moral, cultural, or practical) and that some may never accept this fundamental premise of democracy at all. For those who do, the argument that follows should have relevance. If that seems unsatisfactory, I can grant that is a limitation, but it would take an entirely different book to examine the merits of all the arguments for (and against) inclusion on the basis of equality. Here I will limit our subject by examining its implications, along with the implications of some of the other core assumptions about democracy.

Meaningful Choices

Our second criterion is:

2. Choice: the alternatives for public decision need to be both significantly different and realistically available.

If the people are to govern by exercising choice, then the options from which they choose have to be significantly different. To take an extreme case: if they are to choose between A and B, but A and B are virtually identical, then it does not matter much what they choose. The policy implications are the same. Or, if slightly different, the options may be functionally indistinguishable. It would then seem hard to argue that the public is exercising popular control by choosing between functionally identical options.

In 1950, a committee of the American Political Science Association published what became a famous report "Toward a More Responsible Two-Party System." Early in the report it noted that "Alternatives between the parties are defined so badly that it is often difficult to determine what the election has decided even in broadest terms."[14] The committee's focus was on party platforms because it thought platforms of each party should lay out an agenda for policy and then be responsible for implementing that agenda. That was part of the idea of a "more responsible two-party system" and applied as much to the opposition party as to the party in power.

Now, in a time when sometimes parties do not have "platforms" at all, these expectations seem almost quaint. However, the key point of the report remains relevant. It was that "popular government in a nation of more than 150 million people requires political parties which provide the electorate with *a proper range of choice between alternatives of action*."[15] The presumption was that without reasonably different alternatives to choose between, "popular government" would be impossible.

However, in political science, as spatial models of politics became increasingly influential as a way of thinking about party competition,[16] it became entirely unsurprising that parties would converge on the positions of the median voter. It would seem that to win elections, they have strong incentives to take very similar, if not identical, positions. As Harold Hotelling noted in his original formulation of a spatial model, back in 1929:

> The competition for votes between the Republican and Democratic parties does not lead to a clear drawing of issues, an adoption of two strongly contrasted positions between which the voter may choose. Instead, each party strives to make its platform as much like the other's as possible.[17]

Hotelling's analysis focused on an analogy between parties taking positions and stores deciding where to locate. The stores have an incentive to locate as close to each other as possible. If you envision a spatial dimension for location (for simplicity imagine one dimension or one road) then if they both locate in the middle (the population center or where the median customer [or voter] is), one store (or political party) can capture the market coming from the left to the center and the other the market coming from the right to the center. So it seemed predictable, if not inevitable, that with a two-party system, if one accepts the analogy between commercial locations and party locations on a spatial dimension, both parties would aim for the middle (or the median voter). The common view in the 1950s, the period after the APSA report, that the parties seemed to be as similar on most issues as "Tweedledum and Tweedledee" (characters from Lewis Carroll[18]) seemed confirmed by the basic logic of the situation.

A counter-argument might be that if parties converge on the position of the median voter, that creates a kind of *anticipatory* popular control. Perhaps the voters do not have to actually exercise a choice between different alternatives for the parties to take positions that attempt to satisfy majority opinion. But what majority opinion? On many issues, the public does not have much of an opinion nor does it have relevant information or the motivation to think much about the issues. Perhaps as elections get closer they focus more, if they are paying attention and they think there might be something important at stake. The picture Philip Converse painted in his seminal essay "The Nature of Belief Systems in Mass Publics" still seems relevant. Many citizens "do not have meaningful beliefs, even on issues that have formed the basis for intense political controversy among elites for substantial periods of time."[19] The APSA committee seems wise to have required that voters actually exercise choice between competing parties as a condition for what it called "popular government." Anticipatory attempts to satisfy unfocused "top of the head" impressions of sound bites and headlines hardly seem like a good substitute for the actual exercise of choice. And on the APSA committee's view, to exercise choice there needed to be clear, substantive differences that the parties could be responsible for implementing. The idea was that for voters to exercise choice, American parties in a basically two-party system should be more like European parties in a multi-party system. They needed to have clear programmatic agendas, ideally captured in a party platform with a commitment to realize what is promised to voters.

Now, more than seven decades after the APSA call for reform, there are few if any complaints about the lack of difference between the parties. Indeed, we have demonstrable, extreme partisan polarization on a host of policy issues.[20]

These are differences not only between party elites and their positions, but also between party members (including "leaners" on each side of the partisan divide between the two major parties). There are many explanations for how this situation has arisen, but the results are evident. Some likely factors include the rise of talk radio, cable news, and the partisan enclaves of social media. All have contributed to the decomposition of a shared public sphere.[21] The vast quantity of political opinion and one-sided "information" from blogs, podcasts, and "influencers," spread effectively without the benefit of editors or fact checking, arguably pulls us apart as we withdraw into our respective enclaves.

Furthermore, there are changes in our electoral system in the same period that have affected the incentives for elected office-holders. Note the spread of the mass primary to all levels of public office since reforms of the presidential nomination system beginning with the 1972 McGovern Fraser report.[22] The unexpected consequence of the latter is that to be "primaried" has become a potent verb with a direct object enforcing party discipline by the most right-wing or left-wing factions of the two parties. Why the most polarized factions? Because the most polarized are, on most issues, the voters with the most motivation to turn out in primary elections. The nomination process has arguably become a more potent factor in determining the positions of elected office-holders than the incentives for the general election (to try and move to the middle) since so many candidates are not in competitive districts or competitive states in the general election. The result is that voters are now routinely offered a choice, but in uncompetitive elections where their exercise of choice can make little difference. In grossly uncompetitive general elections or highly gerrymandered districts, the parties may take positions that are significantly different, but the alternatives are not "realistically available."

When the People are Thinking

Our third criterion for popular control is:

3. Deliberation: the people need to be effectively motivated to think about the reasons for and against competing alternatives in a context where they can weigh those arguments on their merits and on the basis of good information.

If democracies are to make a connection between the "will of the people" and what is actually done—a proposition we characterized earlier as the basic normative claim traditionally distinguishing democracies from other systems—then the "will of the people" must have a chance to form and to be expressed. If it is suppressed, distorted, manipulated, effectively crushed as it might otherwise take shape, then there can be no effective connection. We are left only with a mechanics of competition that imitates democratic expectations. For example, in Schumpeter's pure competition model a "synthetic will" is said to emerge as a by-product of party efforts to promote their positions, as if the parties were selling soap or automobiles and creating the market for those products, and proceeding by whatever methods of persuasion are effective and legally permissible. But while this form of "democracy" can perhaps compete with autocracy in terms of its consequences, it fails to make the essential connection to the people ruling in any meaningful sense. Without meaningful opportunities for the "will of the people" to form and be expressed, the "competitive struggle for the people's vote" is reduced to a machine without a soul, without the living spirit of democracy that should animate public decisions.

Perhaps the picture is not consistently so bleak. As Ackerman theorized about "constitutional moments," it is quite possible for the public to engage seriously but episodically. Even if widespread public deliberation is very rare, perhaps it does take place every once in a great while. On such occasions, our democratic machinery is brought to life with a genuine national dialogue that clarifies the public voice for future directions of public policy or, more specifically, clarifies changes in our shared understandings about the Constitution. It does seem plausible, as Ackerman describes, that this happened in the US in the debate over the Founding, over Reconstruction, the New Deal, and the civil rights era. Public opinion was eventually transformed and new understandings about our basic direction arose both in court cases and in public opinion.

Some of these "moments" may take decades. Ben Page and Robert Shapiro depict the transformation in public opinion about the desegregation of schools in the US:

The mere 31% that favored black and white children going to the same schools in 1942 grew to 50% in 1956, 66% in 1963, 71% in 1965, 76% in 1970, an overwhelming 88% in 1980 and 93% in 1985.[23]

The genuine engagement of the public can create, at times, an eventual new consensus on key issues. Even with our flawed institutions, widespread public deliberation can occur, stimulating new, shared understandings about the way forward. On some issues it may even happen rapidly. For example, the new consensus on marriage equality combined a transformation in public opinion[24] with one in legal judgments with great rapidity.[25]

"Democracy Inverted?"

But there is another pattern of concern for proponents of popular rule. The people cannot be said to rule when the direction of causality for substantive opinions is primarily from leaders to followers. As Gabriel Lenz argues in a systematic account, "Voters don't choose between politicians based on policy stances, rather voters appear to adopt the policies that their favorite politicians prefer."[26] He concludes that on our current practices, the "idea of democracy has been inverted." He admits that there are cases of policy voting but these also face challenges when policy views are based on "mistaken beliefs" (perhaps planted by politicians or interest groups) or when "the importance voters place on various policy issues could be manipulated by, for example, media priming."[27] All of these possibilities imply that leaders (including interest groups and policy advocates as well as elected officials) are often more in control of their voters than voters are in control of their leaders. This is not a process of collective decision based on the sincere and thoughtful policy views of the public. That is an aspiration rarely realized in our normal political processes.

A counter-argument might be that even when voters get their policy views from leaders or parties, they have taken ownership of those views, even if it is only because their leaders have endorsed them. Those views have become *their* sincere beliefs. When a party wins based on those views, it arguably has a kind of mandate. Perhaps. But can we say that the people have really exercised choice? My position is that it would be a more convincing kind of choice if the people could have considered arguments for and against the various positions and then come to a considered judgment on the merits. In other words, if they had deliberated. When deliberation is part of a collective decision, it is a form of thoughtful empowerment. In that way it provides a key element of popular control. When the behavior is primarily a matter of follow the leader, then it is much less credible as a form of popular control—precisely because the populace is controlled (at least to a considerable degree).

To What Effect?

Our fourth criterion for popular control is:

4. Impact: the people's choices need to have an effect on decisions (such as who governs or what policies get enacted).

The point of exploring these four criteria for popular control is to clarify when it might be plausible to say that the people rule (at least within some domain of issues for some period). If the public grapples with a real choice, if they deliberate about it, and if all (or nearly all) are included in some way in the process, even these three ambitious criteria together will fall short if the public's conclusions have no effect. To be part of governance, a public deliberation, whether spread widely among the mass public or restricted to a randomly selected microcosm making recommendations, needs to have some effect. It can be an effect on who holds office or on what policies or constitutional changes get enacted. But if it is neither then it might be an effect on the public dialogue or a demonstration of deliberative possibilities. But it would not be an illustration of collective self-rule.

Hence, if the real decisions are made by a military junta regardless of elections, or by religious leaders who retain ultimate control over policy despite the apparatus of electoral democracy, then popular control is obviously undermined.[28] On discrete subjects if deliberative minipublics are convened to contribute to official decisions and their conclusions are ignored, then their contributions to popular control are also vitiated. If elections are held in multi-party regimes with proportional representation for who gets elected to parliament, but essentially the same cabinets are returned from election to election (as the parties negotiate coalition governments), then there is little popular control—at least over the question of who governs.[29]

In sum, the aspiration of democratic systems to achieve popular control can be undermined by lack of inclusion, lack of choice, lack of deliberation about the choices presented, or lack of impact for the decisions made.

The Challenge for Competitive Democracy

What seem to be the prospects, within the general framework of party competition-based democracy, for satisfying all four of these criteria?

In the broadest terms consider three basic kinds of competitive democracy as pictured in Table 2.1. Unless otherwise noted, I will use the term "competitive democracy" to refer to party competition-based democracies (rather than rare non-partisan elections, which have come more and more to mimic party competition-based elections[30]). The first, the "pure competition" model, is the widely influential position articulated by Schumpeter and those who have followed him.[31] It is the "competitive struggle for the people's vote," with few if any guardrails required by the model as to how the competition needs to take place to preserve its democratic character. Schumpeter was even agnostic about who should be included in the demos (the collection of citizens who were included in the democratic process)—a point criticized by Dahl.[32] There were no expectations of anything that we would call public

Table 2.1 Three kinds of competitive democracy.

	Party competition	Liberal institutions	Deliberative institutions
1. Pure competition	+	–	–
2. Liberal democracy	+	+	–
3. Competitive–deliberative	+	+	+

Note: + indicates required by the model, – indicates not required by the model.

deliberation on the pure competition model. On the contrary, from this perspective such expectations would have seemed quaint or naïve leftovers from the supposedly outmoded and misguided "classical" theory. In practice, with our experience of the operation of party competition, we could reasonably expect the competitive pressures of partisanship to overwhelm any nascent efforts at public deliberation.[33]

The second version of competitive democracy, "liberal democracy" or "polyarchy," has some distinctive institutions and legal requirements intended to foster public discussion, freedom of the press, freedom of association, and a shared public sphere, and some "guardrails" of democracy intended to protect the integrity of the electoral process and the non-partisan administration of the rule of law. Hence, the difference in the table between the pure competition model (version 1) and liberal democracy/polyarchy (version 2) is the addition of these familiar "liberal institutions" as a requirement of the model.[34]

However, it has become increasingly clear that the additional institutions identified by "liberal democracy" are insufficient to realize anything like mass public deliberation as an input to popular control, at least on a regular basis. Whatever partial realization of a shared public sphere we may have had before talk radio, cable news, and social media newsfeeds, the classic expectations that falsehoods, mistruths, and distorting half-truths would in time correct themselves has broken down. In our contemporary media environment divided into enclaves, people who prize falsehoods may never hear the corrections. If they do, the emotions that have been stirred up (partly incentivized for profit by various organs of the media) can backfire or at least lead to resistance to any correction.[35] It is now so easy for those who feel intensely to stigmatize others online that our politics seem determined less by how we treat each other than by how we tweet each other.

Given the "audience democracy" of modern mass politics in the large-scale nation state,[36] we need mechanisms to stir involvement of the public in deliberation with diverse others if we are going to revitalize public will formation at the mass level. Hence, the insufficiencies of liberal democracy. It does not seem to do the job even if Dahl hypothesized that such institutions would provide the basis for "enlightened understanding" by the mass public (his proxy for the effect of what we are calling deliberation).

So what more is needed? That is our subject in Chapters 3 and 4. Until then we can note that there seem to be two sorts of institutions that need incorporation into the third model at various places. The first is the deliberative microcosm chosen by lot or random sampling. We will set out some criteria for how these should be conducted and then argue that the Deliberative Polling model offers a good example for the satisfaction of those criteria. Of course, as experimentation continues, there will surely be even better models, but this one provides an example with many applications that will serve our argument. The second institutional need is for mechanisms to scale the deliberative process beyond the confines of random samples but under conditions where the experience can be consequential for the participants and the democracy. We will argue that technology can make such a vision more practical if we have the political will to try and employ it.

If we are right that deliberation is a necessary component of more genuine popular control, then there must be a redesign to achieve it over the long term. Hence, there is a third column in this summary diagram indicating that we will need *deliberative* institutions to be married somehow with the institutions of liberal democracy. This is no easy task. Madison wanted deliberative institutions in his initial aspirations for the Senate, the ratifying conventions, and even the Electoral College. But partisanship, or what he called the "mischiefs of faction," quickly undermined that aspiration.

For the moment we are just identifying a placeholder for the idea that there could be a *"competitive–deliberative"* model of democracy, a model that preserves some of the advantages of party competition-based democracy, but that also systematically incorporates deliberation by the public at key junctures. It will be our task to fill this out in more detail and justify it in light of what we know about deliberative processes and their effects. The result will be a design for what is commonly now called a "deliberative system"[37] in a scheme intended to realize our four criteria for popular control on a regular basis. It will not simply be a blueprint from political theory; it will also draw on several decades of research with empirical applications of deliberation to shed light on design features that could achieve these aspirations. For the moment we will simply label the missing elements "deliberative institutions." Their design and their placement in the decision process will be our theme in Chapter 5. Our over-arching question will be whether or not the resulting design more plausibly fulfils the conditions for popular control than do polyarchy or the pure competition model.

"The Spirit of Party"

When George Washington was finishing his second term as President, he used his "Farewell Address" to the American people to "warn ... in the most solemn manner against the baneful effects of the spirit of party generally."[38] He could see the beginnings of a party system forming and he thought it held great dangers for the Republic.

The very idea of organized parties competing and alternating in power—the essence of later competitive models—posed dangers:

> The alternate dominion of one faction over another, sharpened by the spirit of revenge natural to party discussion, which, in different ages and countries, has perpetrated the most horrid enormities, is itself a frightful despotism ... [and worse] sooner or later, the chief of some prevailing faction, more able or more fortunate than his competitors, turns this disposition to the purpose of his own elevation, on the ruins of public liberty."[39]

Factions and parties (like Madison, he treats the terms synonymously), could "become potent engines by which cunning, ambitious and unprincipled men will be enabled to subvert for themselves the reins of government; destroying afterwards the very engines which have lifted them to unjust domination."[40]

His remedy was not to eliminate faction but to keep it vigilantly in check: "a fire not to be quenched, it demands a uniform vigilance to prevent it bursting into a flame, lest, instead of warming, it should consume."[41] Since his time, we have wrestled with how to control the spirit of party, a problem Madison in *Federalist* 10 termed "curing the mischiefs of faction."[42]

The problem we face with competitive democracy is that the spirit of party can overwhelm the democratic decision process, both in the decisions of representatives (and other office-holders) as they compete for advantage in upcoming elections and in the allegiances of the people. In terms of our criteria, if it is not kept in check it can overwhelm the deliberative process necessary for popular control.

Washington was building upon the *Federalist Papers* and, most obviously, Madison's argument in *Federalist* 10.[43] In fact, Madison had drafted the early version of Washington's Address but instead of giving it after one term, Washington stayed on to deal with international challenges and gave the address at the end of his second term. At that point he had Hamilton help him finish the draft while Madison was beginning to form a political party himself (the Democratic–Republican party, which he co-founded with Jefferson).[44]

While it may seem odd to modern readers to imagine a version of competitive democracy without the spirit of party, without the competitive emotions and inclinations induced by factions, this was the experience of the founders in Virginia. In Richard Hofstadter's assessment the founders had "an example of a partyless government of a free and relatively benign character"[45] in their native Virginia. As one contemporary observer noted after the revolution, reflecting on his colonial experience, "he had never seen anything in the [House of] Burgesses that bore the appearance of party spirit."[46] This kind of partyless government was not notably successful at what we have been calling popular control. Representatives were elected not because of their policy positions but primarily because of their social ones.[47] But it did seem to be a system with a form of competitive elections without the dangers of party-based factions.

Hence, it was not fanciful or unrealistic for Madison to imagine a partyless government with elected representatives. But his aspiration was not only to avoid factions, but also to have representatives who would deliberate on the merits of policy on behalf of the people.

Deliberation was a key part of one of his methods for curing the mischiefs of faction.[48] He applied it to representatives who would "refine and enlarge" the public's views by "passing them through the medium of a chosen body of citizens." It was deliberation not by the people themselves but through their representatives giving voice to what the people would think if they deliberated:

> Under such a regulation, it may well happen that the public voice, pronounced by the representatives of the people, will be more consonant to the public good than if pronounced by the people themselves, convened for the purpose.[49]

Madison's vision was deliberation *through* representatives on behalf of the people without any requirement that the people actually agree with the resulting views.[50] We will encounter a parallel issue with modern deliberative minipublics, which are often criticized when the results of deliberation differ from the views that are actually held by the broader public.[51] In Chapter 5, we will examine ways of closing this gap when we discuss renovating competitive democracy with the addition of deliberative institutions.

Madison thought that when representatives "refine and enlarge the public views," the process provides an antidote to the passions and interests "adverse to the rights of others or to the permanent and aggregate interests of the community." In other words, it provides an antidote to faction. The result would be "the cool and deliberate sense of the community" (as Hamilton phrased it in *Federalist* 71). When the spirit of party is kept in check, representatives can think about the merits of issues rather than just about their political (party) advantage. Of course, elected representatives have a great incentive to get re-elected, and as parties develop they engender a kind of team spirit at both the mass and elite levels.

We will examine evidence about the extent to which deliberation, applied at the level of the mass public rather than to political elites, could contribute to a cure. In other words, we will interrogate deliberative democracy with representative samples of the public to see if Madison's solution, proposed for elites, can be applied to the public. If the results are sufficiently promising, it will lend credibility to the idea of a deliberative–competitive model.

Four Forms of Democratic Practice

I have previously used a version of the scheme in Table 2.2 as a kind of checklist of how different democratic practices fulfill different democratic values. I have now revised the options in two fundamental respects that I will discuss in what follows. In an age of extreme partisan polarization, the connections I previously asserted between the four practices and key democratic values need to be reconsidered.

First, note that these practices rarely stand alone as self-sufficient forms of democracy but are usually combined into decision-making systems. A system can have party-based competitive elections, mechanisms for direct democracy (e.g., referendums), and institutions aimed at achieving deliberative democracy (either by elites or by the people themselves).

Table 2.2 Four forms of democratic practice.

	A	B	C	D
	Competitive democracy	Elite deliberation	Participatory democracy	Deliberative democracy
Equal inclusion	+	?	+	+
Participation	?	?	+	?
Deliberation	?	+	?	+
Non-tyranny	?	+	?	+

The question then is how these processes are best connected so as to achieve a workable system, and aspirationally, a system that realizes popular control.

The scenarios we need to consider help realize some of the values at issue with each practice and can then be evaluated in terms of whether the resulting combined system is likely to realize popular control. If popular control is achieved by the design, is it with a system that is also democratic in that it embodies inclusion on an equal basis, provides active avenues for participation (which, as we noted earlier, can be considered a form of consent), and avoids disqualifying applications of tyranny of the majority?

By competitive democracy I will mean party-competition-based processes, as specified either by Schumpeter (the pure competition model) or by Dahl (the polyarchy or liberal democracy model). Some versions (e.g., Schumpeter's) would be agnostic about participation, and some (e.g., liberal democracy as advocated by Dahl) would embrace it. We can try and make the competitive democracy option as defensible as possible by ignoring Schumpeter's neglect of political equality (a point not shared by many of his followers). So we can designate a commitment to political equality or inclusion on an equal basis as part of model A.

Apathy in Competitive Models

However, there is no necessary commitment to mass participation in the party-competition model. Despite much of our public rhetoric exhorting high turnout, many students and advocates of party competition question whether or not more participation would be better.[52] For example, Bernard Berelson et al. in one of the pioneering voting studies concluded that apathy made a valuable contribution to stability. "Extreme interest goes with extreme partisanship and might culminate in extreme fanaticism that could destroy democratic processes if generalized throughout the community. Low affect toward the election—not caring much—underlies the resolution of many political problems."[53] Samuel Huntington similarly argued: "the effective operation of a democratic political system usually requires some measure of apathy and non-involvement on the part of some individuals and groups."[54] He was afraid of too much political participation overloading the system and undermining its legitimacy. The argument went from Berelson in 1954 to Huntington in 1975 to Richard Posner in 2003 who added that apathy should be interpreted as a sign of "contentment"—it was a sign that the system is working well. Posner cited studies of non-voters to show that their non-participation was not alienation.[55]

The defense of apathy (and the attendant worry about too much mass participation) intersects with the longstanding debate about whether it is "rational" for citizens in mass society to vote at all. Given the minuscule likelihood of one's individual vote affecting the outcome of an election, why go to the time and trouble of voting? And if it is not rational to vote, why spend time and attention considering how you should vote?[56]

The rationality of voting can be rehabilitated by adding a term for civic duty.[57] But how is that civic duty conceptualized and is it something that is widely accepted? If the ethical principle that supports voting is act utilitarian, then it would encounter the same objection that an individual vote has minimal effects. That said, there are other ethical formulations if people are thinking of duty.[58]

It seems more likely that most voters are more motivated by team spirit, or a sense of political identity, than they are by ethical arguments. Hence, the worry on the part of some theorists primarily concerned with a stable system that an aroused citizenry might lead to instability. The concern is that high turnouts must be motivated by angry emotions or mass disaffection. Otherwise, why would people vote? Advocates of competitive democracy do not have a consistent position on the issue (hence the question marks in Table 2.2).

Participation as a Value

We already have a criterion for including everyone ("inclusion on an equal basis"). Why do we also need to consider the value of participation by the mass public? After all, that is another way of including everyone, or at least providing the opportunity for everyone to participate. You can be "included on an equal basis," with equal voting power, by being eligible for being drawn in a random sample that deliberates and makes decisions, or alternatively by actually participating in a collective decision process. In either case, you have a theoretically equal chance of being the decisive voter (even if that chance is nearly infinitesimal). The point is that actual political participation offers something more—the experience of your actions being part of the decision. This experience can come in different forms. It could be relatively anonymous and non-discursive, as in the act of casting a ballot in the privacy of a voting booth. Or it could be the sort of participation Tocqueville found so notable on his trip to America—participation in the New England town meeting and the jury.

Tocqueville wrote in *Democracy in America*: "Town meetings are to liberty what primary schools are to science; they bring it within the people's reach, they teach men how to use and how to enjoy it."[59] His observations stimulated John Stuart Mill, both in his reviews of Tocqueville's two volumes and in his *Considerations on Representative Government*, to think about the educational experience of these novel American forms of public participation. In doing so, Mill sketched a theory about the implications of participation for "public spirited" citizens who would more actively pursue the public interest and participate in democratic processes. If his speculations are well-founded, then participation (or perhaps participation only of a certain kind) can produce other valued effects. Later we will consider some evidence that deliberative participation arguably produces the effects Mill was positing. Those effects will be useful in thinking through how a society might become more deliberative while satisfying the criteria for popular control—a question we will turn to in Chapter 5.

Mill described the effects of participation this way:

> Still more salutary is the moral part of the instruction afforded by the participation of the private citizen, if even rarely, in public function. He is called upon, while so engaged, to weigh interests not his own; to be guided, in cases of conflicting claims, by another rule than his private partialities; to apply, at every turn, principles and maxims which have for their reason for existence the general good . . . He is made to feel himself one of the public and whatever is their interest to be his interest.[60]

Juries and town meetings in the US, like service in parish offices in England, are "school[s] of public spirit" which create among ordinary citizens a sensitivity to the public good, comparable to the effects of participation of the ancient Athenians in the court system and the Assembly.[61]

These observations by Mill helped inspire Carole Pateman's argument about the "educative" effects of political participation in modern times in terms of both public spirit and individual efficacy.[62] But Jane Mansbridge, while convinced that there is a great deal of merit in the argument, questioned whether there is any empirical evidence for the effects of participation. She speculated that if there is such an effect, it would need to be established via a very large, controlled experiment in order to capture very small effects.[63]

Mansbridge's influential article, "On the idea that participation makes better citizens" does not explicitly distinguish discursive participation. Yet the key passages she quotes from Mill, like the ones quoted by Pateman, imply discussion. It is through "political discussion and collective political action that one ... learns to feel for and with his fellow citizens and becomes consciously a member of a great community."[64] The town meeting and the jury are discursive institutions in which people exercise responsibility in light of their discussions. So we will explore whether evidence from organized deliberations, forms of deliberative participation such as Deliberative Polls, have the hypothesized effects. Work by John Gastil and his colleagues on jury service provides further support.[65]

Hence, participation can be valued for its own sake but also instrumentally for its effects on citizens who become more knowledgeable, more aware of public issues, and more efficacious, all of which foster further participation.[66] There is the potential for a virtuous circle, where participation of a certain sort may foster further participation. We return to these questions in more detail in Chapters 3 and 4.

However, the effects of "participation" in a town meeting or a jury—both clearly discursive institutions where balanced, interactive discussion plays a main part—may be very different from the effects of participation in a referendum or ballot initiative in mass society. The social context of relatively small group discussion where competing arguments are engaged is replaced in the initiative or referendum mostly by mere exposure to massive advertising campaigns and emotional appeals. The town meeting and the jury are not perfect by any means,[67] but referendum democracy at the large scale usually lacks the social context that would facilitate any considerable degree of deliberation.

I believe this is basically true, even though statewide initiatives often involve considerable efforts to make information available to voters. Voters commonly have access to voter advice applications, voter handbooks, League of Women Voters guides, and newspaper endorsements. In addition, some jurisdictions have the Citizens' Initiative Review, where a citizens' jury considers the pros and cons of a ballot proposition and selects the strongest arguments on either side, or in some cases votes on a recommendation. However, on the scale of a state such as California or Oregon, all of these laudable efforts, while providing assistance via exposure for those who want it, do not amount to mass discussion of the reasons on either side for a ballot proposition. In addition, these praiseworthy efforts to inform must get the voters' attention in an atmosphere of fierce partisan contestation, often with massive resources spent on competing ads designed to distract and mislead. Hence, any claim about the educative effects of participation have to be contextualized. "Participation" in direct democracy via a New England town meeting is not comparable to participation in the direct democracy of a ballot proposition in California.

Note one further aspect of our political culture surrounding referendums. They tend to be regarded as the last word. There is an assumption that if a referendum produces a result, it has a normative claim to being conclusive. For example, the notorious referendum in the UK on "Brexit" was officially "advisory." And it was certainly flawed, especially in the misleading campaign to portray the result as providing more money for the National Health Service by keeping money that was otherwise sent to the EU ("We send the EU £350 million a week—Let's fund our NHS instead").[68]

But, once the slim win for those campaigning to leave the EU was evident, advocates said "the people have spoken." No matter that they may have been deceived. There was a shared perception that the actual participation of millions in casting a ballot was an affirmation of a public decision that trumped all others.

Hence, in thinking about the design of a deliberative system, we need to account for the sequential placement of any vote by the mass public in the process. If a supposedly deliberative process culminated in a non-deliberative referendum, perhaps with dramatically misleading advertising, then the case for popular control would have been subverted.

Let's return to our inventory of democratic practices and the values that they serve. In Table 2.2, the four values in question are:

1. Inclusion on an equal basis[69]
2. Participation (by the mass public at scale)
3. Deliberation
4. Non-tyranny

We have already discussed equal inclusion, participation, and deliberation. However, "non-tyranny," or avoiding tyranny of the majority (or minority), deserves further discussion. It returns us to the vexing problem of faction. We noted that Madison, at the time of the Founding, tended to treat "faction" and "party" as synonymous. While his definition of faction provides a useful start, he did not consistently view it as synonymous with party. Notably, he later founded a political party himself, and did not always hold to their strict equivalence.[70] One interpretation might be that if the "spirit of party" is uncontrolled it can motivate actions "adverse to the rights of others or to the permanent and aggregate interests of the community."[71] So the question for Madison, and indeed for Washington, was how to *moderate* the spirit of party or check its effects when such motivations are at issue. That problem continues to pose a challenge for us in our current era of extreme partisan polarization.

"Tyranny of the Majority" (and Minority)

As we have already seen, avoiding "tyranny" of the majority (or minority) was a central preoccupation in the debate over the American founding. This is not surprising since a government based on any form of popular rule, however muted or indirect, was a novelty when compared to the forms of government in place at the time. When Franklin emerged from the Constitutional Convention, he was reportedly asked what form of government will it be, a monarchy or a republic? He famously replied, "a republic, if you can keep it."[72] The conditions for "keeping it," or improving it, are another way of framing the challenge that we still face.

The problem of defining the "tyranny of the minority" (or majority) is more analytically challenging than just identifying that majority opinion is overruled, or even that majority opinion is routinely over-ruled. In Levitsky and Ziblatt's very valuable book, *Tyranny of the Minority*, the phenomenon in the title is not actually defined.[73] There are examples, many of them focused on rights deprivations, but without a definition there is no analytical distinction between those particular cases and the long-term pattern that Dahl identified in his *Preface* in 1956, the typical American pattern of "minorities rule" (by which he meant opinion minorities who carry the day through intensity).[74] If that is all that we mean by "tyranny of the minority" then it is routinely characteristic of the US system (and probably others) if you accept Dahl's analysis.

However, there is a current challenge to American democracy that is distinctive and disturbing. It is not just captured by the fact that majorities routinely do not triumph. "Tyranny of the minority" (or the majority) has consequences that require more specification.

Levitsky and Ziblatt's solution to the problem, a solution which they attribute to Madison, is more electoral competition between parties. Whether or not that helps as a solution, it is not Madison's solution. At the time of the *Federalist Papers*, Madison did not even envision political parties. Furthermore, he worried greatly about intense competition between factions.[75] Instead, Madison had another solution, one that has seemed irrelevant since the rise of organized political parties. But it is one that offers promise if it could be applied to the mass public.

We have already noted that Madison's vision required deliberation by representatives (as well as multiple arenas of decision).[76] Intense campaigning by parties would only encourage factions. He hoped that in a large republic "it will be more difficult for unworthy candidates to practice with success the vicious arts by which elections are too often carried."[77] However, this defense, if it were ever true, applies no longer. Presumably his contention was that reaching greater numbers over great distances would make misleading and manipulating the public more difficult. Unfortunately, the modern transformation in our forms of political communication has made it much easier to overcome great distances and to efficiently target large numbers. So Madison's speculation about the comparative difficulty of motivating factions in larger populations may not be so applicable to modern conditions. However, his worry about the "vicious arts" of campaigning in elections seems quite relevant.

Let's distinguish the practice of majority rule applied to the electorate and majority rule applied within representative institutions such as the Senate. As Levitsky and Ziblatt note, Madison rejected supermajority rules in the Senate (and would, on such grounds, have disapproved of the filibuster as in *Federalist* 58). But in order to protect against tyranny of the majority supported by the broader population, he envisioned the Senate standing *against* popular majorities that might motivate faction. In discussing "a well-constructed Senate":

> Such an institution may be sometimes necessary as a defense to the people against their own temporary errors and delusions. As the cool and deliberate sense of the community ought, in all governments, and actually will, in all free governments, ultimately prevail over the views of its rulers; so there are particular moments in public affairs when the people, stimulated by some irregular passion, or some illicit advantage, or misled by the artful misrepresentations of interested men, may call for measures which they themselves will afterward be the most ready to lament and condemn. In these critical moments, how salutary will be the interference of some temperate and respectable body of citizens, in order to check the misguided career and to suspend the blow meditated by the people against themselves, until reason, justice, and truth can regain their authority over the public mind?[78]

Such a protection against misguided popular majorities would have saved Athens from the ignominy of killing Socrates:

> What bitter anguish would not the people of Athens have often escaped if their government had contained so provident a safeguard against the tyranny of their own passions. Popular liberty might then have escaped the indelible reproach of decreeing to the same citizens the hemlock on one day and statues on the next.[79]

Hence, Madison, while an opponent of supermajority rules in the Senate, among the members of the Senate who would supposedly be deliberating,[80] was clearly *not* a supporter of popular majorities in the broader electorate routinely carrying the day. To mobilize a popular majority may require precisely the passions and interests that motivate faction. The deliberations of the Senate or other deliberative institutions can "suspend the blow" that tyrannous factions (even of majorities in the broader population) might otherwise commit.

As we noted, the claim that deliberation via the "refining and enlarging" of public views by representatives would avoid tyranny of the majority was a key part of Madison's solution to the "great desideratum" upon which rested the viability of popular government. The premise was that the "cool and deliberate sense of the community," as expressed by the deliberations of its representatives, would not support tyrannous outcomes. Without a focus on Madison's deliberative theory, the solution in *Federalist* 10 seems unresolvable. In Dahl's modern meditation on Madison and democratic theory, he was forced to conclude: "Like a nagging tooth, Madison's problem of majority tyranny has troubled us throughout these essays."[81]

That core problem has posed a recurrent challenge to the normative claim of democracy over centuries. The people killed Socrates, an example that the Founders cited,[82] and that decision has been used by democracy's critics over centuries.[83] That may well have been Socrates's intention.[84] In the modern era, the American Founders had only recently dealt with the threat of the mob in Shays's Rebellion. They worried that democracy, if factions were not controlled, could do bad things. Governance by angry mobs was something to be feared.

Schumpeter used the problem of tyranny of the majority to discredit any normative claim for democracy, other than that of an instrumental one—a method that should be evaluated in terms of its consequences. On his view, it was not a process that should be valued for its own sake. In setting up his discussion of democracy he invited us to an "experiment":

> Let us transport ourselves into a hypothetical country that, in a democratic way, practices the persecution of Christians, the burning of witches, and the slaughtering of Jews. We should certainly not approve of these practices on the ground that they have been decided on according to the rules of democratic procedure... Democracy is a political *method*, that is to say, a certain type of institutional arrangement for arriving at political—legislative and administrative—decisions and incapable of being an end in itself...[85]

On Schumpeter's view, democracy needs to be evaluated in terms of its effects, compared to other methods, without any independent normative claim about its intrinsic value.

If the recurring fear is that the people can support imposing bad outcomes through the democratic method, can we arrive at any further definition of the kinds of consequences we are concerned about? What kinds of bad outcomes? Madison talked of actions "adverse to the rights of others or to the permanent and aggregate interests of the community." Dahl thought it best to abandon these definitions, given disagreements about rights. He saw no determinate definition of "natural rights"[86] and proposed defining tyranny in terms of the balance of intensities of opinion. His idea was that a workable "modern" definition might be supplied by what he called "severe asymmetrical disagreement" where "a large minority has a strong preference for one of two alternatives and the opposing majority has only a slight preference for the other one."[87] He concludes: "if there is any case that might be considered the modern analogue to Madison's implicit concept of tyranny, I suppose it is this one."[88]

> Intensity is almost a modern psychological version of natural rights. For just as Madison believed that government should be constructed so as to prevent majorities from invading the natural rights of minorities, so a modern Madison might argue that government should be designed to inhibit a relatively apathetic majority from cramming its policy down the throats of a relatively intense minority.[89]

The overall calculation is clearly utilitarian as it depends on "some means... for comparing intensities of preference."[90] As much work with cost–benefit analysis had already demonstrated at the time, there are plausible, if contested, means of doing so.[91] The problem is not whether intensities of preference can be measured, at least roughly; it is what the preferences are about, what actions they support, rather than just how strongly people feel about them.

The balance of intensities does not capture the normative objection to majority tyranny. The cases Schumpeter raised, which seem normatively plausible, involve a procedurally fair determination to take away the rights or destroy the essential interests of a persecuted minority. Dahl's "modern" analogue was that "government should be designed to inhibit a relatively apathetic majority from cramming its policy down the throats of relatively intense minority." In the spirit of Schumpeter's example, if relatively apathetic Nazis (if there could be such a phenomenon) wanted to take away the rights of Jews, assuming the numbers and overall balance of intensities favored the majority, that would fit this "modern analogue" to tyranny of the majority. But suppose the Nazis were more enthusiastic (which only seems to make the example more realistic). That does not alter the normative issue. It is the severe deprivations of rights or the destruction of essential interests imposed on the minority that makes it a case of tyranny of the majority. Not just how strongly they feel about it.

Consider cases where severe asymmetrical disagreement would *not* plausibly constitute "tyranny of the majority," even if the majority overwhelmed the minority in terms of its intensity of feeling and its numbers:

> Suppose there is an ongoing policy of Prohibition. Suppose further that there is a minority of extremely zealous supporters of the policy and that, over time, there also develops a largely apathetic majority that favors repeal. Would it be tyrannous for the less intense majority to overrule such a minority? The members of the minority [the advocates of Prohibition] feel intensely about whether others should be permitted to drink (they will, of course continue to abstain) . . . There is no way in which that minority could claim "a severe deprivation of its natural rights." It is its preferences concerning the behavior of others that is at issue.[92]

Dahl returned to these issues years later in *Democracy and Its Critics* with an explicit invocation of rights (apparently abandoning the intensity-based definition) but on a limited basis. At that point, he was only focused on "primary political rights," those that were "intrinsic to the democratic process."[93]

However, there can obviously be cases of "tyranny of the majority" (or minority) where some suffer severe deprivations that are not, at least in the first instance, about their core political rights. A minority may be persecuted for its religion, its ethnic or racial identity, or its sexual preferences. Or suffer a host of deprivations that are not, in the first instance, about primary political rights, but rather about the rudiments of survival (and only then, secondarily, connected to their core political rights). The problem of tyranny of the majority (or minority) seems to demand an account of more substantive rights that are beyond primary political rights. So we need to think about more than intensity of opinion on either side and more than core political rights to get a viable working account of tyranny of the majority (or minority) and hence of non-tyranny.

In my view, the increased acceptance and refinement of the Universal Declaration of Human Rights provides a good beginning for thinking about the kinds of rights whose severe deprivations might plausibly constitute "tyranny of the majority" (or minority). The Declaration is not perfect; for example, it is insensitive to issues of economic inequality.[94] However, it illustrates, for our purposes here, the kinds of rights whose severe deprivations could be plugged into our definition below.

Hence, for a working definition, we can think of tyranny of the majority (or minority) as the *imposition of severe deprivations of human rights when an alternative choice is available that would not impose such severe deprivations on anyone*. Imposition needs to include not just actions, but also the reasonably foreseeable consequences of inactions. For example, if there is a natural disaster affecting a region or identifiable group and the government refrains from rescue efforts, the inaction can be as devastating (and reasonably foreseeable in its consequences) as an action. There are, of course, innumerable possible inactions. But some will pose likely scenarios leading to reasonably foreseeable severe deprivations.[95] So we need to think about the range of reasonably foreseeable consequences of actions (and inactions) that could lead to severe deprivations.

Another issue is that there may be hard choices, because no matter which option is selected, someone will suffer severe deprivations. Such cases require a further, more developed theory. For our purposes here we can focus on what might be distinguished as "simple tyranny of the majority" (or minority) where someone will suffer severe deprivations when there is an alternative policy choice available that would not impose severe deprivations on anyone. The cases I began with—Schumpeter's "persecution of Christians, the burning of witches, and the slaughtering of Jews"—impose severe deprivations on a minority, clearly drastically affecting their rights (as these would be judged by international standards) while an alternative policy (non-persecution) would not impose severe deprivations on anyone. Fanatics might be very upset, emotions might run strong, but that is why we distinguished sheer intensity of feeling from the consequence of someone experiencing a deprivation of their human rights.[96]

Revising the Scheme

If these reflections are acceptable then we have a working definition of "tyranny of the majority" (and minority). We can now turn to its relation to democratic processes. In this book I have revised the scheme of democratic processes that I have long used in past work.[97] The revised version is pictured in Table 2.2. Note two revisions. Option A, competitive democracy, previously had a "+" on the value of non-tyranny and that has become a "?." There is now ample reason to question whether or not competitive democracies will reliably offer protections against tyranny of the majority (or minority) via constitutional protections. Even if such protections are in place, the "spirit of party" can lead to their being dismantled or reinterpreted or to a neutering of the ability of the judicial system to offer such protections. Hence, the protection is very much in question and we may need further measures.

On a more optimistic note, option D, deliberative democracy, previously had a "?" under non-tyranny and now that has become a "+." I believe that deliberative democracy, when properly implemented, offers significant protection against "tyranny of the majority" (or minority). This claim, which some may see as surprising, as well as related claims about the effects of deliberation, will be our focus later.

While the table is just a shorthand for thinking about our repertoire of democratic processes, the changes signal both significant challenges and opportunities.

The challenge is that intense partisanship, the "spirit of party," can overwhelm the constitutional protections for individual rights that have long been envisioned to provide a bulwark against "tyranny of the majority" (or minority). The spirit of party can overwhelm these protections in at least two ways. First through what in the US has come to be called "popular constitutionalism," the method by which partisan movements change the Constitution, not through the formal amendment process (Article V in the US) but through explicit mobilization for electoral success that gets judges appointed to reinterpret the Constitution to achieve new understandings (within the courts) of our constitutional protections (or their elimination).[98]

I say new understandings, even if the changes are cloaked in a selective "originalism," rewriting the history of old understandings. In this way we are currently living with a Second Amendment reinterpreted in *Heller*, to apply not to militias but to the individual right to bear arms, an interpretation that has continually expanded to include access to modern automated weapons almost without limit (weapons that could not have been imagined at the time of the Second Amendment) producing near-daily atrocities in schools, places of worship, or commercial centers.[99] A similar process has led to the overturning of a half-century of jurisprudence on women's rights to reproductive care and abortion, an overturning rationalized in *Dobbs* through what is arguably a selective originalism—the result of very public political mobilization to change the Constitution by changing how it is interpreted by changing who does the interpreting.

When the mischiefs of faction are unleashed on the judiciary via mobilized efforts to change the *interpretation* of the Constitution, it is hard to avoid concluding that judicial protections for individual rights are very much in question in competitive democracies. Hence the change from "+" to "?" in Table 2.2.

A second way for the judicial protections of individual rights to be undermined in competitive democracies is for there to be partisan political interference with the judiciary's ability to protect or enforce rights. The recent conflict in Wisconsin over control of the state supreme court is a visible reminder.[100] The battle in Israel over dismantling powers of the Supreme Court to override Parliament by interpreting the country's "fundamental law" suggests a parallel problem.[101] There is no doubt that Israel has competitive elections, but in this case, the partisan pressures have ignited a battle to disable the judiciary.

Obviously, we need to think further about how to protect rights in highly competitive democracies. Returning to Madison, let's revisit his "cure" for "the mischiefs of faction." It was a supposition or hypothesis about how he thought deliberation would generally work in the representative institutions proposed in the Constitution. For our purposes, his key conclusion was that majorities achieved through deliberation, in institutions such as the Senate, the Constitutional Convention, the ratifying conventions, even the Electoral College, will not impose tyranny of the majority. Such majorities will not be motivated by passions or interests adverse to the rights of others or to the permanent and aggregate interests of the community. Based on this hypothesis, we will change the "?" under non-tyranny to a "+" for option D "deliberative democracy." But this is an empirical claim about how deliberative democracy is likely to work, probably influenced by Madison's own experience in Virginia, which had representative government without organized political parties at all. The question is whether partisanship can be contained (but not eliminated) among voters, not just among representatives, not when there are no parties, but when the spirit of party is somehow moderated or kept in check at the mass level. Later we will draw on some empirical work with citizens engaging in deliberative processes as part of the empirical evidence buttressing Madison's original supposition. In my view, the more we consider the dynamics of deliberation, the more plausible this supposition becomes.

Near the end of his *Preface*, Dahl provides a useful speculation: "So far as there is any general protection in human society against the deprivation by one group of the freedom desired by another, it is probably not to be discovered in constitutional forms. It is to be discovered, if at all, in extra constitutional factors." Here he alludes to "polyarchal norms" that may prevent groups from taking away the rights of others and respecting the outcomes of the democratic process: "The extent of consensus on the polyarchal norms, social training in the norms, consensus on policy alternatives, and political activity, the extent to which these and other conditions are present determines the viability of a polyarchy itself and provides protections for minorities."[102] These tantalizing suggestions, vague but resonating with our current debate about how to protect democracy, are in the spirit of more recent work by Levitzky and Ziblatt who focus on the deterioration of two key norms in protecting competitive democracy: tolerance and forbearance. Both are vulnerable to being overrun by the competitive pressures of the spirit of party. But both, as we will see, are likely reinforceable by widespread deliberation. As we envisage how to move beyond deliberative microcosms to a more deliberative society, the process of fostering relevant social norms that protect against the excesses of partisanship—what has now come to be called "constitutional hardball"[103]—will need to be part of the discussion.

3
Deliberative Democracy

A Dialogue between Theory and Practice

Our argument thus far has covered four criteria for popular control, three kinds of competitive democracy (see Table 2.1), and four forms of democratic practice (see Table 2.2). My aspiration is to examine the possibilities for a deliberative system built within competitive democracy. Can competitive democracy be reformed (especially via the competitive–deliberative model), to employ the four forms of democratic practice so as to satisfy our four criteria for popular control? Can we imagine designs that mobilize our repertoire of democratic practices so as to restore a plausible version of popular rule?

This argument will come to its climax in Chapter 5. But first we need to examine the design and rationale of *deliberative* institutions. They are the ingredient we are adding to some long and familiar debates. What are they? What might they accomplish, both in theory and in practice? What is there to say in response to the many critics who have burgeoned almost as rapidly as the applications of one design or another have proliferated? I cannot cover all of these issues comprehensively, but will do so from the standpoint of the designs I have advocated (as compared to their rivals) and the reasons (and evidence) I can offer for what they accomplish. It is still early days in the revival of interest in what has come to be called deliberative democracy. But after three decades, there are some points that I believe come into clear focus.

Athenian Democracy: An Early Deliberative System

Our modern challenge is to combine democratic processes into a system that satisfies our proposed criteria for popular control. An instructive example, but one obviously limited to a small-scale society, can be found in ancient Athens. Even though it lacked organized political parties, it grappled with the fundamental problem of curbing the passions and interests that might motivate what Madison, so many centuries later, called the mischiefs of faction. Importantly, for our purposes the Athenians employed recognizably deliberative institutions as their method of cure. The cure was not complete. Indeed, they employed one direct democracy institution, the ostracism, that had no deliberative elements and may have committed great injustices. But the law-making process had important elements for the design of a deliberative system producing, one could argue, a workable system of popular control.

Although Athenian democracy did not operate with what we would call political parties,[1] there was a widely perceived risk that demagogues could use their rhetorical skills to goad the assembly into approving rash or unwise measures. As Hansen explains:

> The Athenians knew perfectly well that a skillful demagogue could win the citizens to his proposal irrespective of whether it was really in their best interest: competition among political leaders could lead to their bidding against each other with promises to the people and to the people being seduced by their promises. There was also a risk of the people, in wrath or in panic, being persuaded into hasty decisions.[2]

The Athenians used arguably deliberative institutions, randomly selected microcosms of the citizenry, of 500 or more, drawn from those who were willing to make themselves available, to limit the risks of irresponsible proposals being passed. Before a proposal could be discussed in the Assembly, it had to be approved by the Council of 500, which deliberated on the agenda. The Council was divided into ten groups of 50, each of which took primary responsibility for a tenth of the year.[3]

The risk of irresponsible proposals, fueled by the rhetoric of the orators to the six thousand or so gathered in the Assembly, was curbed to a degree by a second randomly selected microcosm, the *graphe paranomon*, a special court where members of the Assembly who made irresponsible arguments or proposals could be punished. The court's mandate, again with a jury of 500 or more selected by lot, was broad because irresponsible was a vague charge. But it was designed to discipline the orators in what they advocated in the Assembly.

Lastly, when the Athenians had a chance to redesign their democracy after the disaster of the Peloponnesian war, they added a further microcosm of the public selected by lot, the *nomothetai*. After this reform, a proposal that passed the Assembly did not become a law. It had to pass a further special procedure. A kind of court case with the arguments for and against the proposed law was prepared and a new random sample was selected to hear the arguments on either side and to vote it up or down.[4] Only if it passed by majority vote did it become a law. Harrison suggests that they had "deliberately invented a perfectly democratic brake to slow down the machine."[5] It was designed to maintain "the restored order against the possible ill effects of snap votes in the ekklesia" (the Assembly). A democratic "brake," a description also used by Sinclair,[6] suggests that this was not an impediment to democracy but the use of another kind of democracy, which we would now call deliberative democracy, to tame the dangers of rhetoric in the Assembly.[7] Hansen sees a clear motive for the redesign. "The tendency of the reforms is clear: the Athenians wanted to obviate a return to the political crises and military catastrophes of the Peloponnesian War."[8]

Some have argued that apart from the Council, these institutions (the *graphe paranomon* and the *nomothetai*) were not really deliberative because the 500 or more selected were primarily an audience.[9] They heard the arguments but they did not discuss them. Given what we have learned about deliberation since, there is a case to be made that with extensive discussion the institutions might have been more deliberative. But on our definition of deliberation, there is little doubt that the citizens participating in these institutions were weighing the competing arguments, the arguments for and against the law (or for the *graphe paranomon*, the question of whether a proposal in the Assembly was irresponsible).[10] Throughout this book, we are treating discussion as *instrumental* to this weighing process. As Goodin noted, the deliberation, in theory, could be entirely internal (what he called "deliberation within"). However, discussion of a certain kind has turned out to be the most effective means of *stimulating* the deliberative process.

Let us return to our four criteria for popular control:

1. **Inclusion on an equal basis**: all adult citizens should be provided with an equal opportunity to participate equally in the democratic process.
2. **Choice**: the alternatives for public decision need to be both significantly different and realistically available.
3. **Deliberation**: the people need to be effectively motivated to think about the reasons for and against competing alternatives in a context where they can weigh those arguments on the merits and on the basis of good information.
4. **Impact**: the people's choices need to have an effect on decisions (such as who governs or what policies get enacted).

For the law-making process, Athenian democracy by the fourth century arguably satisfied these four criteria for popular control. The Council of 500 was an institution that satisfied inclusion on an equal basis, as every citizen who was willing to serve had an equal chance of being selected.

The Council would put meaningful choices before the Assembly. Participation in the Assembly was open to every citizen on every day that it met. The Assembly's decisions in passing the proposals were necessary but not sufficient for a proposal to become a law. But once the *nomothetai* met to consider the arguments for and against, if the proposed law passed it would become law. Furthermore, every citizen had an equal chance of being selected for the *nomothetai*, the final stage of decision. Hence, the process embodied inclusion, choice, and deliberation, and it had impact.

There was one institution, not for law-making but for dealing with specific individuals, that lacked deliberation and provided opportunities for severe deprivations to be visited upon specific individuals. The Assembly could decide once a year to hold an ostracism where individuals could write the names of the person to be ostracized on a pottery sherd. No reasons needed to be given. It was a process of mobilization against a particular public figure. It was not a deliberative institution. If enough sherds were submitted with a particular name on them, that person was ostracized for ten years. Even the war hero Themistocles, who defeated the Persians in the battle of Salamis and was later credited by Plutarch with saving Greece from the Persians,[11] was not immune to groups mobilizing to banish him. Recent excavations have found 191 sherds with the handwriting of only 15 people from his ostracism. This may have been a sign of organized mobilization[12] or a case of election fraud. The use of deliberation to limit the mischiefs of faction (to use Madison's phrase) was limited to law-making, not to settling scores toward individuals in a kind of direct democracy.

The Deliberations of a Random Sample: "Usurpation" or the "Will of the People"?

What is the ultimate purpose of inserting deliberative designs into our democratic processes? Some say it is to give voice to "collective wisdom" or the "wisdom of the crowd." On this view, the people, in aggregate, can make wiser or more informed decisions than would most individuals by themselves. This "epistemic" line of argument is sometimes characterized as getting us closer to the truth—providing an alternative to expert guardianship or a benign technocracy of experts.[13] In other words, maybe the people, in aggregate, can be the real experts. Setting epistemic or truth claims to one side, others say the point of deliberative institutions is just to get an unbiased judgment from the public or to provide a method of power sharing to deal with conflict.[14] While I believe there is some merit in these perspectives, our focus here is on fostering *public will formation*: a representation of what the people would really think about an issue if they had the best practical conditions for coming to a considered judgment about what should be done. This public will formation is intended as an input both into the public dialogue and into actual decisions.[15]

I am not claiming that all random samples recruited for deliberation deserve to be listened to or considered an expression of the public will. I will argue that it depends crucially on the design, the sampling, the conditions under which the participants deliberate, and the kinds of data collected to provide a basis for understanding their conclusions and for evaluating the process by which they reached them. But with the right design, properly implemented, the deliberations of a random sample can credibly be employed to estimate the will of the people. When I say "the right design," I do not mean to simply privilege the designs I have been working with as the best possible ones. Rather, I believe they are good approximations of what we need and I have no doubt that as research (and technology) advance, there will be even better ones. But these are good enough to give us a clear picture of what can be accomplished and to identify where further progress can be made.

We live in a time of manipulation, disinformation, and distortion of public opinion both for electoral success and for the advocacy of policies. With the breakdown or decomposition of the public sphere into innumerable enclaves, often of the like-minded, we have extreme partisan polarization, which makes democratic decision-making difficult. Our processes of public will formation, and their distortions, are at the heart of a current and mounting crisis of democratic legitimacy. An overarching question for this book is whether, in the long term and with the right scale of application, deliberative democratic methods could provide an antidote to these deep difficulties.

The design requirements for contributing to public will formation may be different or more demanding than for the other purposes mentioned. I will initially focus on deliberative minipublics, but we will eventually move to the aspiration for mass scaling of something like the same design.

Why should the deliberations of a random sample have any recommending force for policy-makers or the rest of the public? After all, the percentage of the population deliberating under the stipulated "good conditions" is tiny—a few hundred or perhaps a thousand in a modern nation-state, which typically has millions of citizens. Why does this kind of process have a claim on the attention of those who are not doing the deliberating? Or on their policy choices?

On most policy issues of any complexity, most members of the public will not have thought much about the topic. They may have a surface impression of soundbites and headlines, or a sense that bits of information (heuristics such as the positions of the parties or the support of or opposition to prominent people or organizations) incline them to follow such a cue as to whom or what to support. But they are unlikely to have deliberated in any depth about the issues themselves unless there is a really widespread public debate. Even if there were such a debate, they are likely, with our disintegrating public sphere, to have heard mostly one side of the argument. If they consult their friends, they are likely to be talking to those who already agree with them (if they have any opinion at all). The same can be said for their likely media sources and social media feeds. Hence, they are unlikely to have heard, or to have taken seriously, competing sides of any contentious or complicated topic. And if they are exposed to the other side, it may well trigger hostility rather than any thoughtful consideration on the merits.

Despite these well-established limitations of public opinion as we usually find it, Cristina Lafont has argued that deliberative minipublics should not have any appreciable "decisional status." Why count the views of such a tiny group and leave out the views of the vast majority of the citizenry? On her view, these minipublics, whether what I call Deliberative Polls or other designs (citizens' juries, citizens' assemblies, consensus conferences) can usefully contribute to the public dialogue. However, when they affect decisions, they are actually disenfranchising those who have not participated and whose views, whatever they are, have not been taken into account. Lafont argues:

> Once the deliberative filter is deployed—which is the whole purpose of getting deliberative minipublics organized in the first place—the views of participants undergo significant, at times drastic, transformations. But precisely for that reason, it would be a clear case of *usurpation* to claim that the voice of minipublic's participants at the post-deliberation stage is the voice of the people.[16]

Consider a few actual cases of minipublics that have had significant decisional status—influence over the outcome of policy decisions. For reasons that will become clear I will limit my examples here to what I call Deliberative Polls.

Example 1: Texas

Beginning in 1996, each of the regulated electric utilities in Texas, in conjunction with the state Public Utilities Commission, sponsored a series of eight Deliberative Polls in the service territories around the state. Texas was growing rapidly and would need more electricity. How was it to be provided? There were tradeoffs to be considered in terms of the environment, cost, and reliability. Coal was inexpensive but had negative effects on the environment and on public health. Wind power was very clean but was intermittent. Natural gas was cleaner than coal but produced emissions and negative effects on the environment. Conservation, which could be incentivized through investments in "demand-side management," was also a way of addressing the need by cutting the demand. Or the electricity could be imported from Mexico. Nuclear power was not regarded as practical at the time because it was encumbered in litigation. Hence the utilities and stakeholders made a judgment about the range of practical policy options that could be implemented to provide more power. The Public Utility Commission decided that before each utility could file its plan for the future (called an "Integrated Resource Plan"), they needed to consult the public about what mix of these options the public would support. The Commission would hold the utilities to the resulting plans, so the public consultations were not window dressing. They were consequential decisions involving hundreds of millions of dollars of investment in the electricity infrastructure of communities all over the state.

The utilities considered various ways of consulting the public. If they did conventional public opinion polls they knew that the public was not knowledgeable about the competing choices. This view was well based. In fact, some of the initial work in public opinion research on phantom opinions (what Philip Converse called "non-attitudes") came from questions in a panel study about the government's role in electric power. A large percentage of the opinions varied essentially randomly from year to year over a four-year study, leading Converse to conclude that there were no real opinions there.[17] Respondents seemed to select an alternative almost at random because they did not wish to admit that they did not know. So conventional polling, even if done well with good samples so as to be representative of the population, would put phantom opinions in charge of very consequential decisions costing large amounts of money and affecting public policy for years to come.

A second alternative was to conduct focus groups or small discussion groups in which the participants could acquire more knowledge about the choices. But focus groups and other small discussion groups are too small to make any credible claims to representativeness.

A third choice was just to hold public meetings on the options. But the companies and the Commission were well aware that such meetings would be dominated by lobbyists and advocates from organized groups. Whatever the merits of what was advocated, the discussions would not be representative of the public.

Given these alternatives, all eight companies decided to conduct Deliberative Polls. In each case an advisory committee representing the relevant stakeholders was formed: environmental groups, consumer groups, experts or advocates for all the various forms of energy, the large customers, and representatives of the communities that might be affected. This advisory group vetted briefing materials for balance and accuracy that explained the competing policy options and tried to identify the tradeoffs applying to each.[18] A systematic questionnaire was developed about the policy options and the perspectives and values that might bear on support or opposition to those options. Stratified random samples were recruited to deliberate for an entire weekend in small groups with trained moderators. Questions agreed on in the small groups were directed to competing experts in plenary sessions gathering all the groups so that all the participants could hear the answers (and the competing perspectives of the experts) and get the same information. The moderators encouraged the groups to work hard on identifying what they regarded as the most important questions they needed answers to in order to make a decision. At the end of the weekend, the participants took the same questionnaire as on first contact. By using confidential questionnaires, their individual conclusions were protected from the social pressure of a group seeking consensus. If there was a consensus, as turned out to be the case, it was apparent from the data. In each project, the local PBS station covered the proceedings and broadcast a documentary about both the process and its results so that the broader community could have an opportunity to see the discussion and understand the process.

A total of 8,429 randomly selected customers responded to the initial telephone surveys, and 1,493 of them (between 175 and 232 in each Deliberative Poll) took part in the deliberations and completed both pre- and post-deliberation surveys.[19] Averaged over the eight projects, the percentage of the deliberators who were willing to actually pay more on their monthly utility bills to support investments in wind and solar power went from 52% to 84%. And the percentage who were willing to pay more on their monthly utility bills to support investments in energy conservation (demand-side management) went from 43% to 73%. Armed with these results, the Texas Public Utility Commission approved plans requiring significant investments in wind power as well as in conservation. The Commission also used these data to lobby the legislature to approve additional renewable energy portfolios for further investments in wind power. The upshot of this change in the direction of public policy is that Texas went from being last among the fifty states in wind power at the time this process started (1996) to becoming first among the fifty states, surpassing California by 2007.[20]

Given this dramatic shift in public policy, it is undoubtedly the case that the microcosms that were gathered for the Deliberative Polls had considerable "decisional power." It was not unilateral, or conclusive by itself, but an acknowledged part of a decision process shared with institutions and office holders, both governmental (the Commission and the legislature) and the companies.

Consider Lafont's line of argument that unless the broader public actually shares the same considered judgments, the results should not have any impact on policy-making. Without deliberation, they are very unlikely to, as she acknowledges. Mere exposure to the process of deliberation and its results, even via television broadcast, is unlikely to have much effect on public opinion. In fact, if the issues are contentious enough, it may even backfire.[21] As many members of the public get upset by higher taxes, they also get upset by higher utility bills. If a process of actual deliberation could somehow be scaled to the entire community, then there would be reason to believe that deliberations with a representative sample would model where the conclusions of the broader public would go. But for many issues, other than the most consequential, it would hardly seem practical, at least within our current political system, to engage a large percentage of the public in a weekend-long deliberative process on such an issue. This leaves policy-makers with choices like those outlined above: conventional polls that might be representative but not deliberative; focus groups or other small-group discussions that might be deliberative but not representative; and open meetings, which are likely to be neither (if they are populated mostly by advocates and lobbyists with predetermined objectives).[22] An alternative is just ignoring the public altogether. But it is the public who must live with the choices, so why not get their input? And if you are to get their input, why not get it in a representative and thoughtful way?

Is the rest of the community disenfranchised by processes that give some "decisional power" to a deliberative minipublic? Unless one advocates a form of direct democracy in which every decision has to be voted on by the entire public, it is hard to see the argument. And if there were, somehow, a system of continuous direct democracy, it would not engage deliberative judgments unless accompanied by a mechanism of deliberation. Instead, it would be akin to government by initiative increased exponentially.

These Texas Deliberative Polls were both representative and deliberative, so the issue of a clean environment that engaged the public even to the point of wanting to pay more for it on their utility bills would presumably have purchase on the rest of the public if they also engaged with the issue and discussed the tradeoffs applying to the different energy choices.

Lafont says it is "usurpation" to consider the post-deliberation conclusions as the will of the people, as opposed to the opinions of the rest of the public that has not deliberated. However, if one believes previous research and the policy context, much of the public did not really have much of an opinion about these issues. They may have had a vague impression of soundbites and headlines. But most people have never really thought about public utility regulation and the tradeoffs posed by the different energy choices. They certainly had an initial presupposition against higher utility bills, but they had not tested that against any consideration of the community benefits for making investments in renewable energy and conservation.

Hence the considered judgments are standing in the place of phantom opinions or top-of-the-head impressions about a complex policy problem. It is hard to call that "usurpation." It is worth adding that the issue of energy sources for the electric utilities was actually the subject of television advertising and misleading advocacy at the time about the merits of "clean coal." On the expert panels, advocates from the coal industry praised the virtues of clean coal and just how improved it was, only to find themselves sitting next to advocates of natural gas (much cleaner but more volatile in price than "clean coal"), wind power (incomparably cleaner and increasingly cost-effective), and conservation (both clean and cost-effective). The panelists and the briefing materials were able to clarify that so-called clean coal was a modest improvement over dirty coal, but still much more polluting than the other energy sources. So the public arena with television advertising would mislead the public, to the extent the public paid any attention. By contrast, the organized deliberative process allowed the microcosm of the public to engage in competing arguments and weigh their merits. Is it usurpation to substitute the microcosm's considered judgment when a representative sample has been able to consider the merits of the issue as compared to the conclusions that organized interests may try to instill based on whatever partial or misleading information has proven effective in focus group-tested advertising and one-sided advocacy?

Lafont also argues against permitting policy influence for the considered judgments of the microcosm because an individual cannot tell how she would change in the deliberative process. She only knows the aggregate change of the sample (or may know something about subgroups). But the deliberative process, contrary to Lafont, does not ask for "blind deference" to the microcosm's collective considered judgments. Rather, it asks for consideration of conclusions, accompanied by reasons whenever possible. In this case the health and environmental concerns—especially about more use of coal as a source of electricity (despite its low price apart from externalities from pollution)—were evident and shared once people focused on them. Now it is true that some people still supported coal, to pursue this example, because it was, at the time, the cheapest energy source in terms of effects on their utility bills. Hence, an individual might have uncertainty whether or not, after deliberation, she would want to pay a little more on utility bills for cleaner energy. That is perfectly reasonable. But the idea is not to bind each individual. The idea is to inform policy-makers about a collective judgment of what should be done. If one believes in democracy, there is a basis for accepting the recommending force of a collective determination of what should be done—particularly when the process of arriving at this collective determination is part of an official governmental process of consultation advising government officials (in this case the Public Utility Commission).

If that is "usurpation," then what would be the argument if the Public Utility Commission had instead simply engaged a committee of experts to make a recommendation? That is a possible alternative on many policy issues, but it would not represent the public. Is that usurpation? Isn't there a stronger *democratic* case for consulting the public in a representative and informed way than for just engaging expert opinion? After all, the public has values that are at issue in such choices. They have to live with the consequences, pay the bills, breathe the air, live with the reliability or unreliability of the resulting energy system. Shouldn't their values and concerns, once they have had a chance to think about the issue, be part of the process? And if so, shouldn't that input be representative and informed rather than self-selected (and hence unrepresentative) and uninformed?

Example 2: Japan

Consider another case, the Deliberative Poll in Japan on pension reform in 2011. The Democratic Party of Japan (DPJ) Government at the time was on the verge of enacting a reform of the pension system that would, in effect, have substituted private accounts for the kind of "pay-as-you-go" social security system typical in many countries. The proposal had high support in polling at the time, but was described to the public in an arguably misleading way as the "funded" system because each person would have a fund or private account. So polls asking for the level of support for a "funded" system may have been measuring attitudes about financial solidity, not the merits of replacing the government-guaranteed social security system with a system of private accounts. Arguably the proposal had a certain merit, in that Japan is aging so that the ratio of working people to retired is decreasing (with fewer and fewer people of working age having to support more and more retirees in a pay-as-you-go system). Nevertheless, the "funded" system would have required that each person shoulder the risk of the success or failure of his or her investments.

In collaboration with the Center for Deliberative Polling at Keio University led by Professor Yasunori Sone, we helped conduct a national Deliberative Poll in Japan. The pre-deliberation opinions of the participants in the national sample, as in other polls, were clearly in favor of the proposed reform—69% approved. However, during the weekend of deliberation, as participants came to understand that, depending on their choices, they would have to shoulder the risk that their investments might not provide an adequate retirement, support plummeted. Once they understood the proposal and weighed the arguments about it, support dropped by half, to 35%. Instead of supporting private accounts, the deliberators supported an increase in the consumption tax to make the current pay-as-you-go system more financially secure. This option increased from 50% to 75% and opposition to an increase in taxes (provided the increase went to the pension system) decreased from 32% to 19%. Given the collaboration of major media (NHK and Asahi Shimbun), the government was well aware of the precipitous decline in support. The proposal was dropped in favor of an increase in the consumption tax. Was it "usurpation" for the government to pay attention to the Deliberative Poll results, which strongly suggested that the support for private accounts (the "funded" system) was fluid and based on little understanding of what was actually being proposed? The main concern of the public—the provision of a stable and secure basis for retirement—clearly resonated with the government as it made its decision.

These circumstances are not unusual. It is not surprising for major policy changes to be marketed, sometimes with opaque or misleading terms and advocacy. Major financial and political interests were involved in the proposed change to private accounts. The policy proposal was also complex and many members of the public would not have been paying attention in any detail. So what measure of the "public will" should the government pay attention to, particularly on a question that will directly affect the lives, or at least the retirement, of every citizen?

Example 3: Mongolia

Consider the case of Mongolia. In 2015, the capital city, Ulaanbaatar, conducted a Deliberative Poll about the choice among 13 major infrastructure projects. The proposals had long been the subject of public meetings and considerable planning by the city. All of the proposals were popular, but with limited funding and a city with considerable debt, the question was which proposed infrastructure projects should have priority. The city, with our help and that of the Asia Foundation, commissioned a city-wide Deliberative Poll to consider the comparative merit of all 13 proposals. The mayor mentioned in a public interview his particular enthusiasm for one of the proposals: building a metro system (with money to be borrowed from the Japanese). But one proposal that had not gotten much public attention turned out to be the top priority by the end of the process—improved heating for schools. Ulaanbaatar is one of the coldest major cities in the world, and the elementary school children were on multiple shifts in the winter months because few of the schools had proper heating and insulation. The popularity of other proposals dropped; the heating and insulation proposal went to the top; while interest in the metro system, a major image project for the city, declined. As a result of the process, the city provided proper heating and insulation for all the schools (and committed to the other projects in the order preferred by participants after the deliberation). Plans for the metro system were put on hold.

Apart from the Deliberative Poll, the "public will" on these issues about the comparative priority of the proposals had not been engaged and had not been measured. Elites had their opinions. The public had general approval for all the projects. But weighing their comparative merits and the priorities among them requires some kind of informed deliberative process where people compare benefits and costs and how they are distributed. Elites can do this, but to get the public will, the public in some fashion would need to do it. How would it do this? If a deliberative process could be scaled—an issue we will return to—then the "public will" on the comparative priorities of the different proposals could take shape, but only after the mass public had weighed the pros and cons and gotten its questions answered. But such a process does not now exist at scale, and ordinary surveys or even survey experiments are unlikely to provide credible versions of in-depth deliberation (the Deliberative Poll engaged the sample for an entire weekend to understand and evaluate the merits of all the proposals).

Raw public opinion, without some infrastructure of discussion, would likely have just provided a superficial impression based on slogans and news stories. In other words, for the question needing decision, there was not really a judgment by the public about the comparative priorities of the different projects—some affecting the environment, some housing, some heating in schools, some apartment buildings. In that sense, there was no known public will about the comparative priorities to be "usurped" by the deliberative process because the mass public had not engaged in the relevant deliberation to arrive at any such conclusion.

Example 4: Bulgaria

Consider another case where, by contrast, the public did have strong opinions that changed dramatically, and were obviously different from the opinions at the time held by the broader public. Here Lafont might appear to have a stronger argument that the views of the public were "usurped" so as to undermine democracy. In 2007, Bulgaria convened a national Deliberative Poll on policies toward the Roma. The Roma have long been the target of intense discrimination over a broad range of policy areas. This project, convening an excellent national sample of 255 deliberators, drawn from around the country and brought to Sofia, deliberated in a nationally televised convening, attended by the prime minister, on issues such as education, housing, and criminal justice. The Roma were represented in the deliberations in proportion to their representation in the population as estimated at the time (about 6%). After deliberation there were dramatic changes of opinion. For example, the percentage of the sample who thought, "The Roma schools should be closed and *all* the children should be transported by buses to their school [with children from the rest of the population]" went from 42% before deliberation to 66% afterwards. Similarly, the percentage who thought the "Roma schools should be preserved" fell from 46% to 24%. The Roma participants agreed with these changes. The Roma-only schools were drastically underfunded and lacked teachers (the older children were expected to teach the younger ones). During the deliberations, the participants could not help asking what kind of future these children might have.

Given the antipathy toward the Roma, these changes of opinion were regarded as dramatic and surprising.[23] They also helped catalyze the now successful efforts to desegregate the Roma-only schools.

Unlike the other cases mentioned above, the broader population had strong views expressing their well-documented antipathies toward the Roma. Lafont could argue that the government, the media, and civil society were in effect "usurping" the public's actual opinions (contra the Roma) as opposed to the deliberative conclusions supporting desegregation. Why is this not undemocratic?

It depends on the democratic processes and suppositions that are invoked by the claim "undemocratic." The Roma were (and to an important degree still are) an oppressed minority, subject to what, by our previous analysis, would be tyranny of the majority. At the time a majority of the population supported continuing policies that snuffed out the life chances of Roma children, denying them basic rights. As we noted earlier, intentional failures to act can constitute tyranny of the majority as much as can new actions. The combination of neglect and segregation here involved elements of both inaction and action.

Deliberation versus Populism

Just as Madison thought that deliberations in the Senate could stand against tyranny of the majority, and just as the ancient Athenians, on the interpretation of modern scholars, employed the *nomothetai* as a "perfectly democratic brake" on the passions in the Assembly and the *graphe paranomon* on the dangers of the emotions aroused by the orators in the Assembly, we can think of a deliberative microcosm, like the Deliberative Poll on the Roma, as a "perfectly democratic brake" or impediment to the continuing tyranny of the majority that was oppressing the Roma children. On Lafont's view, it is simply undemocratic. On my view it is one process of democracy (the deliberations of a random sample) standing against another process (majoritarian rule in the broader society and its representative institutions). The deliberations revealed the emancipatory potential of a major policy change and contributed to its realization. The ability of deliberative processes to stand against tyranny of the majority embodies an important democratic value.

Lafont considers a version of this argument and rejects it. She reacts to Philip Pettit who poses an interesting hypothetical (reminiscent of the campaign attack on Dukakis with the notorious "Willie Horton" ads). As Lafont puts it, after a horrendous crime "politicians looking for re-election can take advantage of the passion of the citizenry and ask for tougher sentencing in order to make their political opponents look weak":

> They can activate a politics of passion in which they appear as the only individual or the only group really concerned about the horrible crime in question. They can call into existence what Montesquieu called a tyranny of the avengers, letting loose a rule of kneejerk emotional politics that works systematically against the common good [quoting Pettit].[24]

Pettit's solution is to "depoliticize" the decision by the appointment of a minipublic in cooperation with experts to make a deliberative decision about the appropriate levels of sentencing for horrendous crimes. As Lafont grants, an informed deliberation "would move minipublic participants to reject the manipulative proposals of politicians while non-participants would be easily manipulated into embracing tougher sentences."[25]

However, Lafont rejects implementing such a "shortcut" as advocated by Pettit: "Instead of taking the long road of providing the citizenry with information so that they eventually make up their minds on whether to oppose tougher sentencing, he proposes institutionalizing a minipublic as part of a commission in charge of overseeing criminal sentencing."[26]

First, Lafont's counterargument ignores the campaign context, which is part of the official process of making democratic decisions. In a campaign, there is not time for the "long road" of information to have an effect. Second, mere exposure to information rarely has much effect (as contrasted to information when it is part of a deliberative process). So third, the bulk of the population, if left to make a decision, would probably be heavily influenced, as Lafont grants, by the manipulative practices of self-interested (and in this example), demagogic candidates running for office. Pettit's solution of a deliberative minipublic to take the issue out of the political arena is, in my view, a defensible suggestion. Without reforms of the political process, demagogues may distort democracy to yield tyranny of the majority. If we agree with positing non-tyranny as one of our core democratic values, then deliberative processes that stand against tyranny of the majority are an important bulwark for the realization of democratic values.

How about cases where it is not so clear that the deliberations are protecting against tyranny of the majority, but where accepting the deliberative conclusions would require a substantial portion of the population to go along with views they disagree with? Consider two cases where the Deliberative Poll, officially convened by the government, overrode some strong and widely shared views of the public.

After the Fukushima disaster with nuclear power in Japan in 2011, the government faced a crisis in terms of how to provide electric power. Should Japan continue to use nuclear power? To what degree? Or should it phase out nuclear power and substitute other energy sources (renewables, natural gas) and make investments in conservation? These were immense and urgent choices and the government moved to try and get public input in various ways before deciding. They held open meetings around the country but soon found that these were dominated by anti-nuclear activists on one side and employees of the electricity companies on the other. They consulted the public online but self-selection again led to unrepresentative and heated exchanges, perhaps by many of the same people that were in the public meetings. There was conventional public opinion polling, but it was hard to know how much the public knew about the complex energy choices the country faced or how much their answers reflected any engagement with considering the tradeoffs.

Self-selected forums, whether face to face or online, were obviously unrepresentative, even though participants from organized groups routinely attempted to create the impression that they spoke for the concerns of all the people (no matter which side they were on). Good public opinion polling was representative but obviously not deliberative, given the complexities of the choices the country faced from such a major and abrupt change in its energy situation. In this context, the government officially commissioned a national Deliberative Poll.

While the overall challenge was enormously complex, a distinguished scientific committee organized the agenda around three basic options: the so-called 0% option (phase out nuclear power entirely), the 15% option (keep the newer and presumably safer nuclear reactors), and the 25% option (restore nuclear power, over time, to the level of usage it had before the disaster).

Before deliberation, almost half the sample supported the 15% option for continuing nuclear power, but only with the newer reactors. With deliberation, this option went down to 40% while the 0% option went up from 60% to 67%. The government, after a great deal of deliberation, embraced the 0% option to phase out nuclear power entirely. If we presume that the broader public shared the pre-deliberation opinion, with nearly half supporting the 15% option, then this decision imposed the end of nuclear power on about half the country that disagreed).

Lafont's critique would be that the half of the country who disagreed were, in effect, being asked to "blindly defer" to the microcosm's conclusions. First, the argument to go along was not "blind" deference. The process clearly communicated reasons for the conclusions. The participants were asked about four criteria for evaluating the policy options. Their primary concerns coming out of the deliberations were safety and stability of supply. These were broadly shared among the entire sample and in the broader population, but deliberation increased the priority the participants attached to these concerns. Second, the Deliberative Poll was just one step in the official process of making a decision. There was considerable debate within the government before an official decision of the cabinet.

If this is usurpation, what is being usurped? Not the democratically elected government's official decision (since that embraced the deliberative conclusions). Rather, it was only the pre-deliberation views of almost half the population, who supported the 15% option. But the pre-deliberation opinions of the other half (or slightly more) were on the other side of the issue (supporting 0% nuclear). What about them? Given the need for a decision, one side or the other would be overruled.

Furthermore, to insist that a decision require a majority of *pre*-deliberation preferences would be to anoint a process of decision by conventional public opinion polling (or by referendum for mass participation). It would institute a system of continuous plebiscitary democracy. The levels of knowledge and engagement with complex tradeoffs of the mass public in natural settings is notoriously limited. Such a conclusion might seem superficially majoritarian but it would not satisfy our criteria for popular control.

Each democratic alternative should be evaluated based on its achievement of democratic values of the sort pictured in Table 2.2. There we focused on four distinct democratic processes. Competitive democracy (via elections) is only one, deliberations by representatives another, direct participatory democracy a third, and then deliberations by the people themselves (usually implemented in deliberative microcosms selected by random sampling) is yet a fourth. Especially when the deliberations are instituted by an official government process, the conclusions of the random sample need to be considered a distinct embodiment of democracy that can be incorporated into a broader decision process. It is not a mechanism that supplants democracy. It is, in itself, a kind of democracy that serves distinct values that can be incorporated into a system of decision, one that can incorporate other processes that serve other key values.

What if the minipublic is given the final say? In 2017, President Moon of South Korea announced that he would convene a Deliberative Poll to make the final decision about whether or not to restart construction of two nuclear reactors, Shin Gori 5 and 6, that had been partially completed. His party and the other main party had both taken anti-nuclear positions in the election. Public opinion had generally turned against nuclear power since the Fukushima disaster in neighboring Japan. Yet not completing the reactors would have major implications in terms of climate change, cost and reliability. Taking it to a deliberative microcosm like a national Deliberative Poll would provide assurance that the strong cases on both sides received due consideration. While the national sample of 471 was deeply split before deliberation, there was a decisive result afterward; 57% wanted the construction resumed while only 39% wanted it to stay halted after deliberation.[27]

By providing an impartial method where the competing arguments could be considered, a method that was supervised by a balanced scientific advisory committee, the process could break the deadlock and provide the kind of depoliticized resolution that we saw advocated earlier.[28] Would it have been more democratic if President Moon had simply made the decision himself, or done so in collaboration with technical experts? Once again there seems to be a case for thoughtful and representative consultation with the public. While President Moon had the authority to make the decision himself, he officially delegated it to the national Deliberative Poll. He incorporated a distinct decision process into the toolkit of available mechanisms for making the final decision. From my standpoint this is an enhancement of the democratic character of decision, at least on a one-time basis for a very challenging problem.

Institutionalizing Deliberation: The Case of Mongolia

What if the process is not a one-time-only application, but a method that is institutionalized? In Mongolia, after the success of the Ulaanbaatar Deliberative Poll, the Parliament passed a law requiring a national Deliberative Poll before the Parliament considered any proposed changes to the constitution.

This law set out requirements for the non-partisan and professional application of Deliberative Polling: the formation and authority of an Advisory Committee (a "Deliberative Council" independent of the government), the use of a professional survey research organization to select the sample and administer the questionnaires, the standards for the number of people in the sample, and the number who would need to participate. The law also laid out standards for local, regional, and national projects and, most importantly, required Deliberative Polling on constitutional issues before a constitutional amendment could be considered by parliament.[29] Because this is the first institutionalization of Deliberative Polling on a continuing basis, it is worth discussing in somewhat more detail.

In April 2017 the first national Deliberative Poll for the revision of the constitution was held, in conformity with the new law.[30] In preparation for the Deliberative Poll, there were thousands of meetings throughout the country to propose possible topics for constitutional amendments. The Advisory Committee created an agenda of issues in response to this widespread public engagement. The research team created questions and briefing materials based on this agenda.

The sample was recruited by the National Statistical Office (NSO), which does the census. The NSO randomly selected households from randomly selected geographical areas (or strata), and then randomly selected an adult in each of those households to be interviewed. In effect, each adult citizen in the country had an equal random chance of being selected.

1,568 households were selected to cover the entire country. An impressive 96% of the people selected completed the initial interview (1,515 out of 1,568). In conformity with the Law on Deliberative Polling, more than half of those who completed the interview were invited. Out of the 785 who were invited, 669 came to Ulaanbaatar and completed the entire weekend of deliberations. This is an extraordinarily high rate of participation (85% = 669 out of 785). The NSO Report has more data on representativeness and the opinion changes.[31]

The six proposed constitutional amendments generated 18 survey questions about specific aspects of the proposals. Answers to ten of those eighteen questions (55%) changed significantly. It is worth discussing both the significant changes and the proposals that were rated most highly at the end, regardless of change. The highest-rated proposals withstood all the criticisms and still came out at the top of the list. They can be considered the people's considered judgments about what should be done.

Let us start with the opinion changes and then look at the top-rated proposals. Support for two of the most ambitious proposals dropped dramatically with deliberation. The proposal for "Creating a Parliament with two chambers: a people's representative body (People's Great Khural) and legislative body (State Baga Khural)" went from 61% to 30%, a drop of 31 points. With deliberation, the public became more skeptical that "a second chamber would provide effective oversight of the lower house of Parliament." Agreement with this idea dropped from 70% to 38%. More specifically, there was increased agreement with the criticism that "both chambers would be controlled by the same political parties, thereby not providing proper oversight." Those agreeing with this proposition rose from 43% to 56.6% There was also a significant increase, from 48% to 57%, in those who agreed that "adding a second chamber would create too many politicians."

A second major drop in support occurred with the proposal for an indirectly rather than directly elected president who would serve only a single six-year term. There were two components to this proposal—the change in the term and indirect election. Support for "Electing the President for a single six-year term, without reelection" dropped from 61.5% to 41% with deliberation. Support for "Electing the president for a single six-year term by an expanded plenary session of the Parliament that includes Parliament members and the Citizen's Representative Councils of aimags (provinces) and the capital city" started at 36% and ended at 33% (not a significant drop but showing a low level of support after deliberation).

There was also a significant drop in support for one of the arguments in favor of indirect election: "If the President is indirectly elected by the Parliament and the Citizens Representative Councils, then he/she will be someone acceptable to all sides and above the political fray." Agreement with this conclusion dropped from 55% to 38%. On the other hand, there was strong agreement before and after with one of the key arguments in favor of direct rather than indirect election: "If the President is directly elected, s/he can better speak for the interests of all people" (84% before, 80% afterward—no significant change).

By contrast, the deliberators supported an amendment that would increase the power of the Prime Minister: "Granting the Prime Minister the authority to appoint and dismiss the members of his/her Cabinet." This proposal increased significantly from 57% to 73%. Deliberators agreed that "If the Prime Minister cannot even appoint the members of his/her own Cabinet then s/he lacks the authority to get anything done." 68% agreed before and 66% afterwards (not a significant drop).

The Parliament deliberated extensively about these results and eventually passed a constitutional amendment by the two-thirds vote required for passage. Perhaps most notably, the two proposals that were most strongly supported by one of the major parties or the other were both filtered out from the amendment by the Deliberative Poll. The ruling Mongolian People's Party had pressed for the indirect election of the president. This garnered little support in the Deliberative Poll. The main opposition Democratic Party had favored (or many of its members had favored) the proposal for a second chamber. This dropped out of the amendment discussions after the Deliberative Poll. Instead, the amendment included provisions such as those for strengthening the powers of the prime minister and the independence of the judiciary. In sum, the Deliberative Poll had impact on the eventual amendment but some of its impact was in eliminating strongly advocated proposals from final consideration.

In 2023 a new national sample of nearly 800 citizens from throughout the country gathered once again for a long weekend to deliberate about proposed amendment topics. The sample was selected by the National Statistical Office. This highly representative national sample gathered in the Government Palace (the seat of government in Ulaanbaatar) from all over the country.

The Deliberative Council—the independent committee in charge of the process—developed the proposals for deliberation based on 1,100 suggestions from experts, the public, and civil society. Two of the proposals that had very high support at the end of the deliberations provided the basis for the amendment. One was to expand the size of the parliament; the other was to adopt a mixed electoral system, combining majority districts with proportional representation. Expanding the size of the parliament had support from 82% of the participants who had an opinion for or against the proposal after deliberation. Adopting a mixed electoral system for the parliament (with both majority districts and proportional representation) ended with 71% support from those deliberators who had an opinion for or against the proposal by the end of the proceedings.

The new Constitutional Amendment requiring these changes passed Parliament overwhelmingly and became law—a notable result, especially since adding proportional representation might increase representation by third parties (in a Parliament currently dominated by two parties). The Law on Deliberative Polling continues as a meaningful process to bring citizen deliberation to the constitutional amendment process.[32]

In the Mongolia case, it would be difficult to argue that the deliberations usurped the democratic process. Based on the Law on Deliberative Polling, these deliberations were a legally required part of the process of changing the constitution, and they have successfully been used twice to do so.

Deliberative Distortions?

There are two prominent arguments against deliberation that come out of the jury literature. They are empirically based, value-laden criticisms, which address the question why the public and the policy-makers should listen to the results. We should discuss these in some detail because if these two arguments are well-founded, they provide strong reasons against paying attention to the results of deliberation by a microcosm or by any scaled-up version of the same design amongst the broader public.

Domination by the More Advantaged?

The first is the claim that deliberations are likely to be dominated by the more advantaged. While juries do a reasonable job of deciding questions of fact—even complex ones[33]—the critics of deliberation argue that juries often amplify the influence of their most advantaged members. To the extent this is the case, the danger is that deliberation may reflect the power of the more powerful rather than the merits of the arguments being considered. The critique, applied to deliberation in general, is that the more advantaged can be expected to use their better social positions and their greater mastery of the very language and tools of deliberation, to impose their views on everyone else. Critics of the burgeoning applications of deliberation have taken the jury as a test bed for the full range of applications of deliberative democracy. Ideally, as Habermas has posited, deliberative conclusions should reflect the "unforced force of the better argument,"[34] not the force of social deference to the more privileged, or other unequal power dynamics in the deliberations. If the latter were the case, then why listen to the conclusions? They would just reflect the domination of one group over others.

This line of argument against deliberative applications was sparked by Lynne Sanders' now classic article "Against Deliberation":

> American democratic theorists who want to discourage elitism, expand citizen participation, improve the ability of citizens to discuss policy questions, and evaluate political candidates, and before all this, heighten citizen respect for each other, *need to take one problem as primary*. This problem is how more of the people who routinely speak less—who, through various mechanisms or accidents of birth and fortune, are least expressive in and most alienated from conventional American politics—might take part and be heard and how those who typically dominate might be made to attend to the views of others.[35]

Not only will "inequities in class, race, and gender" distort participation in the dialogue according to this argument, but "even if everyone can deliberate and learn how to give reasons, some people's ideas may still count more than others. Insidious prejudices may incline citizens to hear some arguments and not others."

Iris Young extended this case by distinguishing two forms of exclusion. The most obvious is "external exclusion," where some people are simply kept out or are only nominally permitted to participate in what is obviously a rigged process. However, the more insidious form of exclusion is "internal," where "though formally included in a forum or process, people may find that their claims are not taken seriously." This may happen because of who they are, or how they express themselves.[36]

Lupia and Norton eloquently expand on this idea by arguing that "inequality is always in the room":

> "We have spoken before we speak, we have been read before we write. The people who deliberate do so clothed in texts that speak of their place: of their wealth or poverty, their religion, their level of education, their regions, their preferences and politics."[37]

The problem is that those who come into the dialogue unequal cannot, on this view, participate equally, so the results will reflect the domination, either explicit or subtle, by those who are more advantaged. Speaking time, command over the tools of argumentation, the social status and privilege that will lead to deference, the very language and appearance of the more advantaged, will all help replicate privilege through the domination of the deliberations. So instead of the merits of the argument, the results will systematically and predictably reflect the power and influence of the more privileged and their ability to impose their views on everyone else.

To the extent there is an empirical referent for these arguments about the inevitability of domination by the more advantaged in deliberation, it comes from the jury literature. It is certainly true, as Sanders points out, that the first task of a jury is to select a foreman and this choice is, more often than not, an educated white male. Sanders also claims that educated white males talk more and have more capacity to make arguments appropriate for deliberation.[38]

While there is clearly some merit to these critiques, they are applied by the critics broadly to cover *deliberation in general*. Note Sanders' title "Against Deliberation." The other critiques followed in the same spirit. However, our focus here is not deliberation in general but a particular design for deliberative minipublics, the Deliberative Poll. The extent to which deliberative processes may be vulnerable to these problems may depend on the precise design by which the people interact. The Deliberative Poll design differs in important respects from the jury. Juries need to reach a verdict, while the Deliberative Poll collects the final informed judgments in confidential questionnaires precisely in order to shield the opinions from the social pressures that are often required to reach a consensus. Juries are small and despite their aspirations they are hardly representative. Their recruitment is complicated by peremptory challenges motivated by calculations of advantage by each side for the desired verdict. By contrast, Deliberative Poll participants are recruited through stratified random samples whose members are randomly assigned to the small groups. There is no interference with the composition of the groups in order to manipulate the outcome. Deliberative Polls are moderated to ensure balanced consideration of the issues. Juries have only the elected foreman, whose role has a great deal of latitude, varying from jury to jury.

In the case of Deliberative Polls, is there evidence of domination by the more advantaged? An early study by Alice Siu of five US Deliberative Polls included an examination of the talking time for each participant in the small groups—comparing men versus women and white versus non-white participants. There were no significant differences in talking time (number of words) and minutes spoken in terms of gender. In terms of race, the non-white participants actually talked more than the white participants.[39] With moderators and a balanced agenda there was no evidence of domination, in terms of the degree of participation.

Siu also looked at the movements on the policy issues in the small groups, examining whether they were in the direction supported by the more advantaged. The five projects had 99 small groups and 1,474 participants. Considering the more highly educated, those with higher income, and those who were white as the more privileged, Siu concludes "we see no consistent movement toward the more privileged in these Deliberative Polls."[40]

A larger study by Luskin, Sood, Fishkin, and Hahn looked at the small group movements in 21 Deliberative Polls, with 2,744 group–issue pairs. The projects were geographically and substantively quite varied (US, UK, Australia, China, Bulgaria, and EU-wide). They ranged from energy, crime, healthcare, and housing to US foreign policy and the British monarchy. These topics in the 21 Deliberative Polls generated policy indices permitting us to look at whether the more advantaged were able to cause movements on those policy dimensions in the directions they favored. Details on the 21 projects can be found in Table A.1 of Appendix 1. More details about the analyses can be found in Luskin, Sood, Fishkin, and Hahn, "Deliberative Distortions" (2022).[41]

Based on the 2,744 group–issue pairs in 21 Deliberative Polls, each containing 14–30 deliberative groups, discussing 4–12 policy issues, we can examine the extent to which there was any consistent movement in the direction advocated by the more advantaged. For gender, race, and education, we looked at the initial positions of the more advantaged participants (the men, the more educated, and those with higher income).[42] As in Siu's study the idea is that if they were dominating the less advantaged, then the small groups should move in the direction favored by the more advantaged participants.

To make the basic point, we can look at some simplified tables adapted from "Deliberative Distortions." The tables show the percentage of the movements that are in the direction favored by the more advantaged. If they were dominating the opinion change, one would expect that a high percentage of the movements would go in their direction.

More details about these results are in the Appendix. Table A.2 in Appendix 1 shows that only 28% of the group–issue combinations moved in the direction favored by the men. Furthermore, women moved in the directions favored by the men only 42% of the time. There was no consistent movement, either in the samples overall or by the women toward the positions favored by the men. The movements in that direction occurred less than half the time.

Table A.2 in Appendix 1 shows that only 26% of the group–issue combinations moved in the direction favored by the more educated. Furthermore, the less educated moved in the direction favored by the more educated only 42% of the time. As with gender, there was no consistent movement, either in the samples overall or by the less educated toward the positions favored by the more educated.

Turning to income, only 11 of the projects collected data on income. But the result is very similar. Table A.2 shows that only 28% of the group–issue combinations moved in the direction favored by those with higher income. Furthermore, the lower-income participants moved in the direction favored by those with higher income only 35% of the time. Once again, there was no consistent movement, either in the samples overall or by those with lower income toward the positions favored by those with higher income.

The "Deliberative Distortions" paper explores many further complexities, such as the extent of the movements in addition to their frequencies and various ways of comparing the movements of the more and less advantaged. However, these simplified tables make the basic point. Armchair speculations seem to have over-generalized from the critique of juries, and the critique does not apply to deliberative processes in general nor to the Deliberative Polling design in particular. While more experiments are needed disaggregating the components of the deliberative design[43], it seems likely that the elements of balance in moderated civil discussion with diverse others engages those who come in with different views to seriously listen to the voices and concerns of their fellow citizens, no matter how different they are, in gender, education, income, or race (in Siu's study). Without the social pressure to come to an agreement, the process evidently solicits opinions that often reflect change, but not in the predictable pattern the critics expect. The key to the critique is that it be a predictable pattern of small-group deliberation. Hence the relevance of so many group–issue combinations demonstrating that the pattern does not apply reliably at all.

"The Law of Group Polarization"?

There is a second statistical pattern drawn from the jury literature that has been used by critics to undermine the normative claims of deliberation. Like the first, it is held to apply to deliberation in general (although a few exceptions have been noted). Cass Sunstein formulated it as the "law of group polarization." Here is the pattern: 'Polarization means that members of a deliberating group predictably move toward a more extreme point in the direction indicated by the members' predeliberation tendencies.'[44] More specifically, if the issue can be measured along a dimension that has a midpoint, then if the median position of the group is on one side of the midpoint, then, according to this "law," the group will predictably move further toward the extreme in that direction (and if the median position is on the other side, the movement will be in that direction). Sunstein's argument gave birth to his book *Going to Extremes* and to numerous other writings. He documents many cases that have been studied around the world, some with jury-like settings and some with discussions in natural settings. On his view, the pattern seems to pervade every area of life (see his book's appendix documenting this claim).

Sunstein and his collaborators hypothesize two main drivers of this pattern: a "social comparison effect" and an "imbalance in the argument pool." First, people compare their position to that of others in the group and they feel some pressure to go along with the crowd. Second, if most people are on one side of the continuum then there is likely to be an imbalance in the argument pool—more people are likely to express arguments on that side than on the other side, driving opinion in the direction of the dominant perspective.

Sunstein and his colleagues first uncovered the phenomenon in a mock jury experiment, which led them to question the value of deliberation in general:

> Our findings also raise a set of novel issues about deliberation as a whole. Is deliberation anything to celebrate if groups tend to move further in the direction suggested by their original tendency—if (for example) high dollar awards go up, low punishment ratings go down, and groups opposed to gun control and in favor of affirmative action end up thinking a more extreme version of what individual group members originally thought?[45]

The point is that if there is an expected direction of movement that can be predicted on the basis of small-group psychology, then it is harder to claim that the results are determined by an appropriate weighing of the merits.

They illustrated the pattern in a particularly striking experiment in Colorado: "What Happened on Deliberation Day?" Taking the term "Deliberation Day" from Ackerman and Fishkin,[46] they set up an experiment in two localities in Colorado, one primarily liberal (Boulder) and one primarily conservative (Colorado Springs) and with samples that were mostly homogeneous. The groups deliberated briefly on three issues and then tried to arrive at consensus. After agreeing on the consensus, the groups filled out questionnaires similar to those they had filled out pre-deliberation. The result was a strong demonstration of polarization. In Boulder, the group–issue combinations moved in a polarizing direction on Global Warming 60% of the time, on Affirmative Action 80% of the time, and on Civil Unions 100% of the time. In Colorado Springs, the groups moved in a polarizing direction 100% of the time on Global Warming, 100% of the time on Affirmative Action, and 80% of the time on Civil Unions. If the groups started with the median participant on the left, they moved further to the left. If the groups started with the median participant on the right, they moved further to the right.[47] It is hard to imagine a stronger confirmation of the law of group polarization.

However, this design is not what was advocated for Deliberation Day, where the process was modelled on the Deliberative Poll. For Deliberation Day, there was to be no effort to seek consensus before confidential questionnaires. The design is intended to have diversity, not homogeneity, just as in Deliberative Polls.[48] There are elements of balance in the briefing materials, the moderation of the small-group discussions, and the plenary sessions.

Our "Deliberative Distortions" paper tested for polarization just as it did for domination, with the 2,744 group–issue combinations from 21 Deliberative Polls. The results are shown in Appendix 1, Table A.3. Instead of a high percentage of the group–issue combinations moving in a polarizing direction (like the 80% or 90% of the time Sunstein and his collaborators found in Colorado), the pattern prescribed by Sunstein's "law" applied less than half the time (46.7%), with about as much movement in the opposite (depolarizing) direction. Instead of a "law," it was basically a coin flip.

Sunstein and his collaborators acknowledge that one of the factors they changed in the design may have had an effect:

> Deliberators attempted to reach a group decision, and they succeeded in doing so in 83% of group discussions. The effects we describe would likely diminish if experimenters asked deliberators to speak to one another without reaching a decision and then polled privately on their view.[49]

Also, instead of an entire day (or two) of deliberation as in a Deliberative Poll, the participants only deliberated for 15 minutes for each of the three issues. For such complex and controversial issues as the ones they picked (global warming, affirmative action, civil unions) one might think that adequate consideration of competing arguments and tradeoffs would barely get started in such a short period. In any case, the contrast between the non-polarizing results of the Deliberative Poll and Sunstein's demonstration of the "law" is revelatory. The design of the deliberative process matters a great deal for determining whether or not distortions such as domination by the more advantaged or polarization will occur.

No "Shortcuts"?

Having sketched the aspiration for mass deliberation with Deliberation Day, let us return to the usual situation of a minipublic, such as a Deliberative Poll conducted in a context where most of the rest of the public is not engaging in organized deliberation. Can the results provide a "shortcut," or heuristic, as to how people could reasonably decide how to vote, without examining all the issues in depth? Most of us do not have the time and attention to focus on every election or every ballot measure and to study it with the detail it would probably merit. However, we can employ a familiar strategy in ordinary life for many decisions. We can use shortcuts of one sort or another. If those shortcuts were created by the representative and informed conclusions of a deliberative process, they might provide a good basis for voting and improving the democratic process.

That was my original idea when I first proposed the Deliberative Poll in 1988.[50] The original context was to improve the Presidential primary process in the US, where evaluations of many candidates are based on little more than an impression of soundbites and headlines and where the first states in the process (Iowa and New Hampshire at the time) are highly unrepresentative of the rest of the country. We actually conducted a version of the national Deliberative Poll with presidential candidates in January of 1996 and broadcast the process extensively on PBS.[51] However, the project focused on the issues rather than directly on the candidate preferences as I had originally hoped. Even so, the idea was to provide a thoughtful prelude to the primary season that was soon to start.

The applications of Deliberative Polling moved quickly to Australia where the idea was to provide deliberative cues to voters in the national referendum on "the Republic" (the proposal to end the role of the British Monarchy in appointing the Governor General and have an elected president in Australia instead). That project included vote intentions and provided the basis for a project soon after in Denmark for a national Deliberative Poll before the referendum on whether or not the country should join the single European currency.[52]

A similar national broadcast in the UK broadcast the issues and the vote intentions of the sample of a national Deliberative Poll before the 1997 general election. In these early cases, the idea was to have a representative microcosm of voters deliberate about the issues and come to informed conclusions that might help viewers on television and readers in the press come to their own informed conclusions.

This is precisely the idea that Lafont attacks as "usurping democracy" by asking us to "blindly defer" to our *hypothetical* opinions (the opinions we would have if we deliberated).[53] Her argument is that the deliberations create a shortcut that is no substitute for our actually deliberating. First, it supplants what we actually think. Second, we cannot know which side we would be on if we were to deliberate. She thus rejects the relevance of the hypothetical collective judgment, no matter how much more informed or reason-based it might be.

My position is that the creation of a heuristic through a deliberating microcosm is constructive, but second best. It is not a full substitute for actual deliberations by the broader population, first because it is likely to be less consequential in its effect on popular control (mere exposure is likely to have far less effect than actually participating in deliberative discussions), and second, because the best long-term solution for the many problems in our democracy, I will argue, is to create a more deliberative society. As we will see there are many constructive by-products of deliberation—increased efficacy, mutual respect, the creation of more deliberative voters, depolarization of our most extreme partisan differences—that will benefit democracy. So just generating cues will only help modestly with one part of our many problems. Still, I contend it is a constructive step.

Lafont elaborates her argument against voters using shortcuts by critiquing two related arguments by Mackenzie and Warren.[54] They point out that there is almost inevitably a "division of labor" in public opinion. People focus on the topics they find of interest. On the other topics they can use "trusted information proxies," and well-designed deliberative minipublics can serve that function. For Lafont this is just an argument to avoid the hard work of engaging the entire public in serious deliberation. But the problem of engaging the entire public, on most issues, most of the time, is an unsolved problem. Lafont does not solve it. It is an illusory alternative unless we can provide a plausible scenario for accomplishing it. We will address this problem in Chapter 5.

For now, it is worth noting that the two phenomena she decries are ever-present, well studied, and probably inevitable: the "division of labor" in public opinion and the use of heuristics or shortcuts to make decisions in many areas of life, including voting.

A great deal of public opinion research has established that while most people are not focused on most issues on the public agenda, many of those issues are engaged by "issue publics," subsets of the population who care deeply.

Farmers care about farm policy and know a lot more than the rest of the public about it. Jewish and Arab Americans follow the Mideast much more closely than the rest of the population. Most of the organized groups in a pluralist democracy have wider publics, "issue publics" that follow their issues and know more about them than the rest of the population.[55] However, the issue publics are not a solution to the general lack of information or engagement by the public as they are not representative. Farmers follow farm policy because they have a distinct interest, one that will be different from those of consumers, retailers, etc. Jewish and Arab Americans (and neither are monolithic) will have distinctive views on the Middle East and American foreign policy. Issue publics are not a proxy for American public opinion as a whole because they are not representative. But they do reflect a division of labor in which at least some members of the public are paying attention. This specialization seems inevitable in a pluralistic society with different perspectives and interests.

The issue publics do not need shortcuts as they are inclined to put in the hard work to follow an issue in greater depth than other citizens. But the rest of the population may find it reasonable and congenial to use heuristics or shortcuts. These could be expert endorsements of policies or candidates, or messages from organized interests. But another possibility is that cues can be generated by a representative and deliberative process that embodies, in microcosm, recommendations from everyone.

In a now classic article, Arthur Lupia looked at a case of direct democracy in California—a ballot proposition on automobile insurance reform. He wanted to investigate "the extent to which relatively uninformed voters could use information shortcuts to cast the same votes they would have cast if they were better informed." Empirically, he identified voters who "used an information shortcut to emulate the behavior of well-informed voters."[56] The cues from knowledge about the insurance industry's preferences or that of the trial lawyers was effective—for those who had that knowledge—in proxying the votes of those who were more knowledgeable.[57] However, knowing which side is endorsed by whom is a kind of knowledge and it was not widely shared. Perhaps the dissemination of relevant cues can be improved so that the heuristics are more widely available.

John Gastil proposes to put the results of a minipublic deliberation directly on the ballot.[58] That would be an effective form of dissemination. His proposal led to the Citizens' Initiative Review in Oregon and elsewhere, which has put recommendations in the voter handbook that is made available to each voter.

Facilitating Deliberative Cues

To the extent that the dissemination of the cues is effective, does the result contribute to fulfillment of our conditions for popular control? Those conditions included these two criteria (among the four):

Inclusion on an equal basis: all adult citizens should be provided with an equal opportunity to participate equally in the democratic process.
Deliberation: the people need to be effectively motivated to think about the reasons for and against competing alternatives in a context where they can weigh those arguments on the merits and on the basis of good information.

If I am following a heuristic from a random sample, it might be argued that I am not deliberating myself, just following a recommendation. That is what Lafont attacks as "blind deference." I am just unthoughtfully taking instructions as if I were painting a portrait by the numbers without thinking or understanding why the picture is constructed that way.

Yet even if this were entirely correct so that the broad public did not deliberate at all, it would constitute a form of popular control: the cues reach the voters and the voters choose to follow them. But that would be a kind of second-best solution—second best because it did not effectively spread the experience of deliberation.

Is it effective? The outreach to voters from the microcosm can be accomplished in a variety of ways. Televised Deliberative Polls, such as those in the US, Australia, Denmark, and the UK, can put a human face on the issues, by showing the dialogue, in either the plenary sessions or the small groups, or both. In one of the few studies of the effects of broadcasting deliberation, Rasinski et al. (1999) found significant effects on six of 12 policy indices from viewing the first national Deliberative Poll in the US (the 1996 "National Issues Convention" broadcast extensively on PBS before the start of the primary season).[59] By dramatizing the dialogue of participants in evidence-based discussions, the Deliberative Poll apparently had significant effects on the opinions of viewers at home on both foreign and domestic policy issues in the upcoming primary season. Rasinski et al. looked at samples of viewers who were prompted (and not prompted) to view the broadcasts. In a similar way, the written statements in the Citizens' Initiative Review (CIR) seem to have produced some significant effects on voting intention on ballot propositions, as well as on knowledge.

It is worth distinguishing *deliberative cues* from all other cues. In campaigns and elections, there is a near-cacophony of cues given out by candidates, political parties, and other organized interests. Samuel Popkin famously argued that President Ford choking on a tamale (which he did not know to shuck) was an inadvertent televised cue to Mexican-American voters in the Texas primary—a cue that Ford did not, allegedly, know much about their culture or interests.[60] Brady and Sniderman have argued that the "likeability" of a candidate is a cue.[61]

If you find a candidate likeable, you are likely to infer that their policy positions are like your own. Political party is a cue of overwhelming importance in voting. By contrast to all these cues and many others, including accidental ones, we can distinguish "deliberative cues" as those that are generated by a deliberative process that is also designed to make the reasons supporting the cue available.

If a cue is accompanied by reasons, then following it is not "blind deference." It is not "blind" because it is based on the considered judgments of the sample—judgements that are communicated about what is, on balance, most important. But how does it contribute to popular control, even if the justifications are effectively communicated? First, everyone has an equal opportunity (even if very small) of being drawn into the random sample. So it satisfies inclusion on an equal basis. Second, the process, once constituted, is deliberative in determining the conclusions, and deliberative, so far as possible, in communicating the reasons. As we have noted, this solution should be regarded as a second-best compared to everyone actually deliberating themselves, but it is hardly a usurpation of the democratic process by a tiny minority. Rather, the randomly selected microcosm is making a reason-based recommendation to the rest of the electorate, and they are free to balance those reasons against other considerations as they choose. If they consider and follow those reasons, the process is more deliberative than if they just followed the cacophony of other cues, most of which are not reason-based (how likeable is the candidate, the accidental cue of the tamale, blind loyalty to a political party, etc.). Normal political behavior in voting has a lot of "blind deference" when it is not affected by deliberation. By contrast, the recommendations of minipublics can awaken thoughtful choice and agency. If these recommendations to voters occurred in the context of a more deliberative society, then they might be a component in something approaching a "first-best" solution. Sketching that approach is our subject in Chapter 5.

4
Toward a Deliberative–Competitive System

Moderating "the Spirit of Party"

Going as far back as Madison's concern to "cure the mischiefs of faction" and Washington's similar concern to "moderate the spirit of party," there has been a tension at the core of electoral democracy. If we have a democracy with mass elections,[1] we will need political parties,[2] at least according to our experience thus far.[3] However, the partisanship fostered by parties can get out of control, undermining key elements of electoral democracy. When it does, it produces three principal challenges: extreme partisan polarization, distorted public will formation, and the undermining of the essential guardrails of democracy that allow a competitive election system to function. Unless all three of these problems are adequately addressed, it is not credible to conclude that a system with party-based competitive elections satisfies our criteria for popular control.

First, extreme partisan polarization produces deadlock and dysfunction, undermining the legitimacy of the democratic system.[4] Second, the combination of our fractured system of political communication and the partisan incentives for manipulation and distortion with the aim of winning elections (or influencing policy) makes it difficult to assess any firm conclusions about what the people would really want if they focused on the issues (i.e., if they thought about them on their merits, considering the pros and cons of various policies without easily lapsing into just following partisan cues). Extreme partisanship clouds any thoughtful consideration of policy that is independent of party tribalism.

However, without a clear connection to the will of the people there is little to distinguish democracies from a technocracy of elites or some kind of benign autocracy fostering expert decisions without any reference to what the people would really want. Connecting "the will of the people" with what is actually done is supposed to be the key desideratum distinguishing democracy from other forms of government. But the public will can easily get lost in the maze of misleading, one-sided messages or sheer disinformation directed at partisans within the relevant enclaves where the contentious points will not be answered or corrected.

Third, when partisanship gets out of hand, it can motivate attacks on the non-partisan administration of electoral systems, election administration, and the rule of law. "Stop the steal" can become an affirmation of party loyalty disconnected from any evidentiary base. If we cannot trust the results of our elections, then no democratic system relying on party competition to resolve our differences can credibly solve the problem of popular control.

Why not just give up on elections and devise a system of non-partisan, randomly selected microcosms to do the law-making?[5] Perhaps such randomly selected, deliberative gatherings could even indirectly select the key office-holders. At the least, they could replace one or both houses of Congress.[6] But such a radical redesign drops the essential connection that voting provides between citizens and their government. The right to participate and to hold office-holders accountable provides a form of mass consent and, if it can be made to work, it is a valuable mechanism of popular control. Furthermore, to completely replace the institutions of our electoral democracies would be to ignore the path dependence that democratic institutions and practices have developed, particularly in creating norms and expectations about the role of citizens that have come to be popularly accepted. As a result, taking away the voting rights of millions of people would make a transition to any new form of democracy that jettisoned those rights nearly insurmountable.

The alternative advocated here is not a wholesale replacement of our familiar democratic institutions. Instead, it is a series of reforms that *renovates* them so that they better live up to democratic expectations. While the field is still relatively new, we already have dramatic indications of the effects of public deliberation. In this section, I will review some key findings, and then in Chapter 5, sketch some of the potential democratic renovations these findings suggest.

The overall result will be a number of targeted interventions. If we add them up, I believe the impact would be transformative, producing a system that should satisfy our criteria for popular control. But it is a not an all-or-nothing proposition, but rather an agenda of experimentation. Within each domain of decision, each reform is justifiable in its own right. Together they give an overall picture of a set of institutions that are recognizably similar but with enhanced roles for deliberative components to help facilitate thoughtful popular control.

The enhanced role for deliberation depends on some empirical claims. These are that deliberative institutions:

(1) can depolarize our most extreme partisan divisions;
(2) create more deliberative voters, even with a time lag from the deliberations;
(3) help protect the guardrails of democracy, particularly the essential norms of electoral democracy;
(4) provide a method that is scalable, given sufficient political will.

These four claims will provide the foundation for the sketch in Chapter 5 of institutional innovations that will fill out our picture of a more deliberative form of democracy, combining competitive elections and deliberation.

Depolarizing Extreme Partisan Divisions: Results from "America in One Room"

Our test bed for illustrating the effects of deliberation will come from a series of national experiments in the US that took place under the general heading of "America in One Room." We have published detailed empirical analyses of these projects elsewhere, but I will draw on those publications as well as public reports to identify the key points that serve our argument.

The first America in One Room took place with a national sample of more than 500 registered voters recruited by NORC at the University of Chicago that deliberated in a Dallas hotel for an entire weekend. NORC also recruited a control group that did not travel to Dallas, but only answered the same surveys before and after in the same period. The event took place in September 2019, soon before the presidential primary season, and it focused on specific policy proposals in five issue areas. The issue areas were selected on the basis of a previous NORC survey about the topics the public wanted to see discussed in the upcoming campaign:[7] immigration, the economy, health-care, the environment, and foreign policy.[8] Each of the five areas had a number of specific policy proposals. A briefing book was prepared and vetted by a distinguished advisory committee recruited from across the political spectrum.[9] As in other Deliberative Polls, the Advisory Committee vetted the materials for balance and accuracy. The five issue areas yielded 47 specific policy proposals.

The deliberations produced striking depolarization, particularly on the most contested issues. To illustrate, consider the changes by Republicans on immigration policies and the changes by Democrats on the most ambitious social programs.

As you can see in Figure 4.1, support for "forcing undocumented immigrants to return to home countries" fell dramatically among Republicans

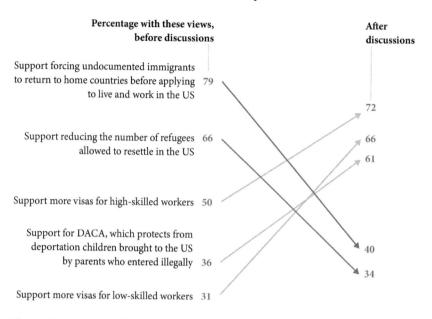

Figure 4.1 How Republicans softened their views on immigration. A selection of positions that were most altered by discussions with people of other viewpoints.

Source: These graphics appeared in James Fishkin and Larry Diamond, "This Experiment Has Some Great News for Our Democracy," *The New York Times*. https://www.nytimes.com/2019/10/02/opinion/america-one-room-experiment.html. Published October 2, 2019. Accessed February 14, 2024.

from 79% to 40%, a drop of 39 points. By contrast only 19% of Democrats supported this before deliberation, dropping slightly to 15% afterwards, while Independents dropped from 49% to 26%. This large movement among the Republicans was also depolarizing in the sense that the mean positions of the two major parties ended up much closer together.[10] Many of the Republicans were initially concerned that undocumented immigrants did not pay taxes and might be a source of crime. However, the evidence-based discussions, building on the briefing materials and the expert panels, made clear that undocumented immigrants pay significant taxes (sales taxes and social security taxes, at least) and they have low crime rates (since they do not want to be swept up by the criminal justice system and possibly get deported). Even though undocumented immigrants were not part of the sample (which included only registered voters and hence US citizens), there were lots of people who were related to or had close ties with immigrants. Their voices and viewpoints were part of the discussions, and over the course of the weekend the temperature cooled on the immigration issue and people who came in with strong opinions left with more understanding and even some empathy for those they disagreed with.[11]

A similar pattern applied to support for reducing the number of refugees allowed to resettle in the US. Republican support dropped a massive 32 points from 66% to 34%, while Democratic support started very low at 17% and went lower to 12% (Independents dropped from 40% to 34%). Again, the mean positions of the two parties greatly depolarized.[12]

There was also a dramatic increase in Republican support for DACA, the Deferred Action for Childhood Arrivals program, which protects people who were brought to the US as children when their parents entered the country illegally. Only 36% of Republicans supported this policy before deliberation. Afterwards, it had risen 25 points to 61%. Democratic support rose from 85% before to 94% after deliberation, and Independents rose from 59% to 75%. Once again deliberation depolarized the gap between Republicans and Democrats, whose mean positions moved significantly closer.[13]

The same pattern held for the other two immigration policy items pictured. Republican support for "more visas for high-skilled workers" increased 22 points from 50% to 72%, while Republican support for "more visas for low-skilled workers" increased 35 points from 33% to 66%. In both cases, Democrats started high and went higher, but the mean positions of Republicans and Democrats depolarized.[14]

Democrats underwent some equally large and depolarizing movements with deliberation, especially on expensive and ambitious social programs.

As you can see in Figure 4.2, one of the more surprising changes was the drop in support among Democrats for increasing the federal minimum wage from $7.25/hr to $15/hr. (Recall that this was in September 2019 before Covid and the subsequent increases in inflation). Democratic support fell from 83% to 59%, a drop of 24 points. Republican support dropped from 21% to 16% (Independents from 48% to 33%). The mean positions of the two parties moved much closer.[15] The sample gathered together respondents from all over the country, and in rural and less developed areas a $15 minimum wage seemed onerous for small businesses, leading to an argument that the minimum wage might best be regulated at the state level.

Two of the changes reflected a concern about government "give aways" in light of the deficit. Democrats worried about some programs that seemed to be appealing ideas in theory but that could explode the budget. One-time Presidential candidate, Senator Corey Booker, had proposed "the government should fund a bond for each child born that will accumulate in value until the child turns 18 to then become usable for higher education or other essentials for a start in life." Support for this proposal among Democrats started at 62% but dropped with deliberation to 21%, a drop of 41 percentage points, the largest of any proposal. Republicans went from 15% to 6%

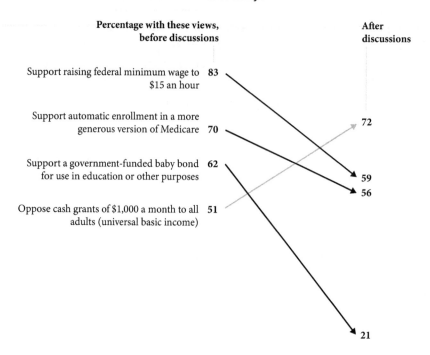

Figure 4.2 The limits of liberalism? Democrats lost enthusiasm for some potentially costly government programs.
Source: Fishkin and Diamond, "This Experiment Has Some Great News for Our Democracy."

and Independents from 43% to 12%. The dramatic drop among Democrats, who worried about the cost despite the positive implications for equal opportunity, produced significant depolarization.[16] Something similar happened with the proposal to provide "cash grants of $1,000/month to all adults (universal basic income)." The percentage *opposing* this proposal went from 51% to 72%, an increase of 21 points.[17] While "universal basic income" was an idea the Democrats found initially attractive, they decided on reflection it was not something the country could afford just now.

These changes are illustrative of the overall pattern.[18] The proposals that most divided the parties were the ones that depolarized. The pattern becomes evident if we distinguish the proposals that exhibited extreme partisan polarization before deliberation. Of the 47 proposals discussed in America in One Room, we classify 26 as instances of extreme partisan polarization between Republicans and Democrats. Our criteria are:

1. At least 15% of each party takes the strongest possible position (0 or 10) at time 1, with these Democrats and Republicans at opposite poles on the proposal.

2. A majority of those party members who take a position at time 1 are on the same side of the scale as those taking the strongest positions in favor or against.

These two criteria combine to identify extreme partisan polarization because those taking the strongest positions are balanced at the two poles, Republicans on one side, Democrats on the other. The majority support, by party, on either side is also symmetrical. A majority of Republicans are on one side and a majority of Democrats are on the other.[19]

The deliberations revolved around five broad issue areas. Each issue area discussed at the event included specific policy proposals (47 in all) under active discussion by presidential candidates or other relevant policy-makers. Some of the proposals were more congenial to Republicans, some more to Democrats. The project briefing materials aimed to concisely present the strongest evidence-based arguments for and against each proposal. A video version of each issue briefing was also prepared and coordinated with the printed versions. The briefing materials were vetted by subject-matter experts with opposing perspectives on the issues and the non-partisan Advisory Committee.

The sample gathered in Dallas on the weekend of September 19–22, 2019, arriving Thursday late afternoon and leaving Sunday after lunch. The agenda alternated small group discussions by issue area and plenary sessions, each lasting 90 minutes and running throughout the weekend. Each of the five issue areas was discussed both in small group discussions and in plenary sessions with experts. Participants remained with the same small group (averaging about 13 persons) throughout the event, enabling them to get to know one another on a personal level over the course of the weekend. In the final questionnaire, completed just before departure, respondents were asked (as they had been in the pre-deliberation survey) to rate each specific policy proposal on a 0 to 10 scale, where 0 was "strongly oppose" and 10 was "strongly favor" (5 being the midpoint). The control group took the same questionnaire in the same approximate time period.

The existing literature offers a basis for sharply contrasting expectations about what is likely to happen when discussion across party lines is engaged on issues of extreme partisan polarization. What will be the effect on issue-based polarization among party members, and, in particular, among those party members taking the most extreme positions? In addition, what is the effect on affective polarization? The increasing dislike of the two parties for each other has added to our evident state of deadlock and division.[20] The growing literature on affective polarization shows that it is distinct from issue-based polarization, so the effects must be evaluated independently.[21]

When members of opposing parties discuss issues that are highly polarized along partisan lines, will the partisan-based polarization on the issues increase or decrease? More specifically, will the mean positions of the members of each party move farther away from each other, or will they move closer together?

There are two main arguments predicting *increased* polarization with cross-party discussion on specific issues that are already highly polarized. The first expects that partisanship is likely to fuel "directional" or "partisan" motivated reasoning. As Taber and Lodge found, partisans "counterargue the contrary arguments and uncritically accept supporting arguments, evidence of a disconfirmation bias." Also, by seeking out supporting arguments they will tend to exhibit confirmation bias.[22] These patterns are both part of *directional* motivated reasoning to support positions they are already invested in.[23] Such processes are likely to push party members to more extreme positions on each side of the polarized divide.[24] Especially on highly polarized issues, mere exposure may have little effect (see the well-established literature on CIE, the "continued influence effect" of misinformation despite exposure to correction[25]) and it will sometimes backfire.[26]

Sunstein's "law of group polarization" provides a second argument that discussion is likely to increase polarization, especially on issues where there are already deep divisions. Because of partisan selectivity, the bias in our social media "news feeds" and the algorithms in our "filter bubbles," partisans are especially likely to get a strong imbalance in the argument pool to which they are exposed.[27] Weighing those unbalanced arguments, the claim is that they are likely to move to further extremes in the direction supported by the imbalance.

With partisan selectivity and the partisan cast of filter bubbles, Republicans live in one social world, Democrats in another. Members of each party are more likely to be in touch with other partisans on their side, so their effective engagement with the argument pool about an issue will be skewed so as to likely increase polarization. Further, the social comparison effect (as they compare their views to their friends and associates and fellow partisans)[28] will create bandwagon effects,[29] a spiral of silence,[30] and added pressure to move to a more extreme position on the side they were already on.

However, these claims about the argument pool apply most clearly to unstructured everyday talk and cross-party encounters in natural settings. Given the latitude jurors have to conduct their deliberations, the jury also produces polarization in mock jury experiments, as Sunstein and his colleagues found.³¹ The deliberative microcosm investigated here, the Deliberative Poll, has a specific design. Consider the argument that this design responds to these dynamics so that organized deliberation may likely *decrease* rather than increase polarization. The design offers a basis for the opposite expectations about both motivated reasoning and the law of group polarization.

"Accuracy-Based" Motivated Reasoning

As Ziva Kunda first hypothesized, there are two distinct kinds of "motivated reasoning"—"directional" and "accuracy-based."³² The argument that polarization will increase on issues of extreme partisan polarization relies on directional motivated reasoning. But if an experimental treatment could encourage the second kind of motivated reasoning—accuracy-based—then reasoning on the merits would likely result. Further, if on issues of extreme partisan polarization, people have arrived at positions without seriously considering (or even encountering) arguments on the other side, then we might well expect accuracy-based reasoning to *de*-polarize by overcoming the legacy of previously one-sided reasoning. The expectation here is not that deliberation will always depolarize, but that it will likely depolarize on issues of extreme partisan polarization.

In a variety of experiments, Kunda concluded that subjects were motivated to be accurate when they "expected to be evaluated, expected to justify their judgments, expected their judgments to be made public or expected their evaluations to affect the evaluated person's life."³³ When people think their views will matter, and when they have to share the reasons supporting their views, they become more attentive to accuracy goals.

These are precisely the motivations that the Deliberative Poll design is created to foster. The task of each of the randomly assigned small groups is to discuss the arguments for and against each policy proposal and then formulate group questions for the balanced panels of competing experts in the plenary sessions, all so that the participants can come to their own individually considered judgments. Groups could also submit additional questions to neutral fact checkers who would reply during the deliberations. The whole design encourages the small groups to seek and weigh relevant information and come to their individual considered judgments.

A parallel argument can be made about how the Deliberative Poll design blunts the directional force of Sunstein's "law of group polarization."³⁴ The design engages the small group discussions with balanced materials, presenting pros and cons for each proposal. On each proposal, the moderators attempt to cover the agenda of competing arguments in the briefing materials and to solicit added arguments from the randomly assigned members of the small groups. Moderators are trained not to give any hint of their own views. The plenary sessions are explicitly balanced with experts representing alternative views (and often the two contending major parties). In this way the problem of imbalances in the argument pool should be minimized. As for the social comparison effect, the participants only express their final judgments in confidential questionnaires. The moderators encourage the participants to consider, and give voice to, the arguments on either side without ever having to express their final decision. There is no "show of hands" or other voting on the proposals. Hence the social pressures to go along with the crowd should be blunted. This process sharply contrasts with juries, which need to reach a verdict, subjecting the jurors to social influence to conform to the views of others.

These aspects of the design can be expected to blunt the dynamics of both directional motivated reasoning and imbalanced argumentation. But blunting the dynamics toward more polarization is not the same as depolarizing. Why would the process actually depolarize on issues of extreme partisan polarization? Our expectation is that partisans have developed their views going into the deliberations on the basis of one-sided argumentation, without ever having taken seriously, or perhaps even considered, the arguments on the other side of the partisan divide. If the design of the treatment can stimulate an accuracy-based motivation and get them engaged with the other side in a substantive way, they are likely to adjust and move somewhat in the direction of the other party.

So far we have been discussing party members for the two main parties. Consider now not just party members in general, but those party members who take the most extreme positions. Should we also expect them to depolarize?

On one hand, some might expect those taking the most extreme positions to be the least likely to depolarize. Their previous thinking has already pushed them as far as possible to the limits of the scale. Their partisan loyalties have likely supported motivated reasoning and imbalanced argumentation in their natural environments. Of all the partisans on either side it seems we should expect them to be the most dug in. Or they may even polarize further to the extent possible.[35] It seems we should expect less depolarization from them than from party members in general.

Still, on the other hand, there is another perspective. If the design of the process stimulates accuracy-based motivated reasoning and balanced argumentation, perhaps those initially taking the most extreme positions will also be susceptible. The very fact that in their natural environments they have arrived at the most extreme positions on the scale may suggest they have been least exposed previously to serious engagement with the other side of the partisan divide. At least on these issues of extreme partisanship, they may be fully as susceptible to depolarization as are the less extreme party members.

There is one more factor that is arguably at work in producing depolarization. We need to consider the role of affect. It could be argued that cross-party discussion on issues of extreme partisan polarization will likely exacerbate affective divisions between the parties, by triggering the dynamics of in-group/out-group identity that increase hostility toward the out-group (in this case, the other party).[36] Stimulating outrage across the partisan divide has become a major part of our political culture in the media, social media, and campaign advertising.[37]

However, the same deliberative design that we believe fosters accuracy-based motivated reasoning and balanced argumentation can also be expected to have an impact on affect. There is a line of research about contact across deep divisions that indicates that under certain conditions, "contact yields liking." Not just any contact but contact satisfying certain conditions. Going back to pioneering work by Gordon Allport, a design that fosters "equal status between groups, common goals, cooperation and institutional support" for the importance of the interactions will likely lead the two groups to a reduction in prejudice.[38] These four conditions are not all essential but in meta-analyses they were held to work best in combination.[39]

The deliberative design employed in "America in One Room" clearly fosters equal status, emphasizing that everyone's opinion counts and deserves to be listened to, and that the participants are meant to cooperate together to consider competing arguments and come to their own informed conclusions, to pose their common questions of greatest concern for presentation on behalf of their group in the plenary sessions. The whole project offered institutional support for these efforts, and the evident media interest in the event added to the sense of informal support for the project.

The contact hypothesis has not previously been applied specifically to the Deliberative Poll treatment for the question of change in affect. However, it has been applied to changes in policy attitudes affecting the Roma in Bulgaria and the Aboriginals in Australia. In those projects the dependent variables were policy proposals affecting the minority groups (more favorable treatment of the Roma or the Aboriginals).[40] Other organized discussions provide support for the contact hypothesis in cases of extreme group division, such as between Israelis and Palestinians.[41]

In other words, the "thermometer ratings" for the party opposite will move higher (or the gap between the in-group and out-group ratings will be lower) after deliberation. The group discussions moderated to ensure mutual respect and a context of equality combined with the common task of formulating questions for the competing experts will lower the temperature of the heated partisan divisions and change the way the in-group feels about the out-group.

This hypothesis applies to party members generally. What of those who take the most extreme positions on either side of the partisan divide? Will they lessen their affective divisions? In theory, the psychology of in-group/out-group division should be even stronger for the "extremists," so one might expect them to be less susceptible to the contact hypothesis. On the other hand, they might be the very people who have had less contact, at least under these constructive conditions, with members of the other party.

In fact, there were striking results in the lowering of affective polarization.[42] We take this as further evidence that the deliberative process cooled the temperature, allowing people to open up and actually listen to each other, rather than retreat to their entrenched positions. The contact hypothesis was arguably at work as they arrived at what Madison called "the cool and deliberate sense of the community."[43]

Overall, there were 26 proposals that fit our criteria for extreme partisan polarization. For party members, Republicans and Democrats moved closer on 22 out of the 26 proposals. In 19, the movements were significant.[44] As noted earlier, both parties showed some equally large movements in a depolarizing direction. For those initially taking the strongest possible positions, either in support or opposition, there was depolarization for 26 out of the 26 proposals. When comparisons to the changes in the control group are taken into account (difference-in-difference analyses) 20 out of the 26 proposals are significant for party members[45] and 26 out of 26 proposals remain significant for those starting at the extremes of the scale.

Creating More Deliberative Voters

A year after America in One Room, we followed up with the participants and the control group to see how they intended to vote (and also, just after the election, to see how they did vote) in the 2020 Presidential election. We were interested in whether or not there was any trace of an effect on their voting. In particular, we were interested in whether or not there were traces of what we could call "deliberative voting"—voting that was arguably connected with their considered judgments following deliberation. We knew that any expectation of an effect was setting a high bar. After all, the deliberations had been a full year earlier. The intervening months subjected everyone (participants, the control group, and the general mass public) to one of the most contentious campaigns on record. Why should we expect a weekend of civil discussion and deliberation on the issues to have any lasting effect after a year of distorted mud-slinging?

The follow-up surveys, just before the 2020 election as well as just after the election, with both the participants and the control group show significant differences in voting behavior for these samples of registered voters.[46]

Figure 4.3 shows the dramatic difference between the treatment and control groups in voting intention just before the election, a full year after the deliberative weekend. The control group had a gap between Joe Biden and Donald Trump at 3.8% (the actual gap in the electorate was about 3%). But the voting intentions of the participants suggest a dramatic effect of the treatment—a gap of 28.2 percentage points between the two major candidates.[47]

How is such an effect possible? The results are surprising because the accepted wisdom in political science has long been that voting behavior, deeply rooted in group attachments, is much more stable, and presumably much harder to change, than political attitudes.[48] We find significant effects on two aspects of voting behavior: who one votes for and whether one votes at all. The second is just as puzzling as the first in that successful interventions on turnout tend to be soon before the election.[49] All of the effects on voting behavior discussed here occur much longer after the intervention. How can deliberation possibly have such effects almost a year later?

Our solution to the puzzle of the delayed effect is that the deliberations gave rise to a latent variable, *an awakening of civic capacities*, that has an effect, in turn, on voting (whether or not one votes at all) and on vote choice (whom one intends to vote for). The people who deliberated over the weekend, as compared to the control group, became more politically engaged. We take significant movement on the polarized policies over the weekend as an indicator that they were deeply involved in the deliberations.[50] Those who deliberated were also more likely to follow the campaign, to have a greater sense of internal efficacy (belief that their political views were "worth listening to"),[51] and to acquire (and continue to acquire) general political knowledge. Deliberative change on the issues following the campaign, feeling that you have views worth listening to, and becoming more knowledgeable are all elements of a coherent civic awakening—a picture of more engaged citizens.

These elements of a civic awakening are roughly similar to those found by Gastil et al. 2002, in their study of the indirect effects on voting from serving

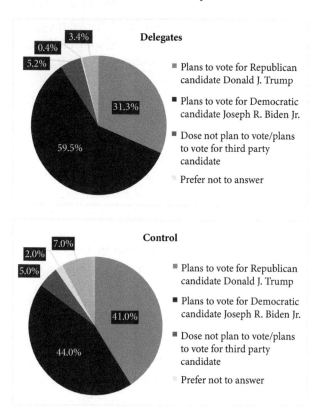

Figure 4.3 Delegates versus control group. If the presidential election were held tomorrow, which candidate would you vote for (or already have voted for)?
Note: Weighted data. Pearson Chi-Square: .000.

on a jury that reached a verdict.[52] They found that the depth of deliberation (which they measured by the number of counts considered at a trial that reached a verdict) was one of the mediators in increasing the likelihood of voting. Our deliberators all considered the same number of policy issues, but we measure "depth of deliberation" through their opinion changes on the deliberative weekend on the issues that were extremely polarized. Gastil et al. also found public affairs media use as measured by "following the campaign," political efficacy, and satisfaction with the deliberative process all connected to the civic awakening from jury service. We use "following the campaign" and gain in general political knowledge as mediators along with internal political efficacy.

In the jury case, the dependent variable was limited to whether or not one voted. In our analysis we are interested both in turnout and in *how* one voted and whether that voting behavior has a connection to one's policy positions.

The latter is essential for considering the broader question of the impact of civic engagement on collective self-government.

Thus far we have traced elements of a civic awakening—greater efficacy, increased knowledge, and closer attention to the campaign among the deliberators. We have also seen indirect effects of the civic awakening on voting at all and voting for Biden. However, we can also explore whether there is a direct effect of their time-3 (the survey just before the election, one year later) policy positions on *how* they voted. Once awakened, are the deliberators more likely to take their policy preferences into account in deciding whom to vote for? In fact, we found a significant direct effect of the policy positions respondents had at time 3 and their willingness to vote for Biden. In short, they made a direct connection between their policy positions at the time of voting and how they voted. Thus, we conclude that the deliberations from a year earlier helped foster more deliberative voters.[53]

Using Technology: Adding the AI-Assisted Moderator

Working with the Helena Group Foundation and other partners,[54] we convened "America in One Room: Climate and Energy" in 2021. It followed the same format as the previous project but the deliberations were conducted entirely online with our AI-assisted Stanford Online Deliberation Platform.[55] We can draw on that project to buttress three points: First, the online deliberations produced depolarization between Republicans and Democrats very comparable to what we found in the original face-to-face America in One Room. Second, they produced an effect on the creation of more *deliberative voters* a year later, parallel to the effect we found from the earlier face-to-face project with human moderators. Third, the online platform suggests a practical mechanism for scaling the deliberations to much larger numbers of people.[56]

NORC at the University of Chicago selected a nationally representative sample of 962 respondents for the deliberations. The agenda focused on 72 substantive questions, while a second representative sample (a pre and post control group of 661) did not deliberate but took essentially the same questionnaire in the same period. Each group completed the survey upon being recruited (in early August) and again at the end of the experiment (in late September), as well as a year later (close to the mid-term Congressional elections).

On 66 of the 72 issue propositions in the survey, the participants changed significantly over the course of the deliberation. Almost all the changes were toward doing more to combat climate change, and these changes were generally in the same direction across party and demographic divides. Democrats were initially more supportive of ambitious policies to address climate change, and Republicans were initially more skeptical (with Independents falling in between the two). However, by the end of the deliberations majorities of Republicans had come to support the general principle of "serious action to reduce greenhouse gases," along with a number of specific proposals to "dramatically accelerate" adoption of renewable sources of energy and to slow deforestation. At the same time, Democrats became more supportive of including a new generation of nuclear power plants in the future energy mix, and a majority of Republicans remained wary of a hard deadline of 2050 for phasing out oil and natural gas.

Figure 4.4 has illustrative cases showing significant changes of opinion, particularly among the Republicans who were initially very skeptical about climate action.[57]

As you can see in the first line plot in Figure 4.4, before deliberation only 35% of Republicans agreed with the basic premise that "rising temperatures are caused by human activities that emit greenhouse gases." After deliberation this percentage rose 19 points to 54%, joining even larger majorities of Independents and Democrats. An almost identical pattern applied to changes in agreement that "To stop the increase in global temperatures humans must reach net zero." Similar changes applied to the elimination of coal by 2035 (Republicans moved from 29% to 52%, joining even larger majorities of Independents and Democrats). While on some items (e.g., eliminating all fossil fuels from electricity generation) the Republican changes fell short of achieving majority support, the pattern of movement was still consistently depolarizing. And on the basic question "We should take serious action to reduce greenhouse gases because waiting is taking irresponsible risk with our kids' future," the same pattern held (Republicans moving 21 points from 36% to 57%, joining even greater majorities of Independents and Democrats).

More generally, we constructed an index of the 27 extremely polarized items in which 15% or more of the respondents took the most extreme possible positions on either side of the 0 to 10 scale.[58] That index showed strong depolarization with deliberation for all 27 of the extremely polarized questions. Once again, issues that were the subject of extreme partisan contention consistently depolarized between Republicans and Democrats as a result of deliberation.

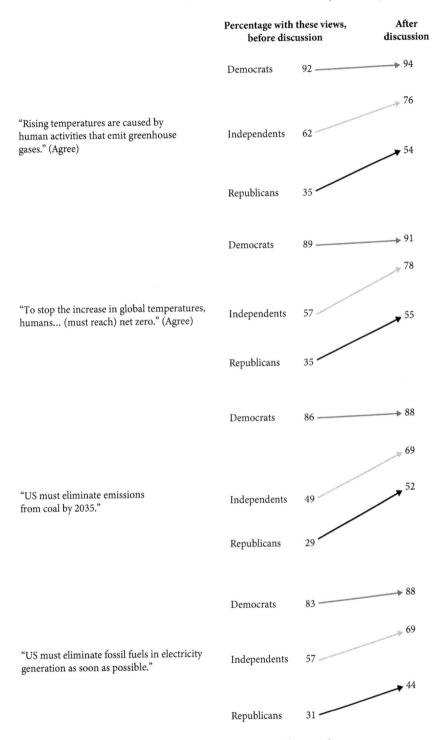

Figure 4.4 Depolarizing changes with deliberation on climate change.

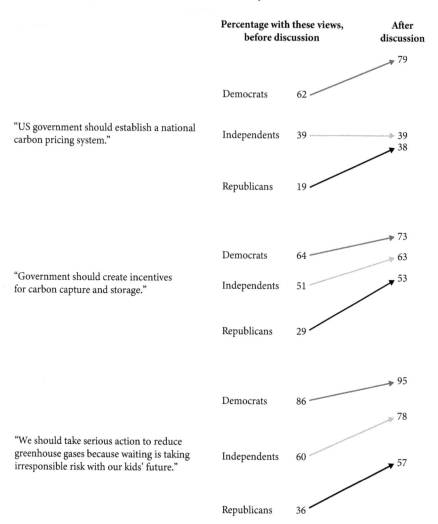

Figure 4.4 Continued

In the follow-up survey a year later, just before the 2022 mid-term elections, we found a "civic awakening" that had an effect on voting roughly parallel to the one we found earlier with the 2019 face-to-face project in the 2020 Presidential election. Deliberation on the weekend led to changes in how much the respondents worried about climate, how many true things they believed about climate, and how knowledgeable about climate they were. We view the scales measuring these three—worry, belief, and knowledge—as measures of a latent *climate engagement dimension*, induced by the deliberations on the weekend and having an effect on climate salience at the time of the election. Climate salience, in turn, then had a direct effect on wanting Democratic control of Congress as a consideration in voting. We measured climate salience by asking how important or unimportant several issues would be in how they planned to vote in the election. The issues included crime, abortion, the cost of living, threats to democracy, jobs and the economy, immigration and the situation at the border, guns, and climate change. The deliberators prioritized climate change fully a year after the deliberations and for those who prioritized climate as a voting issue, there was a strong preference for Democratic control of Congress. This is a striking replication of the long-term effects on deliberative voting that we found in the earlier face-to-face project. Note that these effects were from an online deliberation with the automated platform conducted a full year before a mid-term election. That the treatment was online and that the election was a mid-term would have led most critics to expect little or no effect a full year later. Instead, the results parallel those we found for the face-to-face condition and the presidential election. Deliberation seems to create voters who will act on their considered judgments.

Strengthening the Norms of Electoral Democracy

Electoral democracy requires norms that help safeguard the electoral process. Here we will consider some basic norms about how to ensure access to registration and voting and also how to ensure the counting of votes that have a meaningful chance of playing a role in the process of democratic competition. The norms we will consider are more specific than the general norms that Levitsky and Ziblatt have usefully termed the "guardrails of democracy."[59] Those general norms define a competition in which parties have mutual *tolerance* (so that each can accept the results if the other party comes to power) and *forbearance* (in which each party does not go the full limits of pressing its advantages within the letter of the law, knowing that it might have to live with similar behavior were the other party to come to power). The result is a system that can use competitive elections to settle the question of who governs—at least for now. Rival parties can accept competitive elections in the knowledge that the losers now will likely have a chance to govern in the future because the system offers opportunities for the alternation of power.

Each of these general guardrails obviously requires more specific norms for the conduct of electoral democracy. Many of them are so obvious that they would not normally be in question. But in this period of extreme partisan polarization and intense competition, the specific norms for the conduct of elections have become issues of partisan contention.

In the third iteration of American One Room, focused on democratic reform, we included a number of these items to see if deliberation could strengthen the norms of electoral democracy. At the core of *electoral* democracy is the acceptance that all eligible voters have effective access to the voting process and can be assured that their ballots will be properly counted. Effective access means more than access in theory. It means that there are not arbitrary impediments that make it difficult to register or to cast a vote or to have it properly counted. If voters and competing parties cannot rely on widespread acceptance and implementation of these presumptions then elections will lose their role as a method of settling the question of who comes to power. Rule-based party competition will degenerate into other forms of conflict.

We convened the third America in One Room, this time on democratic reform in the US, in June 2023.[60] When our nationally representative sample of 600 (selected once again by NORC at the University of Chicago) deliberated for a weekend about these issues, Republicans often moved significantly toward initially Democrat positions and Democrats sometimes moved just as substantially toward initially Republican positions. The changes were all consonant with basic democratic values, such as that everyone's vote should count and that our elections need to be administered in a nonpartisan way. In the same period, a comparably sized control group that did not deliberate changed hardly at all on the policy issues.[61]

As you can see in the line plots in Figure 4.5, only 30% of Republicans initially supported providing access to voter registration online, but after deliberations Republicans moved to majority support, joining Democrats (who overwhelmingly supported it at 81%). Republicans abandoned their view that "increasing opportunities for voter registration would open up more opportunities for voter fraud." The percentage of Republicans believing that dropped 26 points (from 56% to only 30%). Republicans similarly abandoned their opposition to restoring federal and state voting rights to convicted felons upon their release from prison. Republican support for restoring voting rights for felons increased dramatically, from 35% to 58%.

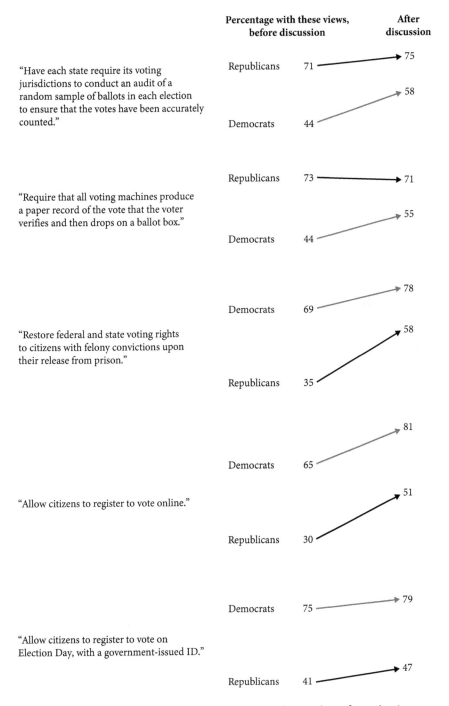

Figure 4.5 Depolarizing changes with deliberation on the conduct of our elections.
While the changes are illustrated with percentages, the means of Republicans and Democrats move closer together with deliberation.

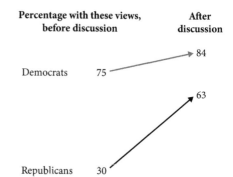

"Allow representatives from political parties and other groups to challenge the eligibility of voters as they cast their ballots at polling places and as officials count the votes at tabulation centers (percentage opposing)."

Figure 4.5 Continued

By contrast, only a minority of Democrats (44%) initially supported the mostly Republican proposal for each state to require its voting jurisdictions to conduct an audit of a random sample of ballots "to ensure that the votes are accurately counted." However, after deliberation Democrats increased their support by 14 points to 58% (joining Republicans who supported it even more strongly at 75%). Getting an accurate count was a goal broadly shared, and audits with a random sample seemed a practical method of assuring everyone about the results. The same goal was served by another, initially Republican, proposal "that all voting machines produce a paper record of the vote that the voter verifies and then drops in a ballot box." Democratic support rose from 44% to 55%, with Republican support staying at over 70%.

Republicans also ended up joining Democrats in *opposition* to the proposal to "Allow representatives from political parties and other groups to challenge the eligibility of voters as they cast their ballots at polling places and as officials count the votes at tabulation centers" (percentage opposing). Democrats went from 75% to 84% opposition while Republican opposition increased dramatically from 30% to 68%, an increase of 38 points. Accurately counting the votes included protecting the process from the actions of intimidating party representatives.

Deliberation also generated bipartisan embrace of two additional reforms to diminish possible partisan bias in electoral administration. Overall public support for "Independent non-partisan redistricting commissions to redraw the boundaries for state legislative and federal congressional districts" increased from 44% to 60%, with Republicans increasing their support from a minority (33%) to a majority (55%). In the discussions this seemed like a practical method at the state level to decrease extreme partisan gerrymandering, which obviously interferes with the ability of the losing side to cast meaningful votes. There was also strong support after deliberation for making the chief election officer in each state (typically the secretary of state) a non-elected, non-partisan official. Support for this reform increased to 54% overall, with Republicans moving from 47% to 54% (and Democrats increasing from 52% to 58%).

Once again, this reform is a thoughtful brake on the spirit of party. It limits the potential for partisan actors to overwhelm the non-partisan administration of elections.

Overall, it should be clear that balanced deliberation can lead to bi-partisan support for the norms of electoral democracy that apply to basic questions such as who should be able to register, how they can register, how the votes are counted, how accuracy in the vote counting can be guaranteed, how partisanship can be kept out of election administration, and how gerrymandering can be curbed so that the votes of all can count. These norms are specific guardrails of electoral democracy that can ensure that elections are meaningful.

Persistence Following Deliberation

These changes on support for the norms governing elections do not just melt away after the deliberations, even in the hot-house environment of our charged political discourse. Three months after America in One Room: Democratic Reform, we did a follow-up survey of the deliberators and the control group. The significant changes on the guardrails of electoral democracy and related issues of electoral reform—such as ranked choice voting and proposals to protect impartial election administration—showed considerable persistence.[62]

Significant findings include:

> **Restore voting rights for felons**: Deliberators were asked whether we should "Restore federal and state voting rights to citizens with felony convictions upon their release from prison." Over the weekend of deliberation, support rose from 50% to 65% for the sample overall, and then three months later, that support was still at 58%, significantly higher than at the start and significantly different when contrasted with changes in the control group (which did not deliberate but just

answered the same questions in the same period).⁶³ Notably, Republicans moved on this question, from a mere 35% support at the start to 57% at the end of the weekend, settling at 48% three months later (a difference from the initial survey of 13 points).

Online voter registration: "Allow citizens to register to vote online." With deliberation, support for this proposal jumped from 45% at the start to majority support at 56%. Republicans moved from 30% to 48% at the end of the weekend, and ended at 38% three months later, a lasting effect of 8 points. These changes were accompanied by a fall in support among Republicans for the idea that 'increased opportunities for voter registration open up more opportunities for voter fraud." Agreement with this claim went from 57% on first contact to 41% by the end of the weekend, ending at 49% three months later (a difference of 8 points from the start).

Partisan challenges to registration and vote counting: "Allow representatives from political parties and other groups to challenge the eligibility of voters as they cast their ballots at polling places and as officials count the votes at tabulation centers." Opposition to this proposal obviously expresses a concern about interference with the registration and vote-counting process. Opposition to this proposal went from 49% at first contact to 72% by the end of the deliberations and settled at 59% three months later, a lasting gain of ten points. Republicans moved from only 31% opposing to 63% opposing by the end of the deliberations, a dramatic 32-point shift. This settled at 59% three months later.

Election audits: "Have each state require its voting jurisdictions to conduct an audit of a random sample of ballots in each election to ensure that the votes have been accurately counted." This is a protection for accuracy in the counting which democrats were initially skeptical about but joined republicans in support of after deliberation. Overall support rose from 57% to 64% on the weekend and stayed at 64% three months later. Republicans went from 73% to 77% after three months while Democrats went from 43% to 55% in the same period.

Non-partisan chief electoral officers: "Have each state make its chief electoral officer (such as secretary of state) a non-partisan, non-elected, professional position." This is a reform intended to protect non-partisan election administration. Overall support went from 49% to 54% and stayed at 54% three months later. Republicans went from 49%

to 55% and settled at 50% three months later. Democrats went from 52% to 59% and were at 60% three months later.

Including everyone's vote: "Making sure everyone who wants to vote can do so." This value-laden goal was shared across the political spectrum and support for it increased significantly from time 1 to time 3. Overall, support for this goal went from 75% to 92% on the weekend, settling at 85% three months later. Republicans went from 72% to 90%, ending up at 81% three months later. Democrats went from 80% to 93%, remaining at 93% three months later.

Keep current system: "Keep the current system of electing representatives from single-member districts" (also known as "first past the post") went from 46% at time 1 to 40% at time 2 to 39% at time 3 (three months later). For Republicans it declined from 60% to 53% at time 3. And for Democrats it declined from 37% to 27% at time 3. These results suggest an increasing openness to other designs for electoral systems. The deliberations stimulated interest and support for both ranked-choice voting and proportional representation.

Ranked-choice voting: This was the system that received the most support. The project explained it this way:

> In this system, voters can rank their choices among a number of candidates. To be elected, a candidate must win a majority of the vote. If no candidate wins a majority of first preference votes on the first ballot, the candidate with the lowest number of votes is eliminated and the second preference votes of their supporters are then counted for the remaining candidates. This process continues in a series of "instant run-offs" until a candidate receives a majority of votes. This system has been used in some American cities and recently in two US states. Voters do not have to rank all the candidates. If they wish they can just choose one. Or they can also identify their second choice, their third choice, etc

Support for ranked-choice voting increased significantly and persisted (in comparison to the control group) at several levels: for Congressional, state, and local elections in the primaries, as well as for general elections at the state and local level. For example: "Congressional elections" (primary stage). Overall, support moved from 44% to 53% at the end of the deliberations, ending at 49% three months later. Republicans moved from 32% to 40%, ending up at 38% three months later, while Democrats moved from 57% to 64% ending up at 62%

three months later. Other results are in the tables. There were similar but smaller movements that persisted in support of proportional representation.

Agreement with the following explanatory variable on what ranked-choice voting does increased and persisted: "Ranked-choice voting will better reflect the public's views on all the candidates." Overall agreement went from 43% to 56% after deliberation and ended up at 51%. Republicans increased from 33% to 36% ending up at 39% while Democrats went from 57% to 71% ending up at 60%.

Also worth noting is the result on **political efficacy**: "I have opinions about politics that are worth listening to." Agreement with this measure of internal political efficacy increased overall, from 65% before deliberation to 75% after, and was still at 74% three months later (with similar movements for Republicans, Democrats, and Independents). In addition to the changes in policy views, the deliberations seemed to create more engaged citizens.

Overall, these lasting effects suggest that deliberation, even merely over the course of a weekend in an online process, can create lasting effects on the guardrails of electoral democracy—our norms of letting everyone register, vote, and have their votes counted accurately without partisan interference. In addition, participants arrived at lasting support for reforms that might better reflect the public views on all the candidates.

Design Criteria for Deliberative Microcosms

The point of Deliberative Polling is to provide an estimate of what the people would really think about an issue if they could weigh the pros and cons of policy proposals on the basis of the best information available, usually over the course of a weekend of discussion in small groups. Hence, the process is designed to satisfy some basic requirements:

1. A stratified random sample must be recruited to deliberate.
2. That sample must be of sufficient size that its representativeness and opinion changes can be evaluated in a statistically meaningful way.
3. Opinions on the policy options as well as on relevant explanatory variables should be collected on first contact and at the end of the deliberative process. The initial opinions should be collected on first

contact so that the estimation of the initial opinions is not contaminated by a partial treatment (the prospective participants starting to change their views and becoming more informed in anticipation of the deliberations).

4. Ideally the project will have a pre–post control group, for two reasons. First, the control, surveyed at the same time as the deliberators, allows one to evaluate the initial representativeness of the sample by comparing the time-1 opinions of the deliberators with those of the control group. Second, the control group, surveyed again at the same time as the deliberators' post-deliberation survey, can provide evidence that the opinion changes are due to the deliberative process rather than events in the wider world. The changes in the treatment group (the deliberators) should be compared with the changes in the control group (difference in difference analysis) in order to assess what changes are due to the deliberative process (rather than changes from events in the wider world).

5. If there is no control group, then the initial attitudinal representativeness can be evaluated by comparing the participants (those who participate in the deliberations) and the non-participants (those who took the initial survey but, for whatever reason, failed to attend). To make this comparison possible, a comprehensive questionnaire on the issues should be administered to all those invited on first contact. Essentially the same questionnaire should also be answered by the participants (and the control group) at the end of the process.

6. An advisory group of relevant stakeholders should be appointed that will vet the selection of policy options and the development of balanced briefing materials. The briefing materials should include pros and cons for each of the policy proposals in the questionnaire.

7. The pros and cons in the briefing materials can be turned into potential explanatory variables that are causally proximate to the deliberative process. They can help reveal the extent to which opinion is moving (or not moving) in response to some key considerations. These explanatory variables are important in understanding why the public changes in the way it does.

8. Knowledge questions should be asked before and after deliberation, both of the treatment group and of the control group. Policy-specific knowledge should be drawn from items in the deliberations, while general political knowledge need not be.

9. Ideally, the deliberations are both unitary and subdivided into small groups. By "unitary" it is meant that if there are n participants deliberating, then all n consider all the options under comparable conditions. If, as in the Deliberative Poll, the participants are randomly assigned to small groups, those groups should meet concurrently with the same agenda. In that way everyone can participate meaningfully, allowing all the participants to independently evaluate all the options, so that all the n from the deliberations can count in the analyses of representativeness (both attitudinal and demographic) and opinion change.
10. Ideally, there are transcriptions of all the small group discussions. These can be analyzed with automated text analysis to provide further evidence about the reasons for support of or opposition to the policy options.
11. If possible, there is a record of the talking time of all participants, to assist in the evaluation of inequalities in participation.
12. There is an opportunity for the small groups to identify key questions on which they want expert input. Questions from the small groups should be answered in plenary sessions where balanced panels of experts (representing different points of view on the policy options) can answer from their perspectives. It is important that this process occur when all the small groups are gathered together, so that all the participants can hear the same answers.

To illustrate the design criteria with an example that arguably satisfies all of them, let's revisit America in One Room: Climate and Energy. This was the largest controlled experiment with in-depth deliberation ever held in the US. It addressed the question: "What would the American public really think about our climate and energy challenges if it had the chance to deliberate about them in depth, with good and balanced information?" If the American people—or in this case, a representative sample of them—could consider the pros and cons of our different energy options, which would they support? Which would they cut back? What possible paths to net zero (the point at which we are not adding to the total of greenhouse gases in the atmosphere) would seem plausible to them? Which proposals would they resist? Can the public arrive at solutions to our climate and energy dilemmas that transcend our great divisions, especially our deep partisan differences? Can they also find common ground across differences in age, race, and region?

NORC at the University of Chicago recruited a national stratified random sample of sufficient size for its representativeness and the opinion changes to be evaluated statistically in a meaningful way. Because all the policy options and explanatory variables were asked at the time of initial contact, there was no issue of a partial treatment (the deliberators beginning to change their views in anticipation of the event) before the participants took the initial survey. Because a control group took the same survey at the time of recruitment and at the end of the deliberations, it is possible to do difference-in-difference analyses of the changes. In this case, because the control group changed hardly at all, despite one of the worst summers for difficult climate disasters on record, the recorded changes were clearly due to the deliberations. A distinguished advisory committee representing diverse policy perspectives vetted the policy options and the briefing materials. Knowledge questions showed significant knowledge gains. All the small group deliberations produced transcripts, which are currently being studied with automated text analysis, and the talking times of each participant in each small group have been recorded. The plenary dialogues proceeded smoothly.

A Contrasting Model

A hint of the importance of some of these design considerations can be gleaned from a prominent citizens' assembly on the same general topic that took place in France in the same period. The sample size for that deliberation was only 150 instead of 1,000. There was no control group, so there is no way of telling whether the changes were due to events in the wider world or to the deliberations. No data are available on the opinion changes because no systematic opinion data were collected at the moment of recruitment before deliberation. Only demographic data were collected. Helene Landemore, an advisor to the French Citizens' Convention on Climate (CCC) describes the sampling as follows:

> The first random sample was created by generating 250,000 phone numbers via a random generator, then texting people to ask whether they would be interested in receiving a call, and then calling people, collecting their information, and eventually forming a stratified random sample of 150 citizens on the basis of that information (along criteria of sex, age, education level, socio-professional category, geographic origin, and territory).[64]

Since the participants were asked to commit themselves for many months of deliberation (as opposed to the weekend on the Deliberative Poll model), it seems reasonable to assume that those who volunteered to participate from the initial 250,000 contacted were more interested in climate change and more concerned to see climate action than the rest of the population. This self-selected group cannot speak for the whole population if they start out with unrepresentative opinions on the issue to be deliberated. Attitudinal representativeness as well as demographic representativeness would seem essential at the start if the deliberative conclusions are to represent what the public would think at the end of the process. This might also be a case where Sunstein's "Law of Group Polarization" might push the opinions even further in the direction of strong climate action.[65] While Sunstein's "Law" (predicting movement toward the extremes depending on the initial composition of the group deliberating) does not apply to the Deliberative Polling model, which asks not for a group decision but only individual opinions, that "Law" does seem to apply to consensus-seeking deliberations such as juries. Since the participants were asked to produce a consensus document, if possible, in the climate change deliberations, the social pressure might be comparable to those in juries. (Sunstein posits two causes for the movement to extremes: the social comparison effect yielding group conformity and the imbalance of the argument pool if more participants are on one side of the issue.) Given the considerable sacrifice in time required to participate in the CCC, one might expect a large imbalance in the argument pool. Then, given the expectation that the participants come to an agreement on recommendations (if possible), the social comparison effect would very probably be engaged. As Sunstein's law would have predicted, the proposals were radical and far-reaching; so much so that the government followed up on very few of them despite initial promises.[66]

A further issue is that the Citizens' Convention for Climate (CCC) did not follow the unitary model of the Deliberative Poll where all the participants deliberate in small groups on the same issues and bring their questions to shared plenary sessions which all attend. Instead, it was "siloed" or subdivided into different groups that discussed different issues. Dimi Courant, an observer of the CCC, explains:

> The CCC had five fixed thematic groups of 30 citizens, so participants did not hear the same experts or deliberate on the same issues. Instead of a collective intelligence of 150, measures were crafted by separate tables of around 5 citizens and then quickly presented to the 25 others in thematic groups. Plenary sessions

with the 150 participants became central in the last two sessions but the deliberation time was drastically reduced. This division of labour means that most citizens voted on measures they had not examined in their own deliberations.[67]

Because of these "silos," the effective sample for deliberating most of the propositions was the 30 people in each thematic group, not the full 150 participants. Whom do these 30 participants represent on a given issue? There do not seem to be any data available to evaluate this, and the sample size for those who effectively deliberated about a given issue would be too small to draw conclusions in any case.

Other citizens' assemblies could easily be cited for the same fundamental problems, even though most are not "siloed" as in the French case. The UK Citizens' Assembly on Brexit had a similar recruitment method without a control and had a sample of only 50 citizens. However, by using the vote in the 2016 Brexit referendum it had a proxy for at least some measure of attitudinal representativeness.[68] The justly famous Irish Citizens' Assembly on abortion had a sample "skewed" in its initial opinions, so far as the key researchers can tell. In an admirable effort to investigate this question, they found the skew in the first questionnaire administered on abortion (the topic of the assembly) in the third weekend of deliberation. In addition, they had a question at the recruitment stage that asked whether participants were in favor of or against changing the constitution. Although a separate national sample at the time showed 22% of the Irish population against changing the constitution, the deliberative sample of 99 persons had only 5%. In short, the opponents of any amendment to change the constitution, including the liberalization of abortion, were very much underrepresented.[69] The researchers rightly point to other elements of balance in the proceedings. Nevertheless, the same question arises: if the minipublic is not like the electorate at the start, why should everyone listen to where it ends up?

None of these criticisms should detract from the spectacular success of the Irish Citizens' Assemblies in engaging citizens to deliberate about an agenda for referendums that then can go on the ballot for all the citizens to vote upon. We will return to this excellent idea in our catalogue of reforms for a more deliberative society in Chapter 5.

In conclusion, I believe these design criteria have implications for the credibility (and interpretability) of the results of any citizen deliberation. The aim should be to create appropriately representative samples and to evaluate the deliberative process in them. To return to Lafont's challenge, if those who are *not* chosen to be in the random sample are not given credible evidence both that the sample is representative at the start and that the deliberations are balanced and thoughtful, then why should the rest of us defer to the sample's conclusions?

The design criteria listed above apply to deliberative microcosms or minipublics that aim to arrive at recommendations that reflect what the public would think under stipulated good conditions for thinking about an issue. The Deliberative Poll, when done well, should satisfy these criteria. Other designs could, in principle, do so as well. As technology for political communication advances, new designs will surely emerge, maybe ones that we cannot even envisage now.

A key question going forward will be whether or not it is practical to scale this design to much larger populations. For scaling, the purpose will not be to represent the public opinion people would have, but rather to provide a social context whereby large numbers of people can arrive at their own considered judgments about what they actually think about key policy isues. This is a key step in creating a more deliberative society.

Is it Scalable?

The online version of Deliberative Polling, and indeed, of other deliberative processes, suggests strategies for more cost-effective and realistic implementations of scaling the deliberative process. The online deliberations implemented in the two projects just discussed—"climate and energy" and "democratic reform"—were conducted via the Stanford Online Deliberation Platform.[70] In theory, it can handle any number of small groups (of approximately ten persons in each group) in synchronous video-based discussions. The process is AI assisted and moderates itself, with a queue for talking time (currently set at 45 seconds per intervention). It nudges speakers who are not participating, intervenes for uncivil language, produces nearly instant transcripts of all the discussions to document the arguments for research purposes, orchestrates the movement of the discussions through an agenda of proposals and initial pros and cons of each proposal, and coordinates each group in identifying its two most important questions for the plenary sessions. Evaluations of the platform by participants show ratings as high as or higher than projects with human moderators.[71] In the climate project, 93% thought the platform provided an opportunity for everyone to participate in the discussions and 92% thought the whole process was valuable. Indeed, we had many requests for repeat participation or the chance to recommend it to a friend (something we have not done for representative samples but which could be done for scaling).⁷²

For scaling deliberation, it would be possible to include those who are recommended by their friends. The goal of scaling is not to get a representative sample to estimate the considered judgments of a population. That is the goal of Deliberative Polling and at least some other minipublics. But scaling can have the goal of affecting the participants by creating more engaged and informed citizens. We envision scaling in two forms. First, as costs plummet with the platform (and even better ones to be developed in the future), we can envision a proliferation of deliberating microcosms (Deliberative Polls or other designs) with good samples. Second, the technology can make scaling easier for those who are not in the random samples. There can be hundreds of thousands or even millions of small groups deliberating on the same model. Their questions can feed into periodic convening of the plenary sessions broadcast online. This scenario is particularly plausible with an institution like Deliberation Day if it were convened before a national election so that the public interest was high.⁷³

5
Institutions for a More Deliberative Society

Two of the historical cases discussed here would seem, at first glance, to be irrelevant to modern democratic reform. First, I have in mind Athenian practices in the fifth and fourth centuries BC. And second, the theory of the role of deliberation put forward by Madison in *The Federalist*, a theory which was quickly overtaken by the emergence of political parties.

The Athenian case would seem irrelevant to modern debates, first because the polity was so small by modern standards and second because the system was so utterly different from modern practices. While the total population of Athens was much larger, the number of adult male citizens (the eligible electorate) ranged between only 30,000 and 60,000.[1] Athens did not have elections for most of the major offices and institutions. It did not have what we would recognize as political parties, although there was some factional behavior.[2] In the 2,400 or so years since, the intermittent struggles around the world with the democratic idea have largely gone in a different direction.[3] Versions of representative democracy with organized political parties, with different electoral systems, with varying degrees of federalism, with presidential or parliamentary systems, were all applied within the framework of party-competition democracy.

Yet there are three lessons we can draw from ancient Athenian practices that are, in fact, relevant to modern democratic reform, even for those democratic systems that operate principally through elections with party competition. First, random samples of adequate size can be used to represent the deliberations of the whole citizenry on issues that are consequential: in Athens this occured in the Council of 500 (which set the agenda for the Assembly), in the courts (which had juries of 500 or more), in the *graphe paranomon* (a special court for prosecuting illegal or irresponsible proposals in the Assembly), and in the *nomothetai* (another court-like institution with a jury of 500 or more that had the final say on whether a proposal from the Assembly could become law).[4] Second, the use of these institutions was so pervasive that together they constituted a kind of rotation method, where each citizen could be expected, in effect, to rule and to be ruled in turn. This experience surely had a socializing effect on all who participated, as J. S. Mill and modern commentators such as Mogens Herman Hansen, Josiah Ober, Jane Mansbridge, and others have speculated.[5] Third, some of the institutions constituted by random selection (from the list of citizens who made themselves available) seem explicitly designed to provide a thoughtful (and democratic) brake on the passions that might be stirred up by orators in the Assembly.[6] Deliberation in an organized setting, as in the Athenian institutions just listed, was seen as an antidote to the passions of what we would now call populism.

These uses of a kind of stratified random sampling (ordered by tribe), often conducted with the *kleroterion* machine built for the purpose, were intended and may have actually served to do what Madison so many centuries later advocated: they helped "cure the mischiefs of faction" through deliberation. In Madison's terms, they helped tame the passions and interests that might motivate factions adverse to the rights of others or to the aggregate interests of the community. For the Athenians, the populist passions in the Assembly, often stirred up by the orators, were a main problem and the cure they tried to implement was some version of deliberation in jury-like institutions selected by lot—before, during, and after the direct democracy in the Assembly.

Just as the Athenian design might seem irrelevant, at first glance, to modern commentators, so does Madison's theory. Madison's vision of the Constitution made no provision for political parties. But his aim was to arrive at the "cool and deliberate sense of the community" through representatives who would "refine and enlarge the public views by passing them through the medium of a chosen body of citizens," as he famously put it. Deliberation by representatives was supposed to provide an important bulwark against tyranny of the majority, as we saw in *Federalist* 10. The ideal was that they would deliberate for the common good rather than just calculate their personal and political interests. As we have argued, it is evident that the deliberations of representatives have since been overwhelmed by "the spirit of party," as Washington warned.

However, we have found that the "cure" which Madison prescribed for representatives,[7] essentially the same cure that the Athenians attempted to implement with random samples of ordinary citizens—deliberation in an organized design—can have the intended effect.[8] This seems amply supported in our modern national deliberative experiments, at least when they are conducted with the design advocated here.

Deliberative institutions can depolarize our most extreme partisan divisions, they can create more deliberative voters (who vote their sincere policy views, even after a considerable passage of time), and they can strengthen norms central to the guardrails of democracy, especially the norms that protect the conduct of elections.

If deliberations on an organized design can have these effects, how can institutions be constructed, compatible with the basic framework of party-competition democracy, to greatly enhance the frequency and scale of such deliberative processes?[9] Some would argue this is a fool's errand. Dennis Thompson, as we noted earlier,[10] argued that deliberation *about* elections could be very productive, but deliberation *in* elections or about matters up for election would be quickly overwhelmed by partisanship. Yet our field experiments were conducted in the US near the start of our elongated primary season and with implications for the effects of deliberation right up until Election Day. Some of them have even been conducted in dialogue with politicians, including presidential candidates, running for office.

The overall result of the sketch I advocate here is a number of targeted, deliberative interventions. If we add them up, I believe the impact would be transformative, producing a system that should satisfy our criteria for popular control. But it is not an all-or-nothing proposition, but rather an agenda of experimentation. Within each domain of decision, each reform is justifiable in its own right. Together they give an overall picture of institutions that are recognizably similar to those we have, but with enhanced roles for deliberative components to help facilitate thoughtful popular control.

Imagine the effects on our individual and collective civic capacities if we could accomplish two goals: first, greatly increase the frequency of deliberations in microcosm. These deliberations with random samples should be on the Deliberative Polling model (or on any other models, existing or developed in the future, that satisfy our design criteria stated earlier). Second, develop strategies for scaling up the model to approximate mass deliberation. We will mention two: spreading deliberation in schools as a form of civic education and convening the entire country in a scaled-up version of innumerable small group discussions on the Deliberative Poll model. That is an aspiration that Bruce Ackerman and I termed "Deliberation Day."[11]

Proliferate Deliberative Minipublics

Let's begin with the first goal, the proliferation of minipublics.

On Major National Issues at the Start of the Primary Season

Many candidates are almost unknown at the start of the presidential selection process, and polling at that point often represents little more than name recognition. In some well-known cases (Jimmy Carter in 1976 emerging in Iowa and Gary Hart in 1984 emerging in New Hampshire), comparatively obscure candidates rose to prominence in early primaries in unrepresentative states, giving them momentum for the primaries that followed. Ideally, a thoughtful consultation on the issues and the candidates with a national sample would better set the stage for initiating momentum. Neither Iowa nor New Hampshire (or South Carolina, for that matter) are representative of the nation. In a multi-candidate field, a strong showing in a national Deliberative Poll as a prelude to the current process might provide a better basis for the emergence of candidates. After all, it would represent the considered judgments of a national sample that these candidates merit support. It would also occur at a time when that judgment could make a difference.

There have been two national pilots of this idea in the US—pilots in the sense that they embody aspects of what might be possible. In 1996, a national Deliberative Poll, with a sample of 466[12] selected by NORC at the University of Chicago, deliberated on the upcoming issues in the presidential primary campaign and engaged in a televised dialogue with presidential candidates hosted by Jim Lehrer. It was partly sponsored by the television network PBS which gave it nine hours of broadcast (including some repeat broadcasts), both distillations of the small group discussions and dialogues with the presidential candidates (who answered questions on the issues agreed in the small groups). There was not an open race on the Democratic side in 1996, but Vice President Al Gore represented the Democrats and four candidates represented the Republican side: Senator Richard Lugar, Senator Phil Gramm, Governor Lamar Alexander, and entrepreneur Steve Forbes. However, the Deliberative Poll questions covered the issues but did not include candidate evaluations.

The second pilot that tested parts of the idea was America in One Room in 2019, before the start of the 2020 presidential primary campaign. We have already described this project in some detail on the issues and on the creation of more deliberative voters, even a year later.[13] But here it is also worth noting its effect on the incentives for candidate behavior in the dialogue with the sample of America.[14]

The Deliberative Polling design had all the candidates answer questions from the entire sample. Instead of normal primary campaign events, where candidates interact with self-selected members of their own party, these candidates were interacting with a microcosm of the entire electorate, including, of course, members of the opposite party. The small groups were randomly assigned so the dialogue on the issues and the question formulations were the result of cross-party dialogue. Instead of a focus on "what is good for my party," the focus was on the general question of "what should be done," and perhaps, "what would be good for the country."

Five candidates appeared individually by video link to answer questions from the sample. Three Republican challengers to then President Donald Trump—former Massachusetts Governor William Weld, former Illinois congressman Joe Walsh, and former South Carolina Governor Mark Sanford. There were two Democratic candidates—Senator Michael Bennet of Colorado and former Housing Secretary Julian Castro.

The transformed political dialogue that this design stimulated is worth noting. Candidates clearly addressed their answers to the entire sample, rather than just their partisan base. Walsh, a former Tea Party ally, affirmed the rights of immigrants to receive due process in their asylum claims. Weld referred to Emma Lazarus (whose poem is inscribed on the pedestal to the Statue of Liberty) in praising the role of immigrants in American society. On the Democratic side, Senator Bennet questioned whether a "one-size-fits-all" approach at the national level was appropriate to raise the minimum wage to $15 an hour. On immigration, Former Secretary Castro argued for a pathway to citizenship for the undocumented who had committed no serious crime. We need immigrants, he argued, to maintain "a young and vibrant work force," to keep the Social Security Trust Fund solvent in the face of a declining birth rate and a coming wave of retirements among baby boomers. This was obviously a way of framing the argument that would appeal across the political spectrum to keep social security afloat. The result was a consistent pattern of Republicans appealing to and getting support from Democrats, and Democrats appealing to and getting support from Republicans. Compared to the control group, there was a remarkable gap of up to thirty points in support from the opposite party for each candidate after deliberation, compared to their support in the control group (who were not part of the deliberations). These striking results are detailed in Appendix 2.[15]

Imagine if a national and highly visible Deliberative Poll on this design were to take place at the start of the primary season before Iowa, New Hampshire, South Carolina and the other early states. The current incentives for extreme rhetoric, which come from candidates focusing exclusively on base voters, would be moderated by this design. The key is that an infrastructure for sponsoring and televising this kind of non-partisan evidence-based dialogue would need to be established.

On Major National and/or Statewide Issues for which there is Stalemate or Deep Division

We have already discussed how South Korea used a national Deliberative Poll to resolve the issue of whether or not to continue construction of two nuclear reactors (Shin Gori 5 and 6) and how national Deliberative Polls in Japan were used to resolve the deeply contested issues of pension reform and the nation's energy choices after the Fukushima disaster. The deliberations of the people provided a clear resolution that could be invoked by politicians as a basis for decision. In both the Japanese and Korean cases, there had been a history of successful and visible deployments of the Deliberative Poll.[16] In the Korean case and the Japanese deliberation on energy choices, the government sponsored an elaborate infrastructure of expert committees to prepare the balanced agenda and the briefing materials. In the Japanese pension case, this infrastructure was provided by civil society and the Center for Deliberative Polling at Keio University (working with media partners). Whatever the sponsorship, these projects arguably had significant effects on policy. Such cases suggest the usefulness of creating a national administrative mechanism, to make it easier to create credible non-partisan deliberations without each effort having to recreate the essential components anew.

Convene Deliberations to Set the Agenda for Ballot Propositions

In the US many states have the initiative whereby signatures must be collected to qualify a proposition to go on the ballot for a statewide (or local) election. For statewide initiatives in large states such as California, the cost of collecting the millions of signatures required[17] is an onerous impediment to public interest ballot propositions getting on the ballot. If it costs $3 million or more to get the signatures, then a public interest group or coalition of non-profits is unlikely to have the resources to mount an effective campaign once its proposal has qualified and it has spent so much just to get on the ballot. This situation leaves the agenda-setting for initiatives mostly in the hands of well-financed interest groups or very wealthy individuals. This situation subverts the goal of the initiative, a key progressive reform, to provide an avenue for self-legislation by the people.

Deliberation could usefully enter at this agenda-setting stage. Suppose that there were periodic convenings of a deliberative microcosm of the state that would vet ballot propositions for which proponents had gathered a much lower minimum level of signatures. The entire process would need to be supervised by a non-partisan commission that appointed experts to vet the briefing materials and supervise the scientific process to ensure an adequate representative sample, etc. A few public service propositions could be selected each cycle to be examined by a Deliberative Poll-type mechanism. Those that are approved would go on the ballot with an explanation that they were selected by a random sample of 500 or so citizens. Over time, such a notation would give the selected propositions added credibility, particularly as the public became more and more used to public deliberation. Why require signatures at all? The process requires proponents who will carry the effort forward after the proposition goes on the ballot. A smaller number of signatures could be thought of as proof that the proponents can be taken seriously to undertake that task.

In 2011, we piloted this idea with a statewide Deliberative Poll, What's Next California?, which gave birth to a proposition that went on the ballot statewide. The sponsoring organization, the non-profit California Forward, successfully got Proposition 31 (an amalgam of a broad range of reform proposals that were supported by the deliberations) on the ballot, but at that point they had no resources left for a campaign. Some elements of the proposition were thought not to be to the advantage of some key special interests and the proposition went down. But we showed that the elements of the proposition, if it had been understood, were popular enough to have passed if people had considered and understood them.[18] If an institution were created to vet the proposals and handle the deliberations, there would be a steady stream of ballot proposals supported by the people, in microcosm, attempting to govern themselves. If the proposals, once on the ballot, were subject to further deliberation during the campaign process, that would make the reform even more effective.

Convene Deliberative Minipublics to Evaluate Ballot Propositions that are on the Ballot

Referendum campaigns have all the characteristics of other large-scale political campaigns in modern competitive democracies: Television advertising, social media, the spread of misinformation/disinformation, and efforts by the proponents and opponents to mobilize voters in the "ground game" to achieve turnout. Sometimes the voters are even more confused than in party-based elections because they don't have an explicit party cue to orient their votes. Referendum campaigns sometimes succeed by mobilizing the angry voices of populism, as in Brexit,[19] or racial bias as in a number of California initiatives, including the notorious Proposition 187 that attempted to expel undocumented immigrant children from the public schools.[20]

In several cases, adequately sized deliberative minipublics have been convened in collaboration with television networks and other media to provide a representative and informed judgment about referendum choices before the election.

In 1999 we worked with the non-profit Issues Deliberation Australia to mount a nationally televised Deliberative Poll before the referendum on whether Australia should become a republic. There was substantial broadcast on the Australian Broadcasting Corporation (ABC) and coverage by a print partner, *The Australian* newspaper,[21] as well as other press. A national random sample of 347 (selected by Newspoll) convened for the weekend of deliberations.

The Australian case set in motion a series of Deliberative Polls in Denmark under the leadership of Kasper Moller Hansen, now of the University of Copenhagen. The first was in 2000 before the referendum on whether or not Denmark should join the single European currency.[22] It was followed by four others sponsored by the Parliament and nationally broadcast, including one before the referendum in 2018 on whether Denmark should join the EU's home and justice legislation.

Denmark's Parliament has sponsored Deliberative Polls about referenda and contested policy issues to assist the public in making informed decisions. In that sense, they were meant to stimulate thought and reflection about the issues rather than simply provide a cue for voting.

Broadcast media is an effective way to put a human face on the issues. Ordinary citizens from across the political spectrum, representing the country in microcosm, are seen grappling with the pros and cons of a referendum or policy proposal and posing questions from their groups about what is most important from their perspectives.

However, there are other ways of effectively reaching voters with the conclusions of a deliberative minipublic before referenda. One proposal, from John Gastil, was to convene a "citizens' panel" before referendums or initiatives and have its recommendations placed on the ballot and in the voter guide.[23] A version of this has been institutionalized in the "Citizens' Initiative Review" (CIR), which convenes a small microcosm on the model of a "Citizens' Jury" to deliberate and make recommendations in the voter's guide. However, the numbers are so small on the Citizens' Jury model that reporting the vote of the jury, at least in close votes, would be statistically meaningless.[24] But if the microcosm were of adequate size and the results were put in the voter guide, as the CIR has usefully pioneered, that would be an effective way of reaching voters. Ideally, such a design could be combined with broadcast media to bring further attention to the issues in the upcoming referendum.

Corporations and Public Deliberation

If we aspire to scale experience with deliberative processes throughout the society, then a potential actor of great importance is the corporation. Large corporations affect large populations—their customers (or the public in general), their shareholders, and their employees. Millions of people live with the results, for better or worse, of corporate decisions motivated primarily by profit, but also sometimes by broader social considerations. There has long been a debate about bringing democratic participation, of some sort, to corporate decision-making.[25] Our narrower question is: Is there a way to incorporate *deliberative* democratic processes, at least on occasion, or on some issues, into corporate decision processes? Are there cases where corporations may have reason to do so?

We have already mentioned the Texas utilities cases, where all eight of the state's then regulated utilities sponsored Deliberative Polls in conjunction with the Public Utilities Commission about "Integrated Resource Planning"—how to deal with future electricity needs. In that case, the regulators required public consultation of some sort by the companies, and because of the large investments at stake, the companies had a need for a rigorously thoughtful and representative process.

Sometimes corporations have found it meaningful to consult the public with Deliberative Polling even outside any specific regulatory requirement. In 2022, Meta consulted a nearly global sample of the world's social media users, consisting of 6,500 deliberators and a comparably sized control group covering nine regions of the world, 32 countries, and 23 languages, about the ground rules for bullying and harassment in the Metaverse. Meta is, of course, a public company, but it was in effect consulting its global customer base about an important set of emergent questions—ground rules for behavior and who should enforce them in the innumerable virtual "worlds" that are rapidly being constructed.[26] The project led to four more about expectations and concerns about AI—in Brazil, the US, Spain, and Germany—with a total of 1,500 participants plus comparable pre–post control groups.[27] These projects gave the company guidance about the novel policy issues it was facing. Most importantly, the guidance was representative and thoughtful from the perspective of the public that would have to live with the results. If this became a new norm for major corporations, it could greatly scale experience with the deliberative process throughout the society.

One could also imagine corporations consulting random samples of their employees for deliberations about novel issues affecting the workplace or worker benefits. Ideally, unions and management and a committee of outside experts could develop and vet briefing materials for such deliberations. There may be cases where the results from deliberations can narrow the issues that might otherwise be subject to collective bargaining and/or strikes.

A last area for reform is the connection to shareholders. Shareholder resolutions often about ESG (environmental, social, and governance) topics are proliferating rapidly.[28] Much of the voting on behalf of shareholders takes place through asset managers voting on behalf of the actual owners of the shares. If the large asset managers were to sponsor online Deliberative Polls to get clarity on what the actual owners of the shares really wanted, then shareholder democracy could be seriously invigorated. Perhaps you, as a shareholder, do not have a clear view about a proxy issue, but then why should you let the asset manager through which you have an account make the decision about what you prefer? Deliberative Polling would empower shareholders, it would spread informed views on public issues, and it would contribute significantly to a more deliberative society. Like the deliberations on ballot propositions for governance, it would spread appropriate heuristics summarizing how the public came out and for what reasons, on shareholder propositions. Such a development could reform shareholder democracy in a way quite parallel to the reform of government by initiatives (accompanied by deliberation) for public policy. If the Securities and Exchange Commission created regulations that would facilitate this kind of consultation, it could spread, just as it spread in Texas after the Public Utility Commission encouraged Deliberative Polls for electricity choices.

Institutionalize Deliberative Minipublics

The deliberative minipublics discussed so far have essentially been one-time events. As we just noted, the eight Texas Deliberative Polls on Integrated Resource Planning for the provision of electricity were quasi-institutionalized by the Public Utility Commission in that each regulated utility was expected to conduct one. However, when the electricity industry in Texas de-regulated, many argued that the market made it unnecessary to consult the public. The public would make its choices in the market. However, an individual choice about whom to buy electricity from is not the same as a public policy choice about the planning for long-term needs with the policy pros and cons and their impact on the community. There is a difference between the considerations at issue depending on whether we are acting as consumers or as citizens. Nevertheless, the quasi-institutionalization of Deliberative Polling was ended by deregulation.

Another example of institutionalization, but in this case actually enshrined in law, is the "Law on Deliberative Polling" in Mongolia.[29] Before the

Parliament can consider a proposal for a constitutional amendment, it must conduct a national Deliberative Poll about the proposal (or proposals). The law lays out very specific criteria for the Deliberative Poll, including sample sizes and sample recruitment, usually under the supervision of the National Statistical Office of Mongolia (which does the Census), an independent Advisory Committee which has control over the agenda and all the basic components of the process. This process has now been used twice to make constitutional amendment recommendations to the Parliament that have actually led to the successful passage of two new amendments to the constitution.[30]

Congress and Public Deliberation

Imagine a mechanism whereby congressional committees and/or the House or Senate as a whole can commission a public deliberation on a deeply contested topic. If there were an arms-length institution that could be entrusted with the production of balanced briefing materials and the scientific management of the deliberative process, Deliberative Polls or other deliberative minipublics could be convened to make recommendations about an agreed policy topic. The Congressional Research Service (Library of Congress) comes to mind as the kind of non-partisan, evidence-based institution that could do it or serve as a model. Such a mechanism would be especially important on difficult issues for which many members might not have a predetermined position. The logic of support for a public deliberation would be similar to President Moon's support for a deliberation on whether to complete the Shin Gori nuclear reactors or the Japanese government's decision to sponsor a national Deliberative Poll to choose among energy options after the Fukushima disaster. When the choice is difficult it may be useful to bring in a nationally representative sample to have a thoughtful public deliberation, to see what the people would really want if they were able to focus on the tradeoffs and become more informed.[31]

Deliberation in the Schools

Imagine if deliberations on the organized design discussed here were a common part of the high-school curriculum in schools around the US. If the deliberations often focused on fundamental issues in American democracy, we have already seen that such deliberations would likely increase support for the guardrails of electoral democracy. Active discussion according to a balanced, organized design is likely to improve learning and also foster democratic norms. The active experience of deliberation is also likely to foster tolerance and mutual respect, as we have seen around the world on highly contentious topics.

A recent comprehensive report, *Educating for American Democracy*, makes the case that "America's Constitutional Democracy Requires Better Civic and History Education."[32] The argument is not just about the need for increased knowledge levels but also, in an age of polarization and contention, the need to foster norms such as "civil disagreement" and "civic friendship." The first—learning to disagree with mutual tolerance based on the merits of the argument—is often a by-product of deliberative democracy. And "civic friendship reminds us that we should all regard one another as fellow Americans capable of sharing ideals, principles, and constitutional forms of self-government even as we vigorously debate our philosophical or policy differences."[33] This kind of mutual trust and respect for those we disagree with is also commonly a result of our deliberative design.

Over the last two decades there have been a number of applications of the Deliberative Polling model in schools. Some have been national deliberations with students randomly selected from across the country. Some have been projects in specific schools or school districts. In many cases students have taken the lead in developing balanced and evidence-based briefing materials for the deliberations following our template. Generally, the results from high-school students are very similar to those from the adult population.[34] It might seem surprising that a widespread curricular reform in high schools around the country could have a long-term effect on democratic norms, preparing the entire population for participation in a more deliberative society. Yet all our experience supports the conclusion that organized deliberation in the schools would likely have such an effect.

Deliberation Day

Most of our discussion thus far has focused on Deliberative Polls that gather stratified random samples of a population to deliberate under stipulated good conditions. We have shown, in a variety of contexts, how these deliberations clarify the public will on an issue, and how they tend to depolarize issues when there is strong partisan contention about them. Such projects constitute advice to policy-makers and to the broader public and civil society. They are representations of what the public really would think if it could discuss the issues in depth and get its questions answered, in an evidence-based way, from different points of view. Sometimes these projects play critical roles in actual decision-making. But the limitation is that the participants are only a minuscule fraction of the entire electorate. That is an advantage in their being cost-effective. But it is a disadvantage in terms of their impact on the broader population.

Deliberation Day is the idea of a national convening for mass participation in many, many small groups, of deliberations conducted on the same model as the Deliberative Poll. Instead of random samples, the participants would, ideally, be the vast bulk of the electorate. When Bruce Ackerman and I made this proposal in 2004, we were thinking of face-to-face deliberations in communities around the country.[35] While we proposed assigning people regionally, there was still a problem that so many areas are red and so many are blue that many of the groups would likely be more homogeneous than most of the small groups in representative microcosms.[36]

However, if the deliberations were to take place on our online platform (or any improved successors to the platform as technology moves apace) then that problem disappears with appropriate algorithms for assignment to the small groups. Participants from far and wide can be assigned to the same small groups of ten or so, and if there are enough small groups then obviously the entire population could participate. Rural and urban and suburban from different states could all be drawn into the same small groups (perhaps from the same or adjacent time zones). Many online plenary sessions with balanced panels of competing experts or advocates could be organized so that the questions from the small groups are answered just as in a Deliberative Poll. The experience can be made very comparable to a Deliberative Poll, except that it is shared by millions. We already have a great deal of evidence that the online platform is evaluated as highly by participants as human moderators and other elements in the face-to-face deliberations. We have also tested the platform in controlled experiments and gotten essentially the same results as human moderators on Zoom calls or human moderators in a face-to-face condition.[37] Hence, we have some assurance that if we scaled the deliberative experience to very large numbers using the online platform (or successors), the deliberative scaling would likely have comparable effects. As a result, the post-deliberation opinions would no longer represent a hypothetical (what the people would think) but instead the far more consequential force of the country's actual judgments.

Imagine a commission or institutional structure to organize Deliberation Day in conjunction with televised Deliberative Polling (a) at the beginning of the primary season, (b) in the general election, and (c) before statewide ballots of special importance (perhaps before major constitutional changes). If the issues are important enough then give everyone a chance to deliberate.

The magic elixir that makes deliberation bring public will formation to life seems to be moderated discussion with diverse others. With technology this can now be achieved effectively and more cost-efficiently than at the time of the original Ackerman and Fishkin proposal.

Deliberation Day and the spread of deliberation in the schools provide two methods of mass scaling that complement the rotation method (the proliferation of many opportunities to be drawn into random samples). The combination of mass scaling and rotation provide the clear prospect of creating a more deliberative society.

Deliberative Referendums for Constitutional Change

The idea of a deliberative referendum suggests one viable approach to instilling deliberation in a constitutional amendment process. The US has arguably the most challenging constitutional amendment process of any democratic republic. Article 5 requires a two thirds vote of each house of Congress and then ratification by three quarters of the states. Or, there is the alternative of a new constitutional convention, never tried, called into being by three quarters of the states and posing the risk of a runaway convention. Recall that our original constitutional convention was supposedly strictly limited in its mandate to revising the Articles of Confederation.[38] In any case our current constitution undergoes dramatic changes outside the formal specifications of Article 5, via constitutional moments, the passage of "super statutes" which provide a normative framework for further judicial interpretation,[39] and the political mobilization for constitutional change that results in the appointment of judges who will reinterpret existing provisions, sometimes radically. This process has come to be called "popular constitutionalism."[40]

Can we imagine a specified procedure that would clearly contribute to popular control, that would embody deliberation at key points? One current example is the Mongolian system, now used successfully for two amendments. The Mongolian system, specified by the Law on Deliberative Polling, is path-breaking as an example of institutionalization, but in an ideal world the reform could be carried even further. Both the participatory and deliberative elements could be further enhanced.

Some key points:

1. In the Mongolian case, there was a large-scale public suggestion process in meetings around the country that put forth proposals to a commission or "Deliberative Council."

2. The Deliberative Council, which is non-partisan and independent of Parliament, distilled these recommendations into a manageable number that could be deliberated on in a national Deliberative Poll.
3. The results of the national Deliberative Poll went to Parliament for debate and consideration.
4. Eventually a new amendment was crafted that passed Parliament by a two-thirds majority.

While this process has many merits as currently conducted,[41] we can imagine further enhancing both the deliberative and participatory components. While there is no history of national referendums in the US, only ballot propositions at the state level, we might imagine a Deliberative Referendum, to be convened twice. It might work like this:

1. An independent commission would be convened by act of Congress.
2. That commission would receive suggestions for a new amendment from state legislatures or from civil society. The commission would select a manageable number of proposals to be considered in a national Deliberative Poll.
3. The commission would report the results to Congress which can formulate a final amendment proposal. That proposal would have to pass both houses of Congress and be signed by the President to be the subject of the Deliberative Referendum
4. There would then be a national referendum accompanied by a national convening of Deliberation Day aimed to effectively stimulate mass participation in a full day of deliberation about the proposed amendment.
5. If the amendment receives a national majority popular vote in the deliberative referendum then it must pass a second time two years later with the same process. If it passes both times it then becomes a new amendment to the constitution.

In between the first and second Deliberative Referendums there would likely be continuing debate and public deliberation. The double vote requirement is a protection against hasty or unwise decisions. There is no danger of a runaway process, as in a new convention, since the amendment as put forward by Congress and the President is the text that is voted on (twice). It embodies a kind of higher lawmaking because there is a strong deliberative element in the agenda-setting and in the evaluation. Most distinctively, it combines mass participation and deliberation to add up to a form of popular control on amendments deemed important enough to justify this elaborate process.[42]

Does Deliberation Serve Social Justice?

When deliberation "cures the mischiefs of faction," as Madison hypothesized, it tends to serve justice. It gives voice to the marginalized, it gives voice to interests and claims to be weighed in the deliberative process (interests that may otherwise have been neglected), and it moderates the passions that would vilify the less well-off. We saw this in the deliberative conclusions about policies toward the Roma in Bulgaria, toward the Aboriginals in Australia, and toward undocumented immigrants in the US (as well as other cases).[43]

Critics of deliberation have long asserted a different picture—that deliberation will simply act as a cover for the more advantaged to dominate the more vulnerable.[44] Critics believe that deliberative processes only mask social conformity and deference to the views of the more advantaged without authentically weighing the force of the better argument. The punchline of the critics' arguments is that the interests (and greater ability to advocate) of the more privileged will supposedly determine the conclusions.

Recall what we found in investigating these claims by looking at the movements of 2,744 group/issue combinations in 21 Deliberative Polls from around the world on a variety of topics.[45] A key question was whether the groups moved on the various issues in the direction advocated by the more advantaged. The clear pattern supports the opposite conclusion. In our study of these many group/issue combinations, the movements were in the direction favored by the men only 28% of the time. They were in the direction favored by the more educated only 26% of the time, and they were in the direction favored by those with higher income only 28% of the time. While the percentage of the movements is only one indicator (a similar conclusion is supported by the magnitudes rather than the frequency of the movements), it shows that the less advantaged arguably had more weight in the discussions rather than less.[46] Perhaps the more privileged had more to learn about the lives of the poor and less educated (and men had more to learn about the lives of women) than the reverse. In a format designed to encourage civil, evidence-based discussion and mutual respect, the perspectives of the disadvantaged were more likely than not to carry the day, whether the issue was crime, housing, healthcare, or topical political issues such as immigration reform. This is evident from the direction of movement of most of the group/issue combinations. It suggests that if we had a more deliberative society we would, as a by-product, eventually have a more just one (at least as evaluated by generally Rawlsian standards focused on the interests of the less well-off or even the least well-off). Such a consequence, by broadly serving the interests of the less advantaged, would also be more enabling for them to be full participants in the deliberative and other political processes. Tantalizingly, these results suggest the possibility of a virtuous circle, at least with ever-greater implementation of deliberation over the long term.

The design of the Deliberative Poll is a successor to a long tradition of attempts to devise a decision procedure for ethics, or ethically charged disagreements. The participants in the Deliberative Poll are a representative sample and have competing value-laden goals: They grapple with the trade-offs posed by issues such as freedom to choose one's own health-care versus a government program that provides for everyone (but which may require some to give up even better coverage in "Medicare for all"), granting rights to the undocumented versus the costs of more generous immigration policies, and the benefits of re-establishing or expanding nuclear power in South Korea or Japan (for clean energy and climate change) versus the risks to safety from a technology whose performance has failed in at least one dramatic case in the region.[47] These are all conflicts among value-laden goals that impinge in different ways on the interests and concerns of different members of the community. How can all these claims be considered impartially?

One strategy would be to abstract from these differences. When John Rawls began to consider decision procedures, he was impressed by the economist John Harsanyi's famous calculation that from behind "a veil of ignorance," in which one could know nothing in particular about one's self or one's social position, there was an argument for average utility as the first principle of decision.[48] However, Rawls did not think that utilitarianism (average or total) was a plausible first principle. It too easily put at risk the life chances of some for the sake of greater benefits to others.

When Rawls first went into these waters, he proposed "An Outline of a Decision Procedure for Ethics,"[49] but the outline did not have the rigorous deductive structure he thought he needed to resolve what he later called 'the priority problem" (to establish a first principle that should always have priority without any need for "intuitionistic" balancing of competing considerations). With the veil of ignorance later built into the "original position" (the design for decision-making on first principles), he was able to achieve the rigor he desired, provided the reader could accept certain assumptions. His proposed conclusion: a general conception of justice in which there was a minimum that needed to be maximized for the share of "primary goods" (the essential goods everyone should want regardless of whatever else they want).

As I have argued in detail elsewhere, this argument is only compelling when the minimum is very stark. In that case, one might not reasonably want to risk falling below such a bare minimum for the sake of possible gains above the minimum. But if the minimum is very stark, and does not keep rising, it leaves most questions of trade-offs among public policies unsettled.

Why not just agree with Rawls on giving priority to *maximin*, a minimum that must keep rising so far as possible? Maximin has many irrationalities, such as preferring less in total, less equally. Furthermore, it can violate a principle of "general advantage," making most people worse off.[50] For the sake of a slight increase in the bottom level, we can prefer making a much more unequal society in which most people are worse off (even though those at the very bottom are a little better off) and there is also less well-being or prosperity all around.

In my view, after decades of debate about what could plausibly come out of the original position, the best seems to be a partial solution, a kind of guaranteed minimum, which would then lead most policy questions up to "intuitionistic" balancing in particular cases. Rawls implies as much with his "four stage sequence" in which the most general principle is first decided and then more and more particular policy choices are introduced with more information taking account of the particular facts at each level of choice.

Rawls redid the argument from his 1971 *Theory of Justice* some years later with more controversial assumptions, attempting to justify what he called "the Priority of Liberty."[51] But the more controversial the assumptions going into the original position, the more easily escapable are the conclusions that come out of it. The argument comes perilously close to assuming what it purports to prove.[52]

My conclusion from decades of debate about "the theory of justice" is that it identifies a priority very usefully distinct from utilitarianism or the general welfare. In that respect it has transformed debate about the first principles of a liberal democratic society. But it has not successfully transformed the question of moral priorities into a calculation of the interests of anyone from behind a veil of ignorance. Interpreted properly, it reveals a very different emphasis than average utility (or classical utilitarianism for that matter), and restores justice versus the general welfare to constituting one of the great tradeoffs to bring to any policy position. These tradeoffs deserve to be the subject of public deliberation, not merely calculation by philosophers or policy experts.

In making this point, note that I am bringing back social context and particularity, the very aspects that Rawls thought we must radically abstract from. However, the limitation of real people deliberating is that they do not solve the issue in general. At best, they solve it for their society in that context of policy debate. If that is the case, why do we need a procedure? Because it systematically brings in voices and perspectives that would otherwise likely be left out. And instead of abstracted voices, the people can speak authentically about their actual experiences. That is what real people do when they share their reasons for supporting or opposing policy proposals that may affect their lives, or their rights, or the viability of their communities.

Deliberation and Future Generations

The methods of deliberative democracy require a dialogue among the living. But what about decisions that impact future generations? Including even those in the distant future? Standard methods of policy analysis simply deal with such issues through a social discount rate. But as social and natural sciences progress, we can be more and more confident about the causal impact of policy decisions now on the further future. As the late philosopher Derek Parfit pointed out, "according to a Social Discount Rate of 5%, one statistical death next year counts for more than a billion deaths in 400 years."[53] He recommended abandoning the social discount rate for the very long term and discounting for the *probability* of effects not for pure time preference. Long-term effects that have a high probability of occurring should not be erased from consideration purely for time preference, even though no one now alive will experience them. These are sometimes called "sleeper effects." For example, we are making policy decisions now on the disposal of nuclear waste, in full knowledge that it will be deadly, if not properly stored, for tens of thousands of years. The almost inevitable short-termism among the living, and especially of most conventional democratic processes, would provide little comfort that the long-term interests of future generations will be adequately safeguarded. The electoral incentives of politicians focus on answering the questions: "What have you done for me lately and what will you do for me shortly?" Voters have short-term time horizons, so politicians face pressures to keep the same focus.

However, there is suggestive evidence that when the public deliberates it is capable of enlarging the time horizon. This was evident for example in America in One Room: Climate and Energy, where the state of the planet in the longer term was the focus—and the motivation—for support of policies now. One of the considerations in support of the many policy options for reducing greenhouse gas emissions was "We should take serious action to reduce greenhouse gases in our atmosphere because waiting to do so is taking an irresponsible risk with our kids' future"[54]—our kids', and presumably their kids' as well. Another suggestive result is that in a Deliberative Poll in South Korea on the storage of spent nuclear fuel, there was a 28-point increase from

32% to 61% in the willingness to pay a significant surcharge on everyone's electricity bills to more adequately store spent nuclear fuel.[55] This is a massive increase in the willingness to pay more now to benefit the long-term future.

In addition to the challenge of the long time intervals involved, deliberations about future generations pose conundrums about the size of our successor populations. Our policies now can have foreseeable effects on how many people will constitute future generations in both the immediate and long term. Sometimes this is a matter of intention. China's famous "one child" policy stemmed population growth but has had drastic effects that continue long after the policy was abandoned. The country will have a dramatically aging population and, likely, a less dynamic economy as the long-term consequence. On the other hand, all over the developing world the education of girls and women has many favorable consequences including a sharp decline in unsustainable birth rates. Evaluation of the long-term consequences of these kinds of choices could be tested in deliberations posing different well-developed scenarios. But this is work still to be done.

By what criteria do we evaluate such choices? There are no obvious general solutions and the field is in controversy among experts. Economists committed to applying cost–benefit analysis, a version of aggregate utilitarianism, can logically be led to endorse immensely large populations that live at a low level of well-being.[56] Another solution is average utility (maximizing the average rather than the total level), which is completely insensitive to the size of populations but which just takes the average level of whatever people happen to exist. But logically, a single-minded commitment to average utility would endorse a very small future population for the entire world if it lived at a high level.[57] Rather than a single canonical principle, we seem to be in a world of tradeoffs applied carefully in context. Deliberative democracy, if applied to specific policy choices, would allow the people of a given society to thoughtfully decide how to deal with such problems. Ideally, an expert commission would convene the deliberations of the people along the lines we have been exploring here. Otherwise, we could easily blunder into the future without any real consideration for the interests of those who will succeed us.

If Deliberation with Random Samples Works So Well, Why Not Just Eliminate Elections?

Some scholars have advocated simply replacing the common apparatus of parties competing in elections with democratic processes focused largely or entirely on "sortition," the practice of convening random samples of the electorate to deliberate.[58] Most of these proposals are based on the citizens' jury or citizens' assembly model, where relatively small samples (50 or up to 150) deliberate for many months to produce a set of agreed recommendations or draft legislation.

We have already discussed the limitations of this model:

1. The samples are too small for the opinion changes and the representativeness (including attitudinal representativeness) to be analyzed in a statistically meaningful way.[59]
2. The citizens' jury and citizens' assembly models aim for an agreed product—a verdict or draft law. Such a process likely distorts the process of public will formation as the participants face social pressure to go along with the consensus. This contrasts with the Deliberative Poll, where the considered judgments are offered in confidential questionnaires to protect the final opinions from social pressure. Hence, there is a likelihood that the very problem the deliberations are intended to solve—defective or distorted public will formation—will be recreated by this design. This argument applies to domination by the more advantaged and to Sunstein's "Law of Group Polarization." Both problems are more likely to occur with anything like the jury model or other consensus-seeking designs.[60]
3. A third limitation is the difficulty of recruiting a representative sample that will be willing to devote months or a year or two to the deliberations. The greater the commitment demanded, the more likely it is that those who agree to participate will have strong views on the subject at the outset, thus raising questions about the representativeness of the sample. Earlier, we saw evidence of this in both the Irish abortion case and the French Citizens' Convention on Climate.[61]

While these models are evolving, it is likely that at least the first two limitations are connected. If an entire group is to produce a consensus document, it will likely encounter some upper limits on size if there is to be genuine and equal engagement by all the members.[62] Of course, the overall group can be subdivided as in the Deliberative Polling design (and in some citizens' assemblies). But then the active drafting of the proposed laws will be by subgroups (or selected subgroups) and the rest of the sample may have limited opportunities to deliberate about the substance at issue (as in the French Citizens' Convention on Climate). However, we can anticipate all kinds of innovations in future versions of these designs. But for the moment we can focus on designs that satisfy all of our criteria.

The Deliberative Polling design satisfies all our criteria, but it is not suitable for replacing the legislature or the executive of any government. It can usefully provide input to such entities. It can support or oppose nuclear power options as with the South Korean and Japanese cases. It can screen proposals—approving some and disapproving others—as it has now twice done for constitutional amendments in Mongolia. But it is not designed to create an entire draft law. Once again, we can note that there is room for future innovation, just as with citizens' assemblies, but for the moment it is not designed to perform such a task.

However, suppose that with innovation there is a version of a deliberating minipublic chosen via random sampling that thoughtfully performs essential government functions such as writing new laws or choosing the President. Could we then do without elections, largely or entirely? As many now advocate, could we replace elections with sortition?

Helene Landemore has ambitiously proposed such a redesign. As with our analysis, she focuses on a design that combines the Athenian ideals of rotation and sortition because it is "the combination of sortition and rotation that ensures equal access to all citizens over time." The challenge is that "if the number of seats and the frequency of rotation are insufficient for everyone to plausibly expect to rule someday, then the comparative advantage of lotteries over elections becomes quite thin."[63] Her solution is to propose "the multiplication of smaller jury-like assemblies (fifty people or fewer) at all levels of the polity, hoping that the statistical representativeness one gets with large, randomly selected assemblies is achieved at the system level." She cites approvingly the permanent council of 29 persons randomly selected in the German-speaking part of Belgium (for 76,000 residents). The idea is that most citizens would have a chance of being chosen over their lifetime. With a proliferation of these many small, randomly selected sites for deliberation, each citizen would have a real chance of substantive involvement in at least some decisions.[64]

Whatever the advantages for the ideal of rotation (giving everyone a chance to participate on some policy at some level at some time in life), such a plan does not satisfy our criteria for popular control. The multiplication of small citizens' assemblies or citizens' juries has the effect of siloing the decision process. Suppose a citizens' assembly decides a controversial issue such as access to abortion or eliminating social security or refusing to fund Medicare expansion, for residents at some level of government (national, state, or local). Perhaps it is a bad draw of the lottery that comes in very unbalanced on that issue. Or perhaps there is a sharply differential response rate from those who feel strongly. The fact that thousands of assemblies meet at different levels on different issues is not much solace to me, if I really care that rights to abortion must be protected, or that the social security system must not be drastically cut, or that the poor must have access to medical care. A simple bad draw of the lottery (or in differential responses to the invitation) could yield such an outcome and make me virtually powerless to do anything about it.[65] It would be little recompense if I am drawn into a different lottery to decide some other issue at some other level, say electricity regulation for my local community. Different siloed "assemblies" for different topics at different levels can leave me with no say at all on whatever issues happen to really matter to me.[66]

Contrast this with the system of deliberative elections outlined earlier in this chapter. On national issues where the parties offer the people meaningful choices, everyone would get a say (a vote) in a system that fosters the creation of deliberative voters. Of course, these choices would be about "packages" of issue positions offered by different parties, but the judgment would still be that, on balance, one package is preferred to another. Perhaps ranked-choice voting and fusion parties can provide further nuance to the choices among packages, and a deliberative infrastructure can make the voting decisions more thoughtful. On our proposal here, the decisions would be shared via more deliberative elections, not siloed as they are farmed out to small deliberative groups in the pure sortition model. To pursue my examples, the elimination of all abortion rights at the national level or the end of social security or the denial of medical care to the poor in a given community would be issues in which we all would have our say. As noted earlier, deliberations would supplement but not replace the electoral processes in which we all get to vote.

The same could be said for the selection of who governs. For example, on my proposal, the President could continue to be elected after a national campaign in which the contrasts are drawn in platforms and the salient issues are discussed in microcosm as well as in the gigantic mobilization of small groups we call Deliberation Day. The opportunities to participate are spread far more widely than in the pure sortition model, but there is a greater opportunity for the people's deliberative choices to have impact and to contribute to collective self-rule for the community as a whole, both about the major policy choices and about who governs. By contrast, in the pure sortition model, the answer to "who governs?" at least at the highest level is an executive "randomly selected from, say, a pool of vetted candidates."[67] This is a random draw limited in some way by vetting. It does not offer the citizenry popular control over the choice of the executive.

The pure sortition model sacrifices the value of participation for the great mass of voters in shared decisions. Instead, it offers participation in a myriad of disconnected decisions that fail to add up to popular control. Based on our empirical findings, we can expect deliberation in whatever context—schools, specific policy issues, Deliberation Day—to have the lasting effect of creating more deliberative voters. Instead of eliminating the opportunity for voters to exercise that capacity (as would happen in the pure sortition model), we should deploy deliberation to make popular control a reality. The people have the capacity to govern themselves. This approach just has to be nurtured by renovated institutions that give it expression.

Recall what Hamilton said in *Federalist* 1 at the beginning of the American experiment:

> [I]t seems to have been reserved to the people of this country, by their conduct and example, to decide the important question, whether societies of men are really capable or not of establishing good government from reflection and choice, or whether they are forever destined to depend for their political constitutions on accident and force.
>
> **(Hamilton, Federalist 1).**

The continuing renovation of the American republic and of other modern democracies should employ, as the American founders hoped, deliberation in the process of transformation and in the structure that results. Each generation should be able to utter the words "we the people" as the subject of an active verb in which they thoughtfully govern themselves.

Appendices

Appendix 1: Analysis across Deliberative Polls in "Deliberative Distortions"

Table A.1 Deliberative Polls analyzed for deliberative distortions

	Topics	n	Country/ countries	City/ region	Year	Mode	Policy Indices	Groups
1	Britain's role in the EU	238	UK		1995	F2F	4	16
2	National Health Service	230	UK		1998	F2F	11	15
3	British monarchy	258	UK		1996	F2F	4	15
4	UK general election	275	UK		1997	F2F	4	15
5	Making Australia a republic	347	Australia		1999	F2F	5	24
6	Crime	299	UK		1994	F2F	5	20
7	EU expansion, pension reform, foreign policy	344	EU*		2007	F2F	7	18
8	How to meet future electricity needs	216	US	CP&L Service Area†	1996	F2F	7	16
9	Prioritizing public works projects	233	China	Zeguo township	2005	F2F	9	16
10	Crime	278	Bulgaria		2007	F2F	5	17
11	Climate change, immigration	348	EU*		2009	F2F	2	25
12	Future of airport, revenue-sharing	132	US	New Haven, CT	2004	F2F	3	16
13	US foreign policy	340	US		2003	F2F	9	24
14	US foreign policy	245	US		2003	OL	9	15
15	US general election	246	US		2004	OL	6	15
16	US presidential primaries	434	US		2004	OL	3	16

Topics		n	Country/ countries	City/ region	Year	Mode	Policy Indices	Groups
17	Housing Policy	239	US	San Mateo, CA	2008	F2F	7	26
18	US foreign policy	454	US		2005	OL	11	30
19	How to meet future electricity needs	230	US	WTU Service Area†	1996	F2F	7	14
20	Economy, foreign policy, the family	466	US		1996	OL	9	30
21	How to meet future electricity needs	232	US	SWEPCO Service area†	1996	F2F	7	14
	Total	6,084					134	397

For mode: F2F means face to face; OL means online.
*All (then 27) Member-States of the EU.
†WTU = West Texas Utilities; CP&L = Central Power & Light; SWEPCO = Southwestern Electric Power.
Source: Appendix Tables A.1–A.3 are adapted from Luskin, Sood, Fishkin, et al., "Deliberative Distortions? Homogenization, Polarization, and Domination in Small Group Discussions."

Table A.2 Domination

A. Movement toward the mean initial position of men (percentage of group–issue movements)

DP		By All	By Women
1	Britain's role in the EU	.109	.234
2	National Health Service	.281	.393
3	British monarchy	.317	.417
4	UK general election	.367	.417
5	Making Australia a republic	.208	.313
6	Crime	.310	.370
7	EU expansion, pension reform, foreign policy	.278	.476
8	How to meet future electricity needs	.250	.417
9	Prioritizing public works projects	.222	.396
10	Crime	.275	.436
11	Climate change, immigration	.220	.400
12	Future of airport, revenue-sharing	.281	.375
13	US foreign policy	.259	.412

Continued

Continued

DP		By All	By Women
14	US foreign policy	.326	.489
15	US general election	.278	.511
16	US presidential primaries	.354	.500
17	Housing policy	.337	.490
18	US foreign policy	.391	.485
19	How to meet future electricity needs	.274	.429
20	Economy, foreign policy, the family	.330	.452
21	How to meet future electricity needs	.262	.381
Mean		**.282**	**.419**

B. Movement toward the mean initial position of the more educated

DP		By all	By less educated
1	Britain's role in the EU	.094	.250
2	National Health Service	.237	.393
3	British monarchy	.350	.483
4	UK general election	.183	.333
5	Making Australia a republic	.292	.479
6	Crime	.160	.350
7	EU expansion, pension reform, foreign policy	.278	.452
8	How to meet future electricity needs	.323	.479
9	Prioritizing public works projects	.153	.341
10	Crime	.118	.309
11	Climate change, immigration	.120	.340
12	Future of airport, revenue-sharing	.188	.406
13	US foreign policy	.247	.505
14	US foreign policy	.343	.388
15	US general election	.318	.477
16	US presidential primaries	.479	.604
17	Housing policy	.327	.495
18	US foreign policy	.352	.445
19	How to meet future electricity needs	.369	.452
20	Economy, foreign policy, the family	.356	.467
21	How to meet future electricity needs	.250	.345
Mean		**.264**	**.419**

C. Movement toward the mean initial position of the higher income

DP		By all Income frequency	By lower income frequency
2	National Health Service	.259	.370
4	UK general election	.200	.317
5	Making Australia a republic	.167	.208
8	How to meet future electricity needs	.271	.500
10	Crime	.350	.435
12	Future of airport, revenue-sharing	.033	.200
13	US foreign policy	.282	.435
14	US foreign policy	.319	.452
15	US general election	.356	.411
16	US presidential primaries	.563	.583
17	Housing policy	.327	.414
Mean		.284	.393

Table A.3 Polarization (percentage of group–issue combinations moving away from the midpoint)

DP		Frequency
1	Britain's role in the EU	.210
2	National Health Service	.376
3	British monarchy	.550
4	UK general election	.383
5	Making Australia a republic	.468
6	Crime	.430
7	EU expansion, pension reform, foreign policy	.379
8	How to meet future electricity needs	.594
9	Prioritizing public works projects	.427
10	Crime	.369
11	Climate change, immigration	.429
12	Future of airport, revenue-sharing	.656
13	US foreign policy	.690
14	US foreign policy	.489
15	US general election	.382
16	US presidential primaries	.596

Continued

Table A.3 *Continued*

DP		Frequency
17	Housing policy	.465
18	US foreign policy	.426
19	How to meet future electricity needs	.622
20	Economy, foreign policy, the family	.230
21	How to meet future electricity needs	.634
Mean		**.467**

Appendices 141

Appendix 2: America in One Room: Presidential candidates

Summary results for presidential candidates who attended America in One Room

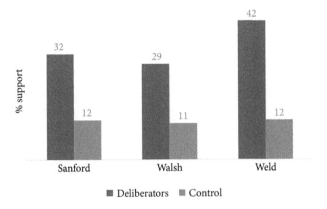

Figure A.1 Republican candidates showed increased support among Democrats
Graphic compares participants after deliberation and control group (without deliberation). There is increased support among deliberators who identify as Democrats for Republican candidates at the America in One Room Deliberative Poll.

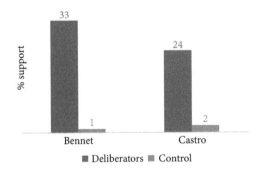

Figure A.2 Democratic candidates showed increased support among Republicans
Graphic compares participants after deliberation and control group (without deliberation). There is increased support among deliberators who identify as Republicans for Democratic candidates at the America in One Room Deliberative Poll.

Endnotes

Chapter 1

1. If deliberation is a kind of "talking cure" for our collective problems, it is obviously quite distinct from psychotherapy, another context where the term has long been used. For various psychotherapy-based models of the "talking cure," see Christopher Marx, Cord Benecke, and Antje Gumz, "Talking Cure Models: A Framework of Analysis," *Frontiers in Psychology* 2017; 8: 1589. DOI: 10.3389/fpsyg.2017.01589.
2. As I argue later, talk is instrumental to the process of weighing competing arguments. In theory there could be, and probably will be, a form of what Robert Goodin calls "deliberation within" (R. Goodin, "Democratic Deliberation Within," *Philosophy & Public Affairs* 2000; 29: 81–109). But thus far, the impact of mere exposure is unimpressive compared to that of discussion. Perhaps some future versions of a more immersive reality will have greater effects. See C. Farrar, J. Fishkin, D. Green, et al., "Disaggregating Deliberation's Effects: An Experiment within a Deliberative Poll," *British Journal of Political Science* 2010; 40: 333–347; and J. Sandefur, N. Birdsall, J. Fishkin, et al., "Democratic Deliberation and the Resource Curse: A Nationwide Experiment in Tanzania," *World Politics* 2022; 74: 564–609 for the condition of mere exposure contrasted with organized discussion in a deliberative process.
3. I take this richly suggestive term from Benedict Anderson who used it for a different purpose (the spread of nationalism). B. Anderson, *Imagined Communities: Reflections on the Origin and Spread of Nationalism* (London: Verso, 1983).
4. For a mixed but worsening picture see L. Diamond, "Democratic Regression in Comparative Perspective: Scope, Methods, and Causes," *Democratization* 2021; 28: 22–42 and Freedom House, *Freedom in the World, 2023.* https://freedomhouse.org/sites/default/files/2023-03/FIW_World_2023_DigtalPDF.pdf.
5. Jan-Werner Muller, *What is Populism?* (Philadelphia: University of Pennsylvania Press, 2016); Larry Diamond, *Ill Winds* (New York: Penguin Press, 2019), ch. 4; Steven Levitsky and Daniel Ziblatt, *How Democracies Die* (New York: Crown Publishing, 2018), chs 5–7; and Steven Levitsky and Daniel Ziblatt, *The Tyranny of the Minority* (New York: Crown Books, 2023), ch. 1.
6. Joseph A. Schumpeter, *Capitalism, Socialism, and Democracy* (New York: Harper Perennial Modern Thought, 2008).
7. Frances E. Lee, *Insecure Majorities: Congress and the Perpetual Campaign* (Chicago: University of Chicago Press, 2016).
8. Levitsky and Ziblatt, *How Democracies Die.*
9. John Stuart Mill, *Considerations on Representative Government* (Amherst, NY: Prometheus Books, 1991 reprint), 56.
10. Ibid.
11. Ibid., 57.
12. Anthony Downs, *An Economic Theory of Democracy* (New York: Harper, 1957).

13. Bernard Manin, *The Principles of Representative Government* (Cambridge; New York: Cambridge University Press, 1997).
14. Daniel A. Bell, *The China Model: Political Meritocracy and the Limits of Democracy* (Princeton: Princeton University Press, 2015).
15. Robert A. Dahl, *Democracy and Its Critics* (New Haven: Yale University Press, 1989), 322–342.
16. Mogens Herman Hansen, *Polis: An Introduction to the Ancient Greek City-State* (Oxford; New York: Oxford University Press, 2006).
17. Randomly sampled from those who said they were available.
18. See Chapter 3, note 7 about the controversy between Hansen and Canevaro on the Nomethetai.
19. For a limitation see Daniela Cammack, "Deliberation and Discussion in Classical Athens," *The Journal of Political Philosophy*: 2021; 29: 135–166. My position is that there can be deliberation without discussion, as suggested by Robert Goodin's "deliberation within," but discussion with the right design greatly enhances deliberation.
20. Mogens Herman Hansen, *The Athenian Democracy in the Age of Demosthenes: Structure, Principles, and Ideology* (Norman, OK: University of Oklahoma Press, 1999), 55.
21. See Josiah Ober, *Democracy and Knowledge: Innovation and Learning in Classical Athens* (Princeton: Princeton University Press, 2008) for a strong case.
22. See Cortland F. Bishop, *History of Elections in the American Colonies* (Buffalo: William S. Hein, 2002). But the elections were public voting, not secret ballots, and often with rewards of alcohol. See Michael Schudson, *The Good Citizen: A History of American Civic Life* (New York: Martin Kessler Books, 1998), 5.
23. Alexander Hamilton, *Federalist* No.71, in Alexander Hamilton, James Madison, and John Jay, *The Federalist Papers*. Isaac Kramnick (ed.) (London: Penguin Books, 1987), 409.
24. Jennifer Tolman Roberts, *Athens on Trial: The Antidemocratic Tradition in Western Thought* (Princeton: Princeton University Press, 1996).
25. Douglass Adair, "'That Politics May Be Reduced to a Science': David Hume, James Madison and the Tenth Federalist," reprinted in Trevor Colbourn (ed.), *Fame and the Founding Fathers* (Indianapolis: Liberty Fund, 1974).
26. Robert Dahl, "The Pseudodemocratization of the American Presidency," *Tanner Lecture Series on Human Values*, 1988, available at: https://tannerlectures.utah.edu/_resources/documents/a-to-z/d/dahl89.pdf.
27. Shanto Iyengar and Stephen Ansolabehere, *Going Negative: How Political Advertisements Shrink and Polarize the Electorate* (New York: Free Press, 1997).
28. David Van Reybrouck, *Against Elections* (London: The Bodley Head, 2013); Helene Landemore, *Open Democracy: Reinventing Popular Rule for the Twenty-First Century* (Princeton: Princeton University Press, 2020).
29. Jason Brennan, *Against Democracy* (Princeton: Princeton University Press, 2016).
30. George Gallup, "Public Opinion in a Democracy," *The Stafford Little Lectures*, Princeton University, 1936.
31. George Gallup, "Testing Public Opinion," *Public Opinion Quarterly* 1938; 2: 8–14.
32. See for example Michael Delli Carpini and Scott Keeter, *What Americans Know about Politics and Why It Matters* (New Haven: Yale University Press, 1997).
33. Robert Goodin, "Democratic Deliberation Within," *Philosophy & Public Affairs* 2000; 29: 81–109.

34. Sandefur, Birdsall, Fishkin, et al., "Democratic Deliberation and the Resource Curse: A Nationwide Experiment in Tanzania," and Farrar, Fishkin, Green, et al., "Disaggregating Deliberation's Effects: An Experiment within a Deliberative Poll."
35. Philip E. Converse "The Nature of Belief Systems in Mass Publics," in David E. Apter (ed.), *Ideology and Discontent* (New York: Free Press, 1964), 206–261.
36. George Bishop, *The Illusion of Public Opinion: Fact and Artifact in American Public Opinion Polls* (Lanham: Rowman and Littlefield, 2005).
37. Richard Morin, "Who Knows? Often, Survey Respondents Have No Opinion—Until the Pollster Prompts Them," *The Washington Post*, September 9, 2001.
38. Kathleen Jamieson, *Dirty Politics: Deception, Distraction, and Democracy* (New York: Oxford University Press, 1993).
39. Trump's priming of immigration apparently emboldened prejudiced expressions more broadly. See Benjamin Newman, Jennifer L. Merolla, Sono Shah, et al., "The Trump Effect: An Experimental Investigation of the Emboldening Effect of Racially Inflammatory Elite Communication," *British Journal of Political Science* 2021; 51: 1138–1159. DOI:10.1017/S0007123419000590.
40. Joseph A. Schumpeter, *Capitalism, Socialism, and Democracy* (New York: Harper and Brothers, 1942), 263.
41. Dahl, *Democracy and Its Critics*, 222.
42. HLA Hart famously noted the eclipse of utilitarianism as an undisputed first principle in the wake of Rawls, Nozick, Dworkin and other rights-emphasizing theorists: There was once "a once widely accepted old faith that some form of utilitarianism, if only we could discover the right form, <u>must</u> capture the essence of political morality." This "old faith" clashed with a new one that somehow emphasized rights and justice. The clash of perspectives persists to this day, in my view, and stands as a challenge to any routine and mechanical application of cost-benefit analysis to resolve our policy disputes. H. L. A. Hart, "Between Utility and Rights," *Columbia Law Review* 1979; 79: 828–846.
43. Timothy Ho, "Explaining Why Cars in Singapore Are So Expensive," *Dollars and Sense* 2023. Available at:https://dollarsandsense.sg/no-nonsense-explanation-on-why-cars-in-singapore-are-so-expensive/
44. Jane Mansbridge, "Everyday Talk in the Deliberative System," in: Macedo S (ed.), *Deliberative Politics* (New York: Oxford University Press, 1999), 211–239.
45. For a mixed picture see Donald Searing, Frederick Solt, Pamela Johnston Conover, et al., "Public Discussion in the Deliberative System: Does It Make Better Citizens?" *British Journal of Political Science* 2007; 37: 587–618.
46. Bruce Ackerman, *We the People* (Cambridge, MA: Belknap Press of Harvard University Press) vol 1, 1991; vol 2, 1998; vol 3, 2014.
47. While there is overlap, Ackerman's moments are different from Huntington's periodic theory of "creedal passions." See Ackerman, *We the People*, Vol. 1 and Samuel Huntington, *American Politics: The Promise of Disharmony* (Cambridge, MA: Harvard University Press, 1981). But this is not surprising as Ackerman is focused on deliberation that might count as "higher lawmaking." Huntington is focused on periods of a roused public.
48. R. Sinclair, *Democracy and Participation in Athens* (Cambridge; New York: Cambridge University Press, 1988), 103.

49. See Manin, *The Principles of Representative Government*, 35, where he weighs conflicting evidence and concludes that, "...selection by lot was regarded as a particularly egalitarian procedure. The problem is knowing to which version of the complex notion of equality it was attached."
50. Hansen, *The Athenian Democracy in the Age of Demosthenes*, 84.
51. Aristotle's Politics 1291b30-8, discussed in Sinclair, *Democracy and Participation in Athens*. For a more detailed description see Yves Sintomer, *The Government of Chance: Sortition and Democracy from Athens to the Present* (Cambridge: Cambridge University Press, 2023), 50–53.
52. "Where there is an established process of election to an office, then, *provided that the election is free* anyone who takes part in the process consents to the authority of whoever is elected to the office" John Plamenatz, *Consent, Freedom and Political Obligation* (London: Oxford University Press, 1968), 170 (emphasis in original). Presumably a "free" election is also one in which participation is uncoerced.

Chapter 2

1. Robert A. Dahl, *A Preface to Democratic Theory* (Chicago: University of Chicago Press, 1956), 128.
2. Ibid., 132.
3. Richard A. Posner, *Law, Pragmatism, and Democracy* (Cambridge, MA: Harvard University Press, 2003), 163.
4. Christopher H. Achen and Larry M. Bartels, *Democracy for Realists: Why Elections Do Not Produce Responsive Government* (Princeton: Princeton University Press, 2016), 7.
5. Ibid., 4.
6. In Chapter 5 I argue that the experience of deliberation can be brought to the schools as a contribution to civic education.
7. I discuss similar criteria in *Democracy When the People Are Thinking: Revitalizing Our Politics through Public Deliberation* (Oxford: Oxford University Press, 2018). But here I use them to make a different argument and I assign them differently to forms of democratic practice.
8. John Stuart Mill, *Considerations on Representative Government*, ch. 7.
9. *Baker v. Carr*, 369 U.S. 186 (1962).
10. John H. Banzhaf III, "Multi-Member Voting Districts: Do They Violate the 'One Man, One Vote' Principle?" *The Yale Law Journal* 1966; 75: 1309–138, especially pp. 1314–1318.
11. William Riker and Peter Ordeshook, "A Theory of the Calculus of Voting," *American Political Science Review* 1968; 62: 25–42.
12. "The democratic ideal ought ideally to be to enfranchise 'all affected interests.' Understood in a suitably expansive 'possibilistic' way that would mean giving virtually everyone everywhere a vote on virtually everything decided anywhere," Goodin, "Democratic Deliberation Within," 68.
13. John Burnheim, *Is Democracy Possible? The Alternative to Electoral Democracy* (Sydney: Sydney University Press, 2006).
14. See "Summary of Conclusions and Proposals," *The American Political Science Review* 1950; 44: 3–4.

15. "Part I. The Need for Greater Party Responsibility," *The American Political Science Review* 1950; 44: 15. Emphasis added.
16. Harold Hotelling, "Stability in Competition," *The Economic Journal* 1929; 39: 41; Duncan Black, "On the Rationale of Group Decision-making," *Journal of Political Economy* 1948; 56: 23–34; and most especially Downs, *An Economic Theory of Democracy*.
17. Hotelling, "Stability in Competition" p. 54.
18. Lewis Carroll, *Through the Looking Glass* (London: Harper Press, 2013), ch. 4.
19. Philip Converse, "The Nature of Belief Systems in Mass Publics (1964)," *Critical Review* 2006; 18: 1–74; Achen and Bartels, *Democracy for Realists*, 32.
20. Frank Newport, "Update: Partisan Gaps Expand Most on Government Power, Climate," Gallup.com, 2023.
21. For a good overview see Cass Sunstein, *#Republic: Divided Democracy in the Age of Social Media* (Princeton; Oxford: Princeton University Press, 2017).
22. Report of the Commission on Delegate Selection and Party Structure as Amended and Adopted by the DNC Executive Committee, March 1, 1974.
23. Benjamin Page and Robert Y. Shapiro, *The Rational Public: Fifty Years of Trends in Americans' Policy Preferences* (Chicago: University of Chicago Press, 1992), 69.
24. See Justin McCarthy, "Record-High 70% in U.S. Support Same-Sex Marriage," Gallup.com 2021, for the trend on marriage equality from 27% support in 1996 to 60% by the time of the Obergefell decision in 2015.
25. See Tom Donnelly, "Judicial Popular Constitutionalism," *Constitutional Commentary* 2015 for a discussion of marriage equality in the framework of constitutional moments, part III.
26. Gabriel Lenz, *Follow the Leader? How Voters Respond to Politicians' Policies and Performance* (Chicago; London: The University of Chicago Press, 2012), 3.
27. Ibid., 9.
28. For a systematic discussion see Steven Levitsky and Lucan Way, *Competitive Authoritarianism: Hybrid Regimes after the Cold War* (Cambridge: Cambridge University Press, 2010).
29. For some striking findings see Arendt Lijphardt, *Patterns of Democracy: Government Forms and Performance in Thirty-Six Countries* (New Haven: Yale University Press, 1999), 7.
30. For evidence that supposedly non-partisan judicial elections are becoming increasingly partisan see Herbert M. Kritzer, "Polarization and Partisanship in State Supreme Court Elections," *Judicature* 2021; 105: 65–75.
31. Schumpeter, *Capitalism, Socialism and Democracy*; Ian Shapiro, *The State of Democratic Theory* (New Haven: Yale University Press, 2006); Richard A. Posner, *Law, Pragmatism, and Democracy* (Cambridge, MA: Harvard University Press, 2003); Achen and Bartels, *Democracy for Realists: Why Elections Do Not Produce Responsive Government*.
32. Dahl, *Democracy and Its Critics*, 121.
33. For a strong statement of this position see Dennis F. Thompson, "Deliberate About, Not In, Elections," *Election Law Journal: Rules, Politics, and Policy* 2013; 12: 372–385.
34. Robert A. Dahl, *Polyarchy* (New Haven: Yale University Press, 1971), 3 and *Democracy and Its Critics*, 220–222.

35. Especially on highly polarized issues, mere exposure may have little effect (see the well-established literature on CIE, the "continued influence effect" of misinformation despite exposure to correction, e.g., Ullrich Ecker, Stephan Lewandowsky, John Cook, et al., "The Psychological Drivers of Misinformation Belief and its Resistance to Correction," *Nature Reviews Psychology* 2022; 1: 13–29, page 15. And it will sometimes backfire—see Brendan Nyhan and Jason Reifler, "When Corrections Fail: The Persistence of Political Misperceptions," *Political Behavior* 2010; 32: 303–30.
36. Bernard Manin, *The Principles of Representative Government* (Cambridge: Cambridge University Press, 1997), 218–235.
37. John Parkinson and Jane Mansbridge (eds), *Deliberative Systems: Deliberative Democracy at the Large Scale* (Cambridge: Cambridge University Press, 2012).
38. George Washington, "Farewell Address," 1796, 16.
39. Ibid.
40. Ibid.
41. Ibid.
42. According to Hofstadter: "Madison, it should be noted, treated the terms party and faction as synonyms" Richard Hofstadter, *The Idea of a Party System* (Berkeley: The University of California Press, 1969), 64. He cites further textual support.
43. James Madison, *Federalist* No.10 in *The Federalist Papers*, Isaac Kramnick (ed.) (New York: Penguin Books, 1987; first published 1788).
44. There is just a hint of concern about parties in the first version drafted by Madison, more in the second version drafted by Hamilton, and still more in the third version finally presented by Washington himself. See Horace Binney, *An Inquiry into the Formation of Washington's Farewell Address*, 1859; (reprinted by Forgotten Books, London 2018). For brief mention of political parties in the first version, see p. 137; for parties in the second version as drafted by Hamilton see pp. 197 and 200; for Washington's final version see pp. 218–219.
45. Hofstadter, *The Idea of a Party System*, 49.
46. Ibid., 48.
47. Ibid., 47.
48. Not "removing the causes" but "controlling the effects." Madison in *Federalist* No. 10.
49. Ibid., 126.
50. For a similar reading of *Federalist* No. 10 see Joseph Bessette, *The Mild Voice of Reason*, 33–39. See also Isaac Kramnick (ed.), "Editor's Introduction," *The Federalist Papers*, 40–43
51. This is a central argument in Cristina Lafont's *Democracy without Shortcuts: A Participatory Conception of Deliberative Democracy* (Oxford: Oxford University Press, 2020) discussed in Chapter 5.
52. See Schumpeter, *Capitalism, Socialism, and Democracy*. Posner for example argues that voter "apathy" should be considered an indicator of "contentment." He cites survey data to dispute that nonvoters are more discontented with the system. Posner, *Law, Pragmatism, and Democracy*, 190. Samuel Huntington, "The Democratic Distemper," *The National Interest*, 1975.
53. Bernard Berelson, Paul Lazarsfeld, and William McPhee, *Voting: A Study of Opinion Formation in a Presidential Campaign* (1954), (Midway reprint edn, Chicago: University of Chicago Press, 1986), 314.

54. Huntington, "The Democratic Distemper."
55. Posner, *Law, Pragmatism, and Democracy*, 190. For a good overview see Kevin Elliot, *Democracy for Busy People* (Chicago; London: University of Chicago Press, 2023), ch. 2.
56. Downs, *An Economic Theory of Democracy*. The equations for the rationality of voting are only balanced in favor of voting by adding a term for civic duty. Perhaps the most compelling version would be some variant of the generalization argument. See Fishkin (note 58 below) on variants of the generalization argument. James Fishkin, *The Limits of Obligation* (New Haven: Yale University Press, 1982). For a systematic critique of the ethics of voting see Donald P. Green and Ian Shapiro, *Pathologies of Rational Choice Theory: A Critique of Applications in Political Science* (New Haven: Yale University Press, 1994), ch. 4.
57. See Riker and Ordeshook, "A Theory of the Calculus of Voting."
58. One could argue on the basis of the generalization argument, "What if everyone did that? What if everyone stayed home," etc. For some complexities see Fishkin, *The Limits of Obligation*, sections 13 and 16.
59. Alexis de Tocqueville, *Democracy in America*, Vol. 1 (New York: Shocken Books, 1961; translated by Henry Reeve), 55.
60. John Stuart Mill, *Considerations on Representative Government*, 79.
61. Ibid., 78.
62. Carole Pateman, *Participation and Democratic Theory* (Cambridge: Cambridge University Press, 1970), 32–33.
63. Jane Mansbridge, "On the Idea that Participation Makes Better Citizens" in: Stephen Elkin and Karol Soltan (eds), *Citizen Competence and Democratic Institutions* (University Park, PA: Pennsylvania State University Press, 1999), 318–319.
64. Ibid., 310.
65. John Gastil, Pierre Deess, and Phil Weiser, "Civic Awakening in the Jury Room: A Test of the Connection between Jury Deliberation and Political Participation," *The Journal of Politics* 2002; 64: 585–595.
66. See the analyses in James Fishkin, Valentin Bolotnyy, Joshua Lerner, et al., "Can Deliberation Have Lasting Effects?" *American Political Science Review* 2024: 1–21.
67. The best assessment of the merits and limitations of the town meeting continues to be Jane J. Mansbridge, *Beyond Adversary Democracy* (New York; Basic Books, 1980). For an assessment of the civil jury system, see this valuable collection: Robert E. Litan (ed.), *Verdict: Assessing the Civil Jury System* (Washington, DC: Brookings, 1983).
68. This claim, emblazoned on the Brexit campaign bus, was a sensational effort to mislead, since it ignored the "rebate" that Mrs Thatcher had negotiated. So there was not a pile of money to be saved and put into the NHS, on anything like the scale alleged.
69. As defined in our first criterion for popular control.
70. See his later "A Candid State of Parties" for acceptance of parties without the pernicious effects in his earlier definition of "faction." James Madison in Gaillard Hunt (ed.), *The Writings of James Madison, Comprising His Public Papers and His Private Correspondence, Including His Numerous Letters and Documents Now for the First Time Printed* (New York: G. P. Putnam's Sons, 1900).
71. Madison, *Federalist* No.10
72. Richard Beeman, "Perspectives on the Constitution: A Republic, If You Can Keep It," National Constitution Center—constitutioncenter.org.

73. Steven Levitsky and Daniel Ziblatt, *Tyranny of the Minority* (New York: Crown, 2023).
74. Dahl, *A Preface to Democratic Theory*.
75. They explain: "Here we return to a basic principle inspired by James Madison and others: Extremist minorities are best overcome through electoral competition. Madison believed that the need to win popular majorities would likely tame the most 'sinister' political tendencies." Levitsky and Ziblatt, *Tyranny of the Minority*, 229–230. They go on to cite the 20th-century political mantra "the cure for the ills of democracy is more Democracy." That was a theme of the Progressives invoked by the McGovern Fraser commission to bring about more mass primaries and was in line with more direct democracy. It was consistent with the animating spirit of "primary, referendum and recall," a quite different direction for political reform than Madison's vision.
76. Note that Madison's attack on supermajority rules was focused at the elite level. At the time of the Founding, he did not envision the filibuster, for example. However, he did envision the Senate standing against popular majorities that might motivate faction. See *Federalist* No. 63.
77. Madison, *Federalist* No. 10, 127.
78. James Madison, *Federalist* No. 63 in Isaac Kramnick (ed.), *The Federalist Papers* (Penguin Books, 1987), 371.
79. Ibid.
80. Madison, *Federalist* No. 58.
81. Dahl, *Preface to Democratic Theory*, 124.
82. Madison, *Federalist* No. 63.
83. Tolman Roberts, *Athens on Trial: The Antidemocratic Tradition in Western Thought*.
84. I. F. Stone, *The Trial of Socrates* (New York: Random House, 1989).
85. Schumpeter, *Capitalism, Socialism, and Democracy*, 242.
86. Dahl, *A Preface to Democratic Theory*, 26.
87. Ibid., 99.
88. Ibid.
89. Ibid., 90.
90. Ibid., 99.
91. I. M. D. Little, *A Critique of Welfare Economics* (Oxford: Oxford University Press, 1960).
92. James Fishkin, *Tyranny and Legitimacy: A Critique of Political Theories* (Baltimore: Johns Hopkins University Press, 1979), 16.
93. Dahl, *Democracy and Its Critics*. "Freedom of speech . . . is necessary both for effective participation and for enlightened understanding; so too are freedom of the press and freedom of assembly. In large democratic systems, the right to form political parties and other political associations is necessary to voting equality, effective participation, enlightenment and final control of the agenda," p. 170. These are references to the elements of his theory of the democratic process in ch. 8.
94. See Samuel Moyn *Not Enough: Human Rights in an Unequal World* (Cambridge, MA: Harvard University Press, 2018).
95. We can leave aside for our purposes here whether the inactions need to be intentional or just failures to realize the evident consequences of a failure to act.
96. The argument has parallels with the classic debate between Hart and Devlin in which Hart argued that offense was not harm, no matter how strongly a moralist such as

Lord Devlin objected to homosexuality. Tyranny of the majority can be imposed on the homosexual minority if it is criminalized (as is apparently happening in contemporary Uganda and Nigeria for behavior that offends but does not directly harm the majority).

97. See, for example, *Democracy When the People Are Thinking*, p. 24.
98. See Reva Siegel, "Constitutional Culture, Social Movement Conflict and Constitutional Change: The Case of the De Facto Era. 2005–06 Brennan Center Symposium Lecture," *California Law Review* 2006; 94: 1323 for the general problem; Reva Siegel, "Dead or Alive: Originalism as Popular Constitutionalism in Heller," *Harvard Law Review* 2008; 122 on Heller; and Reva Siegel, "Memory Games: Dobbs's Originalism as Anti-Democratic Living Constitutionalism—and Some Pathways for Resistance," *SSRN Journal* 2022, DOI: 10.2139/ssrn.4179622 on Dobbs.
99. Siegel, "Dead or Alive."
100. Scott Bauer and David Lieb, "GOP threat to impeach a Wisconsin Supreme Court Justice is Driven by Fear of Losing Legislative Eedge,"*AP News*. https://apnews.com/article/wisconsin-supreme-court-impeachment-republicans-gerrymandering-legislature-21fc8c3cf99623a379cbf4dd01ed0b8c. Published September 10, 2023. Accessed February 10, 2024.
101. Isaac Chotiner, "The Origins of Netanyahu's 'All-Systems Assault' on Israeli Democracy," *The New Yorker* 2023.
102. Dahl, *A Preface to Democratic Theory*, 135.
103. Mark Tushnet, "Constitutional Hardball," *Georgetown Law Faculty Publications and Other Works* 2004.

Chapter 3

1. Hansen notes: "Assembly democracy is inimical to the formation of parties: parties are a child of modern indirect democracy, because they are bound up with elections to representative bodies." However: "there were groupings of political leaders, but they did not have behind them corresponding groups amongst the public who listened and voted." *The Athenian Democracy in the Age of Demosthenes: Structure, Principles, and Ideology*, 306. See also Josiah Ober, *Mass and Elite in Democratic Athens: Rhetoric, Ideology, and the Power of the People* (Princeton: Princeton University Press, 1989), 121.
2. Hansen, *The Athenian Democracy in the Age of Demosthenes*, 307.
3. The best account of the Council of 500 is Josiah Ober, *Democracy and Knowledge: Innovation and Learning in Classical Athens*.
4. Hansen, *The Athenian Democracy in the Age of Demosthenes*, 168.
5. A. R. W. Harrison, "Law-Making at Athens at the End of the Fifth Century B. C.," *The Journal of Hellenic Studies* 1955; 75: 26–35. See p. 35.
6. Sinclair, *Democracy and Participation in Athens*, 84. He emphasizes that by slowing down the passage of new laws it could "prevent change through snap votes or a single stacked meeting."
7. There is a scholarly debate about whether or not the *nomothetai* were selected by lot, and whether or not they operated in the way we have described here. My description is based on the long-accepted view. However, Mirko Canevaro has argued that the evi-

dence is based on a late forgery. See M. Canevaro, "The Authenticity of the Document at Demosth. or. 24.20-3, the Procedures of nomothesia and the so-called ἐπιχειροτονία τῶν νόμων," *Klio* 100, 2018, 70–124. However, Hansen has offered a systematic rebuttal: Mogens Herman Hansen "The Inserted Document at Dem. 24.20–23. Response to Mirko Canevaro" *Klio* 2019; 101(2): 452–472. I accept Hansen's view. But for our purposes we can also say that the benefits of this deliberative design are evident and if it were to turn out to be the case that the Athenians did not actually have such an institution, then maybe they should have had it as an extension of their project to provide a further check on hasty or unwise proposals supported by orators in the Assembly.

8. Hansen, *The Athenian Democracy in the Age of Demosthenes*, 303.
9. Daniela Cammack, "Deliberation and Discussion in Classical Athens," *Journal of Political Philosophy* 2021; 29: 135–66.
10. See George Grote, *A History of Greece* (Cambridge: Cambridge University Press, 2010), 322–323.
11. Plutarch, *Themistocles in Plutarch's Lives with an English Translation by Bernadotte Perrin* (Cambridge, MA: Harvard University Press, 1914). Vol. 2, 1–92.
12. Ober, *Mass and Elite*, 74–75.
13. See Helene Landemore, *Democratic Reason* (Princeton: Princeton University Press, 2012) and Sintomer, *The Government of Chance: Sortition and Democracy from Athens to the Present*, 259–263.
14. See for example, Sintomer, *The Government of Chance*, 121.
15. Habermas distinguishes public opinion and public will formation. Jurgen Habermas, *Between Facts and Norms* (Cambridge MA: MIT Press, 1998), 307–308. However, since the two are inextricably bound and public opinion has become so identified with public polls, I will simplify and use the term public will formation.
16. Lafont, *Democracy without Shortcuts*, 118 (emphasis added).
17. Converse, "The Nature of Belief Systems in Mass Publics."
18. My thanks to Dennis Thomas, a former Chair of the Texas Public Utility Commission, and to the late Will Guild, who conducted the survey work for these utility projects. Robert C. Luskin was also a crucial collaborator on these projects.
19. Rui Wang, James Fishkin, and Robert Luskin, "Does Deliberation Increase Public-Spiritedness?" *Social Science Quarterly* 2020; 101, 2169.
20. Kate Galbraith and Asher Price, "Book Excerpt: How the Public Got Behind Texas Wind Power," *The Texas Tribune* 2013. https://www.texastribune.org/2013/09/17/book-excerpt-how-public-got-behind-tx-wind-power/. Published September 17, 2013. Accessed February 14, 2024.
21. Dennis Chong and James Druckman, "A Theory of Framing and Opinion Formation in Competitive Elite Environments," *Journal of Communication* 2007; 57: 99–118; Nyhan and Reifler, "When Corrections Fail: The Persistence of Political Misperceptions."
22. Most people presumably do not have the time or inclination to attend public meetings about electric utility issues. Hence the turnout for an open meeting will surely be unrepresentative, and dominated by organized interests and lobbyists.
23. Nicholas Wood, "Bulgaria Invites Guests for a Day of Intense Democracy," *The New York Times*. https://www.nytimes.com/2007/05/07/world/europe/07bulgaria.html.

Published May 7, 2007. Accessed February 14, 2024; Nuri Kim, James Fishkin, and Robert Luskin, "Intergroup Contact in Deliberative Contexts: Evidence from Deliberative Polls," *Journal of Communication* 2018; 68: 1029–1051. DOI:10.1093/joc/jqy056.

24. Lafont, *Democracy without Shortcuts*, 131; Phillip Pettit, "Depoliticizing Democracy," *Ratio Juris* 2004; 17: 52–63.
25. Lafont, *Democracy without Shortcuts*, 131.
26. Ibid.
27. See Jieun Park "Deliberative Democracy in South Korea: Four Deliberative Polling Experiments" in Baogang He, Michael Breen, and James Fishkin (eds), *Deliberative Democracy in Asia* (London; New York: Routledge, Taylor & Francis Group, 2022), 154–171; see 164–165.
28. Pettit, "Depolarizing Democracy."
29. An English translation of the Law on Deliberative Polling can be found in the Appendix to Fishkin, *Democracy When the People Are Thinking*, pp. 243–249.
30. The discussion of the constitutional amendment process borrows from James Fishkin and Alice Siu, "Mongolia: Piloting Elements of a Deliberative System," in Baogang He, Michael Breen, and James Fishkin (eds), *Deliberative Democracy in Asia* (London; New York: Routledge, Taylor & Francis Group, 2022), 190–204.
31. National Statistics Office of Mongolia, *Main Findings of the First Nationwide Deliberative Polling on Constitutional Amendment of Mongolia*, 2017, available at: https://drive.google.com/file/d/18IpgAbMfjlezNnlu0gxkpCpZ1Tdu6lN_/view.
32. More details on the second constitutional amendment and how it came about can be found here: https://cddrl.fsi.stanford.edu/news/deliberative-polling-fosters-peace-and-instigates-positive-change-among-people-mongolia.
33. See the landmark findings of Harry Kalven, Jr and Hans Zeisel, *The American Jury* (Boston: Little, Brown & Co., 1966) for a systematic study. For a more recent replication see Theodore Eisenberg, Paula L. Hannaford-Agor, Valerie P. Hans, et al., "Judge-Jury Agreement in Criminal Cases: A Partial Replication of Kalven and Zeisel's The American Jury," *Journal of Empirical Legal Studies* 2005: 171–206. https://doi.org/10.1111/j.1740-1461.2005.00035.x.
34. Habermas, *Between Facts and Norms*, 306.
35. Lynn Sanders, "Against Deliberation," *Political Theory* 1997; 25: 347–76 (emphasis added).
36. Iris Young, *Inclusion and Democracy* (Oxford; New York: Oxford University Press, 2000).
37. Arthur Lupia and Anne Norton, "Inequality is Always in the Room: Language & Power in Deliberative Democracy," *Daedalus* 2017; 146: 64–76.
38. Sanders "Against Deliberation," 12–13.
39. Alice Siu, "Deliberation & the Challenge of Inequality," *Daedalus* 2017; 146: 119–128. See 122.
40. Ibid., 123.
41. Robert Luskin, Gaurav Sood, James Fishkin, and Kyu Hahn, "Deliberative Distortions? Homogenization, Polarization, and Domination in Small Group Discussions," *British Journal of Political Science* 2022; 52: 1205–1225.
42. Given the variety of countries and contexts, education and income were divided at the median for high and low.

43. See Sandefur, Birdsall, Fishkin, et al., "Democratic Deliberation and the Resource Curse: A Nationwide Experiment in Tanzania," and Farrar, Fishkin, Green, et al., "Disaggregating Deliberation's Effects: An Experiment within a Deliberative Poll."
44. Cass Sunstein, "The Law of Group Polarization," in: James Fishkin, Peter Laslett (eds), *Debating Deliberative Democracy* (Malden: Blackwell Publishing Ltd, 2003), 80–101.
45. Ibid.
46. Bruce Ackerman and James Fishkin, *Deliberation Day* (New Haven: Yale University Press, 2004).
47. Ibid. 921.
48. See Chapter 5, n 36 about random assignment within geographical areas to provide diversity in the small groups.
49. David Schkade, Cass R. Sunstein, and Reid Hastie, "What Happened on Deliberation Day," *California Law Review* 2007; 95: 915–940.
50. James Fishkin, "Washington: The Case for a National Caucus," *The Atlantic*, August 1988.
51. See Maxwell McCombs and Amy Reynolds (eds), *The Poll with a Human Face: The National Issues Convention Experiment in Political Communication* (Mahwah, NJ: Lawrence Erlbaum Associates, 1999).
52. It has been followed by a series of national Deliberative Polls in Denmark sponsored by the Parliament and broadcast on television.
53. Lafont, *Democracy without Shortcuts*, 122.
54. M. K. Mackenzie and M. E. Warren, "Two Trust-Based Uses of Mini-Publics in Democratic Systems," in J. Parkinson and J. Mansbridge (eds), *Deliberative Systems: Deliberative Democracy at the Large Scale* (Cambridge: Cambridge University Press, 2012), 95–124.
55. See Converse, "The Nature of Belief Systems in Mass Publics," and Jon Krosnick, "Government Policy and Citizen Passion: A Study of Issue Publics in Contemporary America," *Political Behavior* 1990; 12: 59–92.
56. Arthur Lupia, "Shortcuts Versus Encyclopedias: Information and Voting Behavior in California Insurance Reform Elections," *American Political Science Review* 1994; 88: 63–76. See 63.
57. Ideally, a cue would approximate the views not only of those who were more knowledgeable, but also of those who had actually weighed the pros and cons of the ballot proposition. Hence a cue generated by deliberation of a representative sample might better approximate our criteria for popular control. Nevertheless, those who have become more knowledgeable about the proposition in natural settings may be a good second best, particularly if the knowledge is not completely one-sided.
58. John Gastil, *By Popular Demand: Revitalizing Representative Democracy through Deliberative Elections* (Berkeley: University of California Press, 2000).
59. Kenneth Rasinski, Norman Bradburn, and Douglas Lauen, "Effects of NIC Media Coverage Among the Public," in M. McCombs and A. Reynolds (eds), *The Poll with a Human Face* (Mahwah, NJ: Lawrence Erlbaum Associates, 1999), 155–176. See 157.
60. Samuel Popkin, *The Reasoning Voter: Communication and Persuasion in Presidential Campaigns* (Chicago: University of Chicago Press, 1991), 1.
61. Henry Brady and Paul Sniderman, "Attitude Attribution: A Group Basis for Political Reasoning," *American Political Science Review* 1985; 79: 1061–1078.

Chapter 4

1. A vivid account of the transformation of elections in the US since colonial times can be found in Michael Schudson, *The Good Citizen: A History of American Civic Life* (New York: Martin Kessler Books, 1998).
2. As Madison later realized in helping to found the Democratic–Republican Party.
3. See John H. Aldrich, *Why Parties? A Second Look* (Chicago: University of Chicago Press, 2011), who makes the argument, especially relying on an interpretation of American history, that a political party system is necessary for effective democracy. See p. 311.
4. See Marc J. Hetherington, and Thomas Rudolph, *Why Washington Won't Work: Polarization, Political Trust, and the Governing Crisis* (Chicago: The University of Chicago Press, 2015).
5. Burnheim, *Is Democracy Possible?*; Landemore, *Open Democracy*; David Van Reybrouck, *Against Elections*.
6. See John Gastil and Erik Wright, *Legislature by Lot: Transformative Designs for Deliberative Governance* (London; New York: Verso Books, 2019), and also the proposal of Alexander Guerrero, "Against Elections: The Lottocratic Alternative," *Philosophy & Public Affairs* 2014; 42: 135–178.
7. "2019: The Public's Priorities and Expectations," The Associated Press—NORC Center for Public Affairs Research, 2019. https://apnorc.org/wp-content/uploads/2020/02/2019-The-Publics-Priorities-and-Expectations.pdf.
8. Foreign policy was not a top priority in the NORC study, but it was included since the context was the presidential campaign.
9. The Advisory Committee can be found at the end of the briefing materials available at: https://drive.google.com/file/d/1ja0CIevtWjYVqnmvvHCKmrY-g4AkJbed/view.
10. On a 0 to 10 scale ranging from strong opposition to strong support, the Republican mean moved from 7.930 to 5.320 and the Democratic mean moved from 3.26 to 2.44. Figures 4.1–4.2 and 4.3–4.4 give an overall picture of the changes but not the movements of the mean position of the parties. We consider depolarization as the movement closer together of the mean responses of the members of each party on the 0 to 10 scale. See James Fishkin, Alice Siu, Larry Diamond, et al., "Is Deliberation an Antidote to Extreme Partisan Polarization? Reflections on 'America in One Room,'" *American Political Science Review* 2021; 115: 1464–1481 for further details.
11. CNN broadcast a distillation of the immigration discussion, available at: https://www.youtube.com/watch?v=FhNWKaLUWKw. The significant drop in affective polarization is an indication of the cooler temperature fostered by the dialogue as people learned to listen to each other. Note the spontaneous embrace of the strongest advocates on either side near the end of the video. See Fishkin et al. "Is Deliberation an Antidote to Extreme Partisan Polarization?" for the affective polarization results. The discussion here of "America in One Room" draws extensively on this article and our collaborative work. That work was published under a Creative Commons Attribution 4.0 International (CC BY 4.0: https://creativecommons.org/licenses/by/4.0/).
12. On a 0 to 10 scale ranging from strong opposition to strong support, the Republican mean moved from 7.05 to 4.72 and the Democrat mean from 3.3 to 2.39.

13. On a 0 to 10 scale, ranging from strong opposition to strong support, the Republican mean moved from 4.64 to 6.11 and the Democrat mean from 8.74 to 9.25. The gap in the mean positions of the two parties closed from 4.1 to 3.14.
14. See Fishkin et al. "Is Deliberation an Antidote?"
15. The gap between the mean positions of Republicans and Democrats went from 5.04 points to 3.77 on the 0 to 10 scale.
16. The difference in the mean position of Democrats and Republicans on the 0 to 10 point scale went from 4.14 before deliberation to 2.16 after deliberation.
17. The gap between the mean positions of the parties went from 3.11 to 2.02 on the 0 to 10 scale.
18. This discussion of America in One Room distills the essential points in Fishkin et al. "Is Deliberation an Antidote?"
19. Party membership is based on the standard battery of party self-identification for the two major parties. Independents were asked whether they lean Republican or Democrat. Results for party members plus leaners are presented in tables. See "Participants by Party ID Issues Scale" at https://deliberation.stanford.edu/news/america-one-room-results.
20. Hetherington and Rudolph, *Why Washington Won't Work*.
21. Shanto Iyengar, Yphtach Lelkes, Matthew Levendusky, et al., "The Origins and Consequences of Affective Polarization in the United States," *Annual Review of Political Science* 2019; 22: 129–146.
22. Charles Taber and Milton Lodge, "Motivated Skepticism in the Evaluation of Political Beliefs," *American Journal of Political Science* 2006; 50: 755–769. See p. 755.
23. Ziva Kunda, "The Case for Motivated Reasoning," *Psychological Bulletin* 1990; 108: 480–498.
24. James Druckman, Erik Peterson, and Rune Slothuus, "How Elite Partisan Polarization Affects Public Opinion Formation," *American Political Science Review* 2013; 107: 57–79; Thomas Leeper and Rune Slothuus, "Political Parties, Motivated Reasoning, and Public Opinion Formation," *Political Psychology* 2014; 35: 129–156; Matthew Levendusky, James Druckman, and Audrey McLain, "How group discussions create strong attitudes and strong partisans," *Research & Politics* 2016; 3:205316801664513.
25. Ullrich Ecker, Stephan Lewandowsky, John Cook, et al., "The Psychological Drivers of Misinformation Belief and its Resistance to Correction," p. 15.
26. Chong and Druckman, "A Theory of Framing and Opinion Formation in Competitive Elite Environments," and Brendan Nyhan and Jason Reifler, "When Corrections Fail: The Persistence of Political Misperceptions." In a later study, Nyhan and others found the backfire effect difficult to replicate. See Brendan Nyhan, Ethan Porter, Jason Reifler, et al., "Taking Fact-Checks Literally But Not Seriously? The Effects of Journalistic Fact-Checking on Factual Beliefs and Candidate Favorability," *Political Behavior* 2020; 42: 939–960. However, they found misinformation persists despite exposure to correction, a result consistent with the continued influence effect (CIE).
27. Sunstein, *Going to Extremes*; Eli Pariser, *The Filter Bubble: What the Internet Is Hiding from You* (London: Viking, 2011).
28. Solomon Asch, "Opinions and Social Pressure," *Scientific American* 1955; 193: 31–35.
29. Robert Goidel and Todd Shields, "The Vanishing Marginals, the Bandwagon, and the Mass Media," *The Journal of Politics* 1994; 56: 802–810.

30. Elizabeth Noelle-Neumann, *The Spiral of Silence: Public Opinion, Our Social Skin* (Chicago: University of Chicago Press, 1984).
31. David Schkade, Cass R. Sunstein, and Daniel Kahneman, "Deliberating about Dollars: The Severity Shift," *Columbia Law Review* 2000; 100: 1139, and Schkade, "What Happened on Deliberation Day?"
32. Kunda, "The Case for Motivated Reasoning."
33. Ibid., 481.
34. Sunstein, "The Law of Group Polarization," 55–57.
35. Magdalena Wojcieszak, "Deliberation and Attitude Polarization," *Journal of Communication* 2011; 61: 596–617.
36. Henri Tajfel, *Human Groups and Social Categories: Studies in Social Psychology* (Cambridge; New York: Cambridge University Press, 1981).
37. Jeffrey Berry and Sarah Sobieraj, *The Outrage Industry: Political Opinion Media and the New Incivility* (Oxford; New York: Oxford University Press, 2014); Diana Mutz, *In-Your-Face Politics: The Consequences of Uncivil Media* (Princeton: Princeton University Press, 2015).
38. Gordon Allport, *The Nature of Prejudice* (Cambridge, MA: Perseus Books, 1954).
39. Thomas Pettigrew and Linda Tropp, "A Meta-Analytic Test of Intergroup Contact Theory," *Journal of Personality and Social Psychology* 2006; 90: 751–783; Kristin Davies, Linda Tropp, Arthur Aron, et al., "Cross-Group Friendships and Intergroup Attitudes: A Meta-Analytic Review," *Personality and Social Psychology Review* 2011; 15: 332–351; Miles Hewstone and Hermann Swart, "Fifty-odd Years of Inter-group Contact: From Hypothesis to Integrated Theory," *British Journal of Social Psychology* 2011; 50: 374–386.
40. Nuri Kim et. al, "Intergroup Contact in Deliberative Contexts: Evidence from Deliberative Polls."
41. Ifat Maoz, "An Experiment in Peace: Reconciliation-Aimed Workshops of Jewish-Israeli and Palestinian Youth," *Journal of Peace Research* 2000; 37: 721–736.
42. See Fishkin et al., "Is Deliberation an Antidote?"14.
43. Madison, *Federalist* No. 63, 371.
44. Significance at least at the .05 level with two-tailed tests.
45. For some further complexities, see Fishkin et al. "Can Deliberation Have Lasting Effects?" This count includes the Trans Pacific Partnership (TPP) question because the two parties moved to the same side. Republicans moved or depolarized so much that they crossed the midpoint to the same side as the Democrats.
46. In this section I draw directly on some of the discussion in Fishkin, Bolotnyy, Lerner, et al., "Can Deliberation Have Lasting Effects?" and on James Fishkin, Belotnyy, Lerner, et al., "Scaling Dialogue for Democracy: Can Automated Deliberation Create More Deliberative Voters?" Perspectives on Politics, forthcoming. "Can Deliberation Have Lasting Effects?" DOI:10.1017/S0003055423001363 was published under a Creative Commons Attribution 4.0 International (CC BY 4.0, https://creativecommons.org/licenses/by/4.0/).
47. For a similar table with recollected vote after the election, see table A7 in the Appendix of Fishkin, Bolotnyy, Lerner, et al., "Can Deliberation Have Lasting Effects?"
48. See Angus Campbell, *The American Voter* (1960) (Chicago: University of Chicago Press, 1980); Donald Green, Bradley Palmquist, and Eric Schickler, *Partisan Hearts and Minds:*

Political Parties and the Social Identities of Voters (New Haven; London: Yale University Press, 2002); Achen and Bartels, *Democracy for Realists*.

49. See for example Donald Green and Alan Gerber, *Get Out the Vote: How to Increase Voter Turnout* (Washington, DC: Brookings Institution Press, 2019).
50. We measured movement on the 26 extremely polarized items with a policy-based score (PBS). For details see Fishkin, Bolotnyy, Lerner, et al., "Can Deliberation Have Lasting Effects?"
51. We have focused on internal or self-efficacy rather than external efficacy for a long-term effect, as one's sense of developing "opinions worth listening to" is not dependent on the contested and changing political context of a hotly contested campaign. After a year of no-holds-barred campaigning, it is hard to imagine citizens agreeing that "Public officials care about what people like me think" (the standard external efficacy question that we included). But it is possible to imagine that deliberators might continue to believe "I have opinions about politics that are worth listening to" (a standard measure of internal efficacy that we included).
52. John Gastil, Pierre Deess, and Phil Weiser, "Civic Awakening in the Jury Room: A Test of the Connection between Jury Deliberation and Political Participation." These are also suggestive connections to the construct of "political capital" in Lawrence Jacobs, Fay Cook, and Michael Delli Carpini, *Talking Together: Public Deliberation and Political Participation in America* (Chicago: University of Chicago Press, 2009), which includes political efficacy, political attention, and general political knowledge among other variables. But this is from a single cross-sectional survey, not an experiment (exploring the effects of attending public meeting).
53. The direct effects can be found in table 8 of Fishkin, Bolotnyy, Lerner, et al., "Can Deliberation Have Lasting Effects?"
54. The Greater Houston Partnership and California Forward were among the other funders for the climate and energy project.
55. The Stanford Online Deliberation Platform is a collaboration at Stanford between the Deliberative Democracy Lab (http://deliberation.stanford.edu) and the Crowdsourced Democracy Team (https://voxpopuli.stanford.edu/) directed by Professor Ashish Goel in Management Science and Engineering).
56. This discussion of America in One Room: Climate and Energy draws in detail on Fishkin et al., "Scaling Dialogue for Democracy: Can Automated Deliberation Create More Deliberative Voters?" and the materials posted at: https://deliberation.stanford.edu/news/america-one-room-climate-and-energy#DETAILED especially James Fishkin and Larry Diamond "Is the Climate Crisis Just Too Hot for Us to Handle?" *The American Purpose* November 5, 2021 available at: https://www.americanpurpose.com/articles/is-the-climate-crisis-just-too-hot-for-us-to-handle/.
57. Two of the seven illustrations in Figure 4.4 appeared in Fishkin and Diamond, "Is the Climate Crisis too Hot to Handle?" Reproduced with permission. While the changes are illustrated with percentages the means for Republicans and Democrats move closer together with deliberation.
58. This was what we call a "policy-based score" (PBS), a policy index for polarized issues. We used this method in two articles Fishkin, Bolotnyy, Lerner et al., "Can Deliberation Have Lasting Effects?" and Fishkin et al., "Scaling Dialogue for Democracy: Can Automated Deliberation Create More Deliberative Voters?" The PBS especially reflects the work of our collaborator Valentin Bolotnyy of Stanford.

59. Levitsky and Ziblatt, *How Democracies Die*.
60. This was a Helena project with additional support from Porticus, the Skoll Foundation, the Thiry-O'Leary Foundation, and other donors.
61. See https://deliberation.stanford.edu/a1r.
62. The changes for policy proposals reported here are significant from time 1 (initial contact) to time 3 (three months after the deliberations) compared to the changes in the control from time 1 to time 3 (difference in difference analysis available here under "Follow-Up Study": Results of America in One Room: Democratic Reform| Deliberative Democracy Lab (stanford.edu). https://deliberation.stanford.edu/sites/g/files/sbiybj21211/files/media/file/a1r-dr-followup-diff-of-diff-treatment-v-control.pdf
63. Ibid.
64. Helene Landemore, *Open Democracy*, 93.
65. Sunstein, "The Law of Group Polarization."
66. Dimitri Courant, "The promises and disappointments of the French Citizens' Convention for Climate," *Deliberative Democracy Digest* 2021.
67. Ibid.
68. Alan Renwick, Sarah Allan, Will Jennings, et al., "What Kind of Brexit do Voters want? Lessons from the Citizens' Assembly on Brexit," *Political Quarterly* 2018; 89: 649–658. I am indebted to Jane Suiter for bringing this case to my attention.
69. David Farrell, Jane Suiter, Kevin Cunningham, et al., "When Mini-Publics and Maxi-Publics Coincide: Ireland's National Debate on Abortion," *Representation* 2023; 59: 55–73.
70. See https://deliberation.stanford.edu/tools-and-resources/online-deliberation-platform.
71. See Fishkin et al., "Scaling Dialogue for Democracy," appendix, table 1 for evaluations.
72. In a pilot with volunteers from civic groups, Net Zero Together explored the willingness of participants who deliberated together on the platform about climate change to recommend the process to their friends. See Zabrae Valentine and Peter Weber, *Testing Scalability of Civic Deliberation to Support Informed & Inclusive Civic Engagement: Lessons Learned from the July 2022 "Table Talks Project" Pilot*, 2022, https://deliberation.stanford.edu/news/what-table-talks-project. See p. 26. 65% would recommend the process to others and 55% would do it again if other topics were available.
73. Ackerman and Fishkin, *Deliberation Day*.

Chapter 5

1. Hansen, *The Athenian Democracy in the Age of Demosthenes*, 55. He says the total population is "unknown" but clearly much larger than the number of adult male citizens.
2. Ober, *Democracy and Knowledge*, 101. See also Hansen, *The Athenian Democracy*, 306.
3. The exceptions are well-documented in Sintomer, *The Government of Chance*, especially ch. 2.
4. Here I am following Hansen rather than Canevaro. See Hansen, *The Athenian Democracy*, and Canevaro, *The Authenticity of the Document at Demosth*.
5. John Stuart Mill, *Considerations on Representative Government*, 78–80; Hansen, *The Athenian Democracy*, 320; Ober, *Democracy and Knowledge*, 274; Mansbridge, "On

the Idea That Participation Makes Better Citizens," 291–328; and Carole Pateman, who, building on Mill, called it the "educative function of participation" (in Pateman, *Participation and Democratic Theory*, 42–43).
6. A. R. W. Harrison, "Law-Making at Athens at the end of the Fifth Century B.C.," *The Journal of Hellenic Studies* 1955; 75: 26–35. See p. 35.
7. In the *Federalist* No. 10, Madison talked of deliberation as a "cure." "The scheme of representation" "promises the cure for which we are seeking" to the problem of majority faction. His explanation was the deliberation of representatives who would "refine and enlarge the public views."
8. The Athenian institutions did not, of course, always achieve their intended effect. For example, George Grote noted that the *graphe paranomon* was sometimes used to discredit opponents and tie them up in legal issues. See his classic *A History of Greece from the Time of Solon to 403 bc* (condensed and edited with notes and appendices J. M. Mitchell and M. O. B. Caspari (London: Routledge and Sons, 1907, reprinted 1930), p. 323.
9. This chapter takes up a challenge posed by Simone Chambers: "More and more deliberative democratic theory looks at and investigates alternatives or supplements to mass democracy in the form of innovative small-scale deliberative experiments, rather than ways of making mass democracy itself more deliberative. Today, deliberative democratic theory pays almost no attention to elections campaigns, referendums, or broad questions of public opinion formation." See Simone Chambers, "Rhetoric and the Public Sphere: Has Deliberative Democracy Abandoned Mass Democracy?" *Political Theory*, 2009; 37: 323–350. See p. 331.
10. Dennis F. Thompson, "Deliberate About, Not In, Elections."
11. Ackerman and Fishkin, *Deliberation Day*.
12. For an overview, see the edited volume about the event, McCombs and Reynolds (eds), *The Poll with a Human Face*.
13. See Fishkin, Bolotnyy, Lerner, et al., "Can Deliberation Have Lasting Effects?"
14. This discussion of the candidates is based on James Fishkin and Larry Diamond, "Presidential Candidates Advance by Being Divisive. We Can Do Better than That," *USA Today*. https://www.usatoday.com/story/opinion/2019/12/05/presidential-candidates-skipped-partisanship-gained-strength-column/4310114002/. Published December 5, 2019. Accessed February 23, 2024. Also available at https://drive.google.com/file/d/10D-akmNwMXGIj_uMVI_ct7KzQJgUque4/view.
15. For the representativeness of the treatment and control groups and comparisons of the changes see sections 1 and 2 of the online appendix for Fishkin et al. "Is Deliberation an Antidote?"
16. http://deliberation.stanford.edu (see separate pages for Japan and South Korea and the links there); Park, "Deliberative Democracy in South Korea: Four Deliberative Polling Experiments"; and Yasunori Sone, "Democracy and Deliberative Polling in Policymaking in Japan," in Baogang He, Michael Breen, and James Fishkin (eds), *Deliberative Democracy in Asia* (London; New York: Routledge, Taylor & Francis Group, 2022).
17. In California a proposition to change the law requires valid signatures equaling 5% of the vote in the last gubernatorial election. To change the constitution, the requirement is 8%.

18. See James Fishkin, Thad Kousser, Robert C. Luskin, et al., "Deliberative Agenda Setting: Piloting Reform of Direct Democracy in California," *Perspectives on Politics* 2015; 13: 1030–1042.
19. Claus Offe, "Referendum vs. Institutionalized Deliberation: What Democratic Theorists Can Learn from the 2016 Brexit Decision," *Daedalus* 2017; 146: 14–27.
20. Daniel Martinez HoSang, *Racial Propositions: Ballot Initiatives and the Making of Postwar California* (Berkeley: University of California Press, 2010), ch. 6.
21. The project was conceived and led by Dr Pam Ryan of *Issues Deliberation Australia*. See https://deliberation.stanford.edu/news/deliberative-pollingr-referendum-make-australia-republic. For some background on the referendum, see John Uhr, "Making Sense of the Referendum," Parliament of Australia 1999: https://www.aph.gov.au/~/~/link.aspx?_id=96091033C7CC4B31B896512CEE31B5CA&_z=z.
22. Kasper M. Hansen, *Deliberative Democracy and Opinion Formation* (Odense: University Press of Southern Denmark, 2004).
23. Gastil, *By Popular Demand*, p. 161.
24. See my critique of the Citizens' Initiative Review (CIR) tabulation of majority and minority support for a medical marijuana proposition with 13 in favor and 12 against in *Democracy When the People Are Thinking*, p. 165. The CIR has since dropped publicizing the vote tabulation for and against for such small samples, now focusing very usefully on substantive statements about the citizens' views in favor of and against the proposals, as well as a list of key findings.
25. See Robert A. Dahl, *A Preface to Economic Democracy* (Berkeley: University of California Press, 1985). For a recent proposal that emphasizes bicameral governance of firms (workers represented by one chamber and shareholders by the other), see Isabelle Ferreras, Tom Malleson, and Joel Rogers (eds), *Democratizing the Corporation: The Bicameral Firm and Beyond* (London: Verso, 2024). The Bicameral proposal would democratize corporate governance, but it is not explicitly a proposal for more deliberation.
26. See the report: James Fishkin, Alice Siu, Samuel Chang, et al., *Meta Community Forum: Results Analysis*, Deliberative Democracy Lab, 2023. https://cddrl.fsi.stanford.edu/publication/metaverse-community-forum-results-analysis.
27. For the Metaverse project, see https://cddrl.fsi.stanford.edu/news/results-first-global-deliberative-pollr-announced-stanfords-deliberative-democracy-lab. For the generative AI projects, see https://deliberation.stanford.edu/meta-community-forum-generative-ai-results.
28. See Lindsay Stewart, "Proxy-Voting Insights: How Differently Do The Big Three Vote on ESG Resolutions," *The Harvard Law School Forum on Corporate Governance*, 2023, https://corpgov.law.harvard.edu/2023/07/03/proxy-voting-insights-how-differently-do-the-big-three-vote-on-esg-resolutions/.
29. See appendix in Fishkin, *Democracy When the People Are Thinking* for an English translation.
30. See the discussion of Mongolia in the sections "Institutionalizing Deliberation: the Case of Mongolia" in Chapter 3 and "Deliberative Referendums for Constitutional Change" in Chapter 5.
31. Such a deliberation should not be confused with town halls sponsored by individual members of Congress with random samples. The samples would need to be represen-

tative and the agenda balanced with opportunities both for small group discussions and plenary sessions with competing experts, all to ensure balance. Such a design is importantly different from the "deliberative town halls" organized by Michael Neblo and his collaborators. Those that take place in single congressional districts are dialogues with the representative. While there are questionnaires before and after, they show systematic movement in the direction advocated by the representative. Is that balanced deliberation or what Neblo et al. call "deliberative persuasion"? See Michael Neblo, Kevin Esterling, and David Lazer, *Politics with the People: Building a Directly Representative Democracy* (Cambridge; New York: Cambridge University Press, 2018), p. 85.
32. Educating for American Democracy (EAD). *Educating for American Democracy: Excellence in History and Civics for All Learners.* iCivics, 2021. https://www.educatingforamericandemocracy.org. See p. 4.
33. Ibid., p. 30.
34. For a compendium of national and local US projects in the schools with links to detailed reports see: https://deliberation.stanford.edu/projects/organization/deliberation-schools. See also Patricia G. Avery, "Deliberation as a core part of teacher education and civics classrooms," *Enseñanza de las Ciencias Sociales* 2011; 10: 11–21 for a separate international effort to bring deliberation to the schools with a different model.
35. See Ackerman and Fishkin, *Deliberation Day*.
36. Ibid., 265, note 12: "While Deliberation Day will take place in local communities, it will employ random assignment within convenient geographical areas in order to engage people in conversation beyond their normal interlocutors."
37. Kimmo Grönlund, Kaisa Herne, James Fishkin, et al., "Good deliberation regardless of mode? An experimental comparison of automated online moderation, human online moderation, and face-to-face moderation in a Deliberative Poll." Paper prepared for the meetings of the American Political Science Association, Philadelphia, September 2024.
38. Such a convention can be called into being by two-thirds of the states, and if a proposed amendment is proposed by the convention it must be ratified by three fourths of the states.
39. The classic account is William N. Eskridge Jr. and John A. Ferejohn, "Super-Statutes," *Duke Law Journal* 2001; 50: 1215–1276.
40. See Reva Siegel, "Constitutional Culture, Social Movement Conflict and Constitutional Change: The Case of the De Facto Era. 2005–06 Brennan Center Symposium Lecture," *California Law Review* 2006; 94: 1323 for the general problem; Reva Siegel, "Dead or Alive: Originalism as Popular Constitutionalism in Heller," *Harvard Law Review* 2008; 122" on Heller; and Reva Siegel, "Memory Games: Dobbs's Originalism as Anti-Democratic Living Constitutionalism—and Some Pathways for Resistance, *SSRN Journal* 2022, DOI: 10.2139/ssrn.4179622 on Dobbs.
41. See https://cddrl.fsi.stanford.edu/news/deliberative-polling-fosters-peace-and-instigates-positive-change-among-people-mongolia.
42. This proposal is a variation of proposals I consider in *Democracy When the People Are Thinking* (part IV, section 11).
43. Nuri Kim et. al. (2018) "Intergroup Contact in Deliberative Contexts: Evidence from Deliberative Polls." For more details see https://deliberation.stanford.edu/news/deliberative-pollingr-policies-toward-roma-bulgaria, and https://deliberation.stanford.edu/news/deliberative-pollingr-reconciliation-australia.

44. Variations of this argument can be found in Sanders, "Against Deliberation"; Lupia and Norton, "Inequality is Always in the Room"; Iris Marion Young, *Intersecting Voices* (Princeton: Princeton University Press, 1997).
45. Robert Luskin, Gaurav Sood, James Fishkin, et al., "Deliberative Distortions? Homogenization, Polarization, and Domination in Small Group Discussions."
46. See Tables A1 to A3 in Appendix, and for more details, Robert Luskin, Gaurav Sood, James Fishkin, et al., "Deliberative Distortions? Homogenization, Polarization, and Domination in Small Group Discussions."
47. The Fukushima disaster, which was the subject of a national, government-sponsored Deliberative Poll. See https://deliberation.stanford.edu/news/deliberative-pollingr-energy-and-environmental-policy-options-japan.
48. John Rawls, *A Theory of Justice* (Cambridge: Harvard University Press, 1971), 164–165.
49. John Rawls, "Outline of a Decision Procedure for Ethics," *The Philosophical Review* 1951; 60: 177.
50. Douglas Rae, "Maximin Justice and an Alternative Principle of General Advantage," *American Political Science Review* 1975; 69: 630–647.
51. In essence the key revision was to assume "a model conception of a moral person" that prized liberty and then derived the priority of liberty from that assumption. For my broader argument about Rawls see James Fishkin, *The Dialogue of Justice: Toward a Self-Reflective Society* (New Haven: Yale University Press, 1992), 82–96.
52. See my *Dialogue of Justice*, 93–96.
53. Derek Parfit, *Reasons and Persons* (Oxford: Oxford University Press, 1986), 482.
54. https://deliberation.stanford.edu/news/america-one-room-climate-and-energy#EXECUTIVE.
55. Jieun Park, "Deliberative Democracy in South Korea: Four Deliberative Polling Experiments." See p. 163.
56. Parfit's repugnant conclusion, *Reasons and Persons*, p. 388.
57. An argument Parfit frames as "only France survives," *Reasons and Persons*, p. 421.
58. These include: David Van Reybrouck, *Against Elections*; John Gastil and Erik Olin Wright *Legislature by Lot: Transformative Designs for Deliberative Governance*; Alexander Guerrero, "Against Elections: The Lottocratic Alternative"; Landemore, *Open Democracy*; and numerous others.
59. See Chapter 4.
60. Sunstein, *Going to Extremes*.
61. The evidence is incomplete because most of these processes do not collect attitudinal data at recruitment. See the discussion in Chapter 4.
62. Dahl famously offered simple calculations about the vanishingly small talking time per person as group size increases. See Dahl, *Democracy and Its Critics*, 227.
63. Landemore, *Open Democracy*, 91.
64. Alexander Guerrero had earlier proposed a siloed design with a smaller number of larger assemblies, apparently all at the national level. These are 300-person, randomly selected "single-issue legislatures" that meet for three years. With the smaller number, the proposal does not address the challenge of fulfilling the rotation method. But with the larger number in each assembly or legislature, each could make a more adequate claim to representativeness via stratified random sampling. See Guerrero, "Against Elections: The Lottocratic Alternative." David Van Reybrouck, *Against Elections*, 149 had earlier

proposed building up to a "historic transformation" in which selection by lot would replace the entire legislative process.
65. I would, apparently, have the option of starting a signature campaign for an initiative that would go either to the legislature (presumably chosen randomly) or to a mass popular vote. Referendums would be "by construction deliberative" (p. 150), but designing the wording in a deliberative manner, presumably by a random sample, does not bring deliberation to the process of voting in them. See my discussion earlier in the chapter for proposals about how to do that.
66. In theory this can happen on occasion with elections, even deliberative ones, but one could expect the competing party packages to cover the most salient issues.
67. Landemore, *Open Democracy*, 145.

References

Achen, C. H. and Bartels, L. M. *Democracy for Realists: Why Elections Do Not Produce Responsive Government*. Princeton: Princeton University Press, 2016.
Ackerman, B. A. *We the People, Vol. 1: Foundations*. Cambridge, MA: Belknap Press of Harvard University Press, 1991.
Ackerman, B. A. *We the People, Vol. 2: Transformations*. Cambridge, MA: Belknap Press of Harvard University Press, 1998.
Ackerman, B. A. *We the People, Vol. 3: The Civil Rights Revolution*. Cambridge, MA: Belknap Press of Harvard University Press, 2014.
Ackerman, B. A. and Fishkin, J. S. *Deliberation Day*. New Haven: Yale University Press, 2004.
Adair, D. "'That Politics May Be Reduced to a Science': David Hume, James Madison, and the Tenth Federalist." In: Colbourn, T. (ed.). *Fame and the Founding Fathers*. Indianapolis: Liberty Fund, 1974; 3–36.
Aldrich, J. H. *Why Parties? A Second Look*. Chicago: University of Chicago Press, 2011.
Allport, G. W. *The Nature of Prejudice*. Cambridge, MA: Perseus Books, 1954.
American Political Science Association, Committee on Political Parties. "'Toward a More Responsible Two-Party System,' Part I: The Need for Greater Party Responsibility." *The American Political Science Review* 1950; 44: 15–36.
Anderson, B. *Imagined Communities: Reflections on the Origin and Spread of Nationalism*. London: Verso, 1983.
Asch, S. E. "Opinions and Social Pressure." *Scientific American* 1955; 193: 31–35.
Associated Press—NORC. "What Americans think about the Economy." 2018.
Associated Press—NORC. *2019: The Public's Priorities and Expectations*. Associated Press—NORC Center for Public Affairs Research, 2019.
Avery, P. G. "Deliberation as a core part of teacher education and civics classrooms." *Enseñanza de las Ciencias Sociales* 2011; 10: 11–21.
Banzhaf, J. F. "Multi-Member Electoral Districts. Do They Violate the 'One Man, One Vote' Principle?" *The Yale Law Journal* 1966; 75: 1309.
Bauer, S. and Lieb, D. A. "GOP Threat to Impeach a Wisconsin Supreme Court Justice is Driven by Fear of Losing Legislative Edge." *AP News*. https://apnews.com/article/wisconsin-supreme-court-impeachment-republicans-gerrymandering-legislature-21fc8c3cf99623a379cbf4dd01ed0b8c. Published September 10, 2023. Accessed February 14, 2024.
Beeman, R. "Perspectives on the Constitution: A Republic, If You Can Keep It." National Constitution Center—constitutioncenter.org.
Bell, D. *The China Model: Political Meritocracy and the Limits of Democracy*. Princeton: Princeton University Press, 2015.
Berelson, B., Lazarsfeld, P. F., and McPhee, W. N. *Voting: A Study of Opinion Formation in a Presidential Campaign*. Chicago: University of Chicago Press, 1986.
Berry, J. M. and Sobieraj, S. *The Outrage Industry: Political Opinion Media and the New Incivility*. Oxford; New York: Oxford University Press, 2014.
Bessette, J. M. *The Mild Voice of Reason: Deliberative Democracy and American National Government*. Chicago: University of Chicago Press, 1994.
Binney, H. *An Inquiry into the Formation of Washington's Farewell Address*. London: Forgotten Books, 2018.

Bishop, C. F. *History of Elections in the American Colonies.* Buffalo: William S. Hein, 2002.
Bishop, G. F. *The Illusion of Public Opinion: Fact and Artifact in American Public Opinion Polls.* Lanham: Rowman & Littlefield, 2005.
Black, D. "On the Rationale of Group Decision-making." *Journal of Political Economy* 1948; 56: 23–34.
Brady, H. E. and Sniderman, P. M. "Attitude Attribution: A Group Basis for Political Reasoning." *American Political Science Review* 1985; 79: 1061–1078.
Brennan, J. *Against Democracy.* Princeton: Princeton University Press, 2016.
Burnheim, J. *Is Democracy Possible? The Alternative to Electoral Democracy.* Sydney: Sydney University Press, 2006.
Cammack, D. "Deliberation and Discussion in Classical Athens." *Journal of Political Philosophy* 2021; 29: 135–166.
Campbell, A. and University Of Michigan (eds). *The American Voter.* Chicago: University of Chicago Press, 1980.
Canevaro, M. "The Authenticity of the Document at Demosth. or. 24.20–3, the Procedures of *nomothesia* and the so-called ἐπιχειροτονία τῶν νόμων." *Klio* 2018; 100: 70–124.
Carroll, L. *Through the Looking Glass.* London: Harper Press, 2013.
Chambers, S. "Rhetoric and the Public Sphere: Has Deliberative Democracy Abandoned Mass Democracy?" *Political Theory* 2009; 37: 323–350.
Chong, D. and Druckman, J. N. "A Theory of Framing and Opinion Formation in Competitive Elite Environments." *Journal of Communication* 2007; 57: 99–118.
Chotiner, I. "The Origins of Netanyahu's 'All-Systems Assault' on Israeli Democracy." *The New Yorker*, March 7, 2023.
Committee on Political Parties, "Toward a More Responsible Two-Party System: A Report of the Committee on Political Parties; Summary of Conclusions and Proposals." *The American Political Science Review* 1950; 44: 1–14.
Converse, P. E. "The Nature of Belief Systems in Mass Publics." In: Apter D. E. (ed.). *Ideology and Discontent.* New York: Free Press, 1964, 206–261.
Converse, P. E. "The Nature of Belief Systems in Mass Publics (1964)." *Critical Review* 2006; 18: 1–74.
Courant, D. "The Promises and Disappointments of the French Citizens' Convention for Climate." *Deliberative Democracy Digest*, 2021.
Dahl, R. A. *A Preface to Democratic Theory.* Chicago: University of Chicago Press, 1956.
Dahl, R. A. *Polyarchy: Participation and Opposition.* New Haven: Yale University Press, 1971.
Dahl, R. A. *A Preface to Economic Democracy.* Berkeley: University of California Press, 1985.
Dahl, R. A. "The Pseudodemocratization of the American Presidency." 1988. The Tanner Lectures on Human Values delivered at Harvard University April 11 and 12, 1988 available at https://tannerlectures.org/wp-content/uploads/sites/105/2024/06/dahl89.pdf
Dahl, R. A. *Democracy and Its Critics.* New Haven: Yale University Press, 1989.
Davies, K., Tropp, L. R., Aron, A., Pettigrew, T. F., and Wright, S. C. "Cross-Group Friendships and Intergroup Attitudes: A Meta-Analytic Review." *Personality and Social Psychology Review* 2011; 15: 332–351.
Delli Carpini, M. X. and Keeter, S. *What Americans Know about Politics and Why It Matters.* New Haven: Yale University Press, 1997.
Diamond, L. "Democratic Regression in Comparative Perspective: Scope, Methods, and Causes." *Democratization* 2021; 28: 22–42.
Diamond, L. *Ill Winds: Saving Democracy from Russian Rage, Chinese Ambition, and American Complacency.* New York: Penguin, 2019.
Donnelly, T. "Judicial Popular Constitutionalism." *Constitutional Commentary*, 2015.
Downs, A. *An Economic Theory of Democracy.* New York: Harper, 1957.

Druckman, J. N., Peterson, E., and Slothuus, R. "How Elite Partisan Polarization Affects Public Opinion Formation." *American Political Science Review* 2013; 107: 57–79.

Ecker, U. K. H., Lewandowsky, S., Cook, J., Schmid, P., Fazio, L., Brashier, N., Kendeou, P., Vraga, E., and Amazeen, M. "The Psychological Drivers of Misinformation Belief and its Resistance to Correction." *Nature Reviews Psychology* 2022; 1: 13–29.

Educating for American Democracy (EAD). *Educating for American Democracy: Excellence in History and Civics for All Learners.* iCivics, 2021.

Eisenberg, T., Hannaford-Agor, P. L., Hans, V. P., Waters, N L., Munsterman, G. T., Schwab, S. J., and Wells, M. T. "Judge–Jury Agreement in Criminal Cases: A Partial Replication of Kalven and Zeisel's *The American Jury.*" *Journal of Empirical Legal Studies* 2005; 2: 171–207.

Elliott, K. J. *Democracy for Busy People.* Chicago; London: University of Chicago Press, 2023.

Eskridge, W. N. and Ferejohn, J. "Super-Statutes." *Duke Law Journal* 2001; 50: 1215.

Farrar, C., Fishkin, J. S., Green, D P., List, C., Luskin, R. C., and Levy Paluck, E. "Disaggregating Deliberation's Effects: An Experiment within a Deliberative Poll." *British Journal of Political Science* 2010; 40: 333–347.

Farrell, D. M., Suiter, J., Cunningham, K., and Harris, C. "When Mini-Publics and Maxi-Publics Coincide: Ireland's National Debate on Abortion." *Representation* 2023; 59: 55–73.

Ferreras, I., Malleson, T., and Rogers, J. (eds). *Democratizing the Corporation: The Bicameral Firm and Beyond.* London: Verso, 2024.

Fishkin, J., Bolotnyy, V., Lerner, J., Siu, A., and Bradburn, N. "Can Deliberation Have Lasting Effects?" *American Political Science Review* 2024: 1–21.

Fishkin, J., Belotnyy, V., Lerner, J., Siu, A., and Bradburn, N. "Scaling Dialogue for Democracy: Can Automated Deliberation Create More Deliberative Voters?" *Perspectives on Politics* (forthcoming).

Fishkin., J and Diamond, L. "Opinion | This Experiment Has Some Great News for Our Democracy." *The New York Times.* https://www.nytimes.com/2019/10/02/opinion/america-one-room-experiment.html. Published October 2, 2019a. Accessed February 14, 2024.

Fishkin, J. and Diamond, L. "Presidential Candidates Advance by Being Divisive. We Can Do Better than That." *USA TODAY.* https://www.usatoday.com/story/opinion/2019/12/05/presidential-candidates-skipped-partisanship-gained-strength-column/4310114002/. Published December 5, 2019b. Accessed February 23, 2024.

Fishkin, J. and Diamond, L. Is the Climate Crisis Just Too Hot for Us to Handle? *American Purpose,* 2021.

Fishkin, J., Siu, A., Diamond, L., and Bradburn, N. "Is Deliberation an Antidote to Extreme Partisan Polarization? Reflections on 'America in One Room.'" *American Political Science Review* 2021; 115: 1464–1481.

Fishkin, J., Kousser, T., Luskin, R. C., and Siu, A. "Deliberative Agenda Setting: Piloting Reform of Direct Democracy in California." *Perspectives on Politics* 2015; 13: 1030–1042.

Fishkin, J., Siu, A., Chang, S., Ciesla, E., and Kartsang, T. *Meta Community Forum: Results Analysis.* Deliberative Democracy Lab, 2023.

Fishkin, J. S. *Tyranny and Legitimacy: A Critique of Political Theories.* Baltimore: Johns Hopkins University Press, 1979.

Fishkin, J. S. *The Limits of Obligation.* New Haven: Yale University Press, 1982.

Fishkin, J. S. "The Case for a National Caucus." *The Atlantic,* 1988: 16–18.

Fishkin, J. S. *The Dialogue of Justice: Toward a Self-Reflective Society.* New Haven: Yale University Press, 1992.

Fishkin, J. S. *Democracy and Deliberation: New Directions for Democratic Reform.* New Haven: Yale University Press, 1991.

Fishkin, J. S. *When the People Speak: Deliberative Democracy and Public Consultation*. Oxford: Oxford University Press, 2011.

Fishkin, J. S. *Democracy When the People Are Thinking: Revitalizing Our Politics through Public Deliberation*. Oxford: Oxford University Press, 2018.

Fishkin, J. S and Siu, A. "Mongolia: Piloting Elements of a Deliberative System." In: He, B., Breen, M. G., and Fishkin, J. S. (eds). *Deliberative Democracy in Asia*. London; New York: Routledge, Taylor & Francis Group, 2022, 190–204.

Freedom House. *Freedom in the World, 2023*, 2023.

Galbraith, K. and Price, A. "Book Excerpt: How the Public Got Behind Texas Wind Power." *The Texas Tribune*. https://www.texastribune.org/2013/09/17/book-excerpt-how-public-got-behind-tx-wind-power/. Published September 17, 2013. Accessed February 14, 2024.

Gallup, G. "Public Opinion in a Democracy." 1939. Pub. under the University extension fund, Herbert L. Baker foundation, Princeton university, 1939: 15 pages. Available at: Public Opinion in a Democracy - George Gallup - Google Books

Gallup, G. "Testing Public Opinion." *The Public Opinion Quarterly* 1938; 2: 8–14.

Gastil, J. *By Popular Demand: Revitalizing Representative Democracy through Deliberative Elections*. Berkeley: University of California Press, 2000.

Gastil, J, Deess, E. P., and Weiser, P. "Civic Awakening in the Jury Room: A Test of the Connection between Jury Deliberation and Political Participation." *The Journal of Politics* 2002; 64: 585–595.

Gastil, J. and Wright, E. O. *Legislature by Lot: Transformative Designs for Deliberative Governance*. London; New York: Verso, 2019.

Goidel, R. K. and Shields, T. G. "The Vanishing Marginals, the Bandwagon, and the Mass Media." *The Journal of Politics* 1994; 56: 802–810.

Goodin, R. E. "Democratic Deliberation Within." *Philosophy & Public Affairs* 2000; 29: 81–109.

Green, D. P. and Gerber, A. S. *Get Out the Vote: How to Increase Voter Turnout*. Washington, DC: Brookings Institution Press, 2019.

Green, D. P, Palmquist, B., and Schickler, E. *Partisan Hearts and Minds: Political Parties and the Social Identities of Voters*. New Haven; London: Yale University Press, 2002.

Green, D. P. and Shapiro, I. *Pathologies of Rational Choice Theory: A Critique of Applications in Political Science*. New Haven: Yale University Press, 1994.

Grönlund, K., Herne, K., Fishkin, J., Huttunen, J., Jäske, M., Lindell, M., Siu, A., Backström, K., and Vento, I. "Good deliberation regardless of mode? An experimental comparison of automated online moderation, human online moderation, and face-to-face moderation in a Deliberative Poll." Annual Meeting of the American Political Science Association. Philadelphia, 2024.

Grote, G. *A History of Greece*. Cambridge: Cambridge University Press, 2010.

Guerrero, A. A. "Against Elections: The Lottocratic Alternative." *Philosophy & Public Affairs* 2014; 42: 135–178.

Habermas, J. *Between Facts and Norms: Contributions to a Discourse Theory of Law and Democracy*. Cambridge, MA: MIT Press, 1998.

Hamilton, A., Madison, J., and Jay, J. *The Federalist Papers*. Kramnick, I. (ed.). London: Penguin, 1987.

Hansen, K. M. *Deliberative Democracy and Opinion Formation*. Odense: University Press of Southern Denmark, 2004.

Hansen, M. H. *The Athenian Democracy in the Age of Demosthenes: Structure, Principles, and Ideology*. Norman, OK: University of Oklahoma Press, 1999.

Hansen, M. H. *Polis: An Introduction to the Ancient Greek City-State*. Oxford; New York: Oxford University Press, 2006.

Hansen, M. H. "The Inserted Document at Dem. 24.20–23. Response to Mirko Canevaro." *Klio* 2019; 101: 452–472.

Harrison, A. R. W. "Law-Making at Athens at the End of the Fifth Century B.C." *The Journal of Hellenic Studies* 1955; 75: 26–35.

Hart, H. L. A. "Between Utility and Rights." *Columbia Law Review* 1979; 79: 828.

Hetherington, M. J. and Rudolph, T. J. *Why Washington Won't Work: Polarization, Political Trust, and the Governing Crisis*. Chicago: University of Chicago Press, 2015.

Hewstone, M. and Swart, H. "Fifty-odd years of Inter-group Contact: From Hypothesis to Integrated Theory." *British Journal of Social Psychology* 2011; 50: 374–386.

Ho, T. "Explaining Why Cars in Singapore Are So Expensive." *Dollars and Sense*, 2023. Available at: https://dollarsandsense.sg/no-nonsense-explanation-on-why-cars-in-singapore-are-so-expensive/

Hofstadter, R. *The Idea of a Party System: The Rise of Legitimate Opposition in the United States, 1780–1840*. Berkeley: University of California Press, 1976.

HoSang, D. *Racial Propositions: Ballot Initiatives and the Making of Postwar California*. Berkeley: University of California Press, 2010.

Hotelling, H. "Stability in Competition." *The Economic Journal* 1929; 39: 41.

Hunt, G. (ed.). *The Writings of James Madison, Comprising His Public Papers and His Private Correspondence, Including His Numerous Letters and Documents Now for the First Time Printed*. New York: G. P. Putnam's Sons, 1900.

Huntington, S. "The Democratic Distemper." *The Public Interest*, New York, Fall 1975; 9–38.

Huntington, S. *American Politics: The Promise of Disharmony*. Cambridge, MA: Harvard University Press, 1981.

Iyengar, S. and Ansolabehere, S. *Going Negative: How Political Advertisements Shrink and Polarize the Electorate*. New York: Free Press, 1997.

Iyengar, S., Lelkes, Y., Levendusky, M., Malhotra, N., and Westwood, S. "The Origins and Consequences of Affective Polarization in the United States." *Annual Review of Political Science* 2019; 22: 129–146.

Jacobs, L. R., Cook, F. L., and Delli Carpini, M. X. *Talking Together: Public Deliberation and Political Participation in America*. Chicago: University of Chicago Press, 2009.

Jamieson, K. H. *Dirty Politics: Deception, Distraction, and Democracy*. New York: Oxford University Press, 1993.

Kalven, Jr. H. and Zeisel, H. *The American Jury*. Boston: Little, Brown & Co., 1966.

Kim N., Fishkin J. S., and Luskin, R. C. "Intergroup Contact in Deliberative Contexts: Evidence from Deliberative Polls." *Journal of Communication* 2018; 68: 1029–1051.

Kritzer, H. M. "Polarization and Partisanship in State Supreme Court Elections." *Judicature* 2021; 105: 65–75.

Krosnick, J. A. "Government Policy and Citizen Passion: A Study of Issue Publics in Contemporary America." *Political Behavior* 1990; 12: 59–92.

Kunda, Z. "The case for motivated reasoning." *Psychological Bulletin* 1990; 108: 480–498.

Lafont, C. *Democracy without Shortcuts: A Participatory Conception of Deliberative Democracy*. Oxford: Oxford University Press, 2020.

Landemore, H. *Democratic Reason: Politics, Collective Intelligence, and the Rule of the Many*. Princeton: Princeton University Press, 2012.

Landemore, H. *Open Democracy: Reinventing Popular Rule for the Twenty-First Century*. Princeton: Princeton University Press, 2020.

Lee, F. E. *Insecure Majorities: Congress and the Perpetual Campaign*. Chicago; London: University of Chicago Press, 2016.

Leeper, T. J. and Slothuus, R. "Political Parties, Motivated Reasoning, and Public Opinion Formation." *Political Psychology* 2014; 35: 129–156.

Lenz, G. S. *Follow the Leader? How Voters Respond to Politicians' Policies and Performance*. Chicago; London: University of Chicago Press, 2012.

Levendusky, M. S., Druckman, J. N., and McLain, A. "How Group Discussions Create Strong Attitudes and Strong Partisans." *Research & Politics* 2016; 3(2): 1–6.

Levitsky, S. and Way, L. A. *Competitive Authoritarianism: Hybrid Regimes after the Cold War*. Cambridge; New York: Cambridge University Press, 2010.

Levitsky, S. and Ziblatt, D. *How Democracies Die*. New York: Crown, 2018.

Levitsky, S. and Ziblatt, D. *Tyranny of the Minority*. New York: Crown, 2023.

Lijphart, A. *Patterns of Democracy: Government Forms and Performance in Thirty-Six Countries*. New Haven: Yale University Press, 1999.

Litan, R. E., Brookings Institution, American Bar Association (eds). *Verdict: Assessing the Civil Jury System*. Washington, DC: Brookings Institution, 1993.

Little, I. M. D. *A Critique of Welfare Economics*. Oxford: Oxford University Press, 1960.

Lupia, A. "Shortcuts Versus Encyclopedias: Information and Voting Behavior in California Insurance Reform Elections." *American Political Science Review* 1994; 88: 63–76.

Lupia, A. and Norton, A. "Inequality is Always in the Room: Language and Power in Deliberative Democracy." *Daedalus* 2017; 146: 64–76.

Luskin, R. C., Sood, G., Fishkin, J. S., and Hahn, K. S. "Deliberative Distortions? Homogenization, Polarization, and Domination in Small Group Discussions." *British Journal of Political Science* 2022; 52: 1205–1225.

Mackenzie, M. K. and Warren, M. E. "Two Trust-Based Uses of Mini-Publics in Democratic Systems." In: Parkinson, J. and Mansbridge, J. J. (eds). *Deliberative Systems: Deliberative Democracy at the Large Scale*. Cambridge: Cambridge University Press, 2012; 95–124.

Manin, B. *The Principles of Representative Government*. Cambridge; New York: Cambridge University Press, 1997.

Mansbridge, J. "On the Idea that Participation Makes Better Citizens." In: Elkin, S. L. and Soltan, K. E. (eds). *Citizen Competence and Democratic Institutions*. University Park, PA: Pennsylvania State University Press, 1999, 291–328.

Mansbridge, J. "Everyday Talk in the Deliberative System." In: Macedo, S. (ed.). *Deliberative Politics*. New York: Oxford University Press, 1999, 211–239.

Mansbridge, J. J. *Beyond Adversary Democracy*. New York: Basic Books, 1980.

Marx, C., Benecke, C., and Gumz, A. "Talking Cure Models: A Framework of Analysis." *Frontiers in Psychology* 2017; 8: 1589.

Maoz, I. "An Experiment in Peace: Reconciliation-Aimed Workshops of Jewish-Israeli and Palestinian Youth." *Journal of Peace Research* 2000; 37: 721–736.

McCarthy, J. "Record-High 70% in U.S. Support Same-Sex Marriage." Gallup.com, 2021.

McCombs, M. and Reynolds, A. (eds). *The Poll with a Human Face: The National Issues Convention Experiment in Political Communication*. Mahwah, NJ: Lawrence Erlbaum Associates, 1999.

Mill, J. S. *Considerations on Representative Government*. Amherst, NY: Prometheus Books, 1991.

Morin, R. "Who Knows? Often, Survey Respondents Have No Opinion—Until the Pollster Prompts Them." *The Washington Post*. https://www.washingtonpost.com/archive/2001/09/10/who-knows/7f4204ab-b7ee-4d3e-959f-e722ee92bc31/. Published September 9, 2001. Accessed February 25, 2024.

Müller, J.-W. *What Is Populism?* Philadelphia: University of Pennsylvania Press, 2016.

Mutz, D. C. *In-Your-Face Politics: The Consequences of Uncivil Media*. Princeton: Princeton University Press, 2015.

National Statistics Office of Mongolia. Main Findings of the First Nationwide Deliberative Polling on Constitutional Amendment of Mongolia, 2017.

Neblo, M., Esterling, K. M., and Lazer, D. M. J. *Politics with the People: Building a Directly Representative Democracy*. Cambridge; New York: Cambridge University Press, 2018.

Newman, B., Merolla, J. L., Shah, S., Lemi, D. C., Collingwood, L., and Ramakrishnan, S. K. "The Trump Effect: An Experimental Investigation of the Emboldening Effect of Racially Inflammatory Elite Communication." *British Journal of Political Science* 2021; 51: 1138–1159.

Newport, F. "Update: Partisan Gaps Expand Most on Government Power, Climate." Gallup.com, 2023.

Noelle-Neumann, E. *The Spiral of Silence: Public Opinion, Our Social Skin*. Chicago: University of Chicago Press, 1984.

Nyhan, B., Porter, E., Reifler, J., and Wood, T. "Taking Fact-Checks Literally But Not Seriously? The Effects of Journalistic Fact-Checking on Factual Beliefs and Candidate Favorability." *Political Behavior* 2020; 42: 939–960.

Nyhan, B. and Reifler, J. "When Corrections Fail: The Persistence of Political Misperceptions." *Political Behavior* 2010; 32: 303–330.

Ober, J. *Mass and Elite in Democratic Athens: Rhetoric. Ideology and the Power of the People*. Princeton: Princeton University Press, 1989.

Ober, J. *Democracy and Knowledge: Innovation and Learning in Classical Athens*. Princeton: Princeton University Press, 2008.

Offe, C. "Referendum vs. Institutionalized Deliberation: What Democratic Theorists Can Learn from the 2016 Brexit Decision." *Daedalus* 2017; 146: 14–27.

Page, B. I. and Shapiro, R. Y. *The Rational Public: Fifty Years of Trends in Americans' Policy Preferences*. Chicago: University of Chicago Press, 1992.

Parfit, D. *Reasons and Persons*. Oxford: Oxford University Press, 1986.

Pariser, E. *The Filter Bubble: What the Internet Is Hiding from You*. London: Viking, 2011.

Park, J. "Deliberative Democracy in South Korea: Four Deliberative Polling Experiments." In: He, B., Breen, M., and Fishkin, J. S. (eds). *Deliberative Democracy in Asia*. London; New York: Routledge, Taylor & Francis Group, 2022; 154–171.

Parkinson, J. and Mansbridge, J. J. (eds). *Deliberative Systems: Deliberative Democracy at the Large Scale*. Cambridge: Cambridge University Press, 2012.

Pateman, C. *Participation and Democratic Theory*. Cambridge: Cambridge University Press, 1970.

Pettigrew, T. F. and Tropp, L. R. "A Meta-analytic Test of Intergroup Contact Theory." *Journal of Personality and Social Psychology* 2006; 90: 751–783.

Pettit, P. "Depoliticizing Democracy." *Ratio Juris* 2004; 17: 52–65.

Plamenatz, J. P. *Consent, Freedom and Political Obligation*. London: Oxford University Press, 1968.

Plutarch. *Themistocles in Plutarch's Lives with an English Translation by Bernadotte Perrin*. Cambridge, MA: Harvard University Press, 1914.

Popkin, S. L. *The Reasoning Voter: Communication and Persuasion in Presidential Campaigns*. Chicago: University of Chicago Press, 1991.

Posner, R. A. *Law, Pragmatism, and Democracy*. Cambridge, MA: Harvard University Press, 2003.

Rae, D. "Maximin Justice and an Alternative Principle of General Advantage." *American Political Science Review* 1975; 69: 630–647.

Ranney, A. *Curing the Mischiefs of Faction: Party Reform in America*. Berkeley: University of California Press, 1975.

Rasinski, K., Bradburn, N., and Lauen, D. "Effects of NIC Media Coverage Among the Public." In: McCombs, M. and Reynolds, A. (eds). *The Poll with a Human Face*. Mahwah, NJ: Lawrence Erlbaum Associates, 1999, 155–176.

Rawls, J. "Outline of a Decision Procedure for Ethics." *The Philosophical Review* 1951; 60: 177.

Rawls, J. *A Theory of Justice*. Cambridge, MA: Harvard University Press, 1971.

Renwick, A., Allan, S., Jennings, W., McKee, R., Russell, M., and Smith, G. "What Kind of Brexit do Voters want? Lessons from the Citizens' Assembly on Brexit." *Political Quarterly* 2018; 89: 649–658.

Riker, W. H. and Ordeshook, P. C. "A Theory of the Calculus of Voting." *American Political Science Review* 1968; 62: 25–42.

Roberts, J. T. *Athens on Trial: The Antidemocratic Tradition in Western Thought*. Princeton: Princeton University Press, 1996.

Sandefur, J., Birdsall, N., Fishkin, J., and Movo, M. "Democratic Deliberation and the Resource Curse: A Nationwide Experiment in Tanzania." *World Politics* 2022; 74: 564–609.

Sanders, L. M. "Against Deliberation." *Political Theory* 1997; 25: 347–376.

Schkade, D., Sunstein, C. R., and Hastie, R. "What Happened on Deliberation Day?" *California Law Review* 2007; 95: 915–940.

Schkade, D., Sunstein, C. R., and Kahneman, D. "Deliberating about Dollars: The Severity Shift." *Columbia Law Review* 2000; 100: 1139.

Schudson, M. *The Good Citizen: A History of American Civic Life*. New York: Martin Kessler Books, 1998.

Schumpeter, J. A. *Capitalism, Socialism, and Democracy*. New York: Harper and Brothers, 1942.

Searing, D. D., Solt, F., Conover, P. J., and Crewe, I. "Public Discussion in the Deliberative System: Does It Make Better Citizens?" *British Journal of Political Science* 2007; 37: 587–618.

Shapiro, I. *The State of Democratic Theory*. Princeton: Princeton University Press, 2006.

Siegel, R. B. "Dead or Alive: Originalism as Popular Constitutionalism in Heller." *Harvard Law Review* 2008; 122;191–245.

Siegel, R. B. "Constitutional Culture, Social Movement Conflict and Constitutional Change: The Case of the De Facto Era. 2005–06 Brennan Center Symposium Lecture." *California Law Review* 2006; 94: 1323.

Siegel, R. B. "Memory Games: Dobbs's Originalism as Anti-Democratic Living Constitutionalism—and Some Pathways for Resistance." *Texas Law Review* 2023; 101: 1127–1204.

Sinclair, R. *Democracy and Participation in Athens*. Cambridge; New York: Cambridge University Press, 1988.

Sintomer, Y. *The Government of Chance: Sortition and Democracy from Athens to the Present*. New York: Cambridge University Press, 2023.

Siu, A. "Deliberation & the Challenge of Inequality." *Daedalus* 2017; 146: 119–128.

Siu, A. and Stanisevski, D. "Deliberation in Multicultural Societies." In: Nabatchi, T., Gastil, J., Leighninger, M., and Weiksner, G. M. (eds). *Democracy in Motion*. Oxford; New York: Oxford University Press, 2012, 83–99.

Sone, Y. "Democracy and Deliberative Polling in Policymaking in Japan." In: He, B, Breen, M, and Fishkin, J (eds). *Deliberative Democracy in Asia*. London; New York: Routledge, Taylor & Francis Group, 2022, 136–154.

Stewart, L. "Proxy-Voting Insights: How Differently Do the Big Three Vote on ESG Resolutions." The Harvard Law School Forum on Corporate Governance, 2023.

Stone, I. F. *The Trial of Socrates*. New York: Random House, 1989.

Sunstein, C. "The Law of Group Polarization." In: Fishkin J. S. and Laslett P. (eds). *Debating Deliberative Democracy*. Malden: Blackwell Publishing Ltd., 2003, 80–101.

Sunstein, C. R. *Going to Extremes: How Like Minds Unite and Divide*. Oxford; New York: Oxford University Press, 2009.

Sunstein, C. R. *#Republic: Divided Democracy in the Age of Social Media*. Princeton; Oxford: Princeton University Press, 2017.

Taber, C. S. and Lodge, M. "Motivated Skepticism in the Evaluation of Political Beliefs." *American Journal of Political Science* 2006; 50: 755–769.

Tajfel, H. *Human Groups and Social Categories: Studies in Social Psychology*. Cambridge; New York: Cambridge University Press, 1981.

Thompson, D. F. "Deliberate About, Not In, Elections." *Election Law Journal: Rules, Politics, and Policy* 2013; 12: 372–385.

Tocqueville, A. de. *Democracy in America, Vol 1*. New York: Shocken Books, 1961.

Tushnet, M. "Constitutional Hardball." *Georgetown Law Faculty Publications and Other Works*, 2004.

Uhr, J. "Making Sense of the Referendum*." *Parliament of Australia*, 1999.

Valentine, Z. and Weber, P. Testing Scalability of Civic Deliberation to Support Informed & Inclusive Civic Engagement: Lessons Learned from the July 2022 "Table Talks Project" Pilot, 2022. Report Submitted to the Deliberative Democracy Lab at Stanford University available at: https://drive.google.com/file/d/1EosyBFUtSxqN3B2qnZh_ZHoUdCSHDXqu/view

Van Reybrouck, D. *Against Elections*. London: Bodley Head, 2013.

Wang, R., Fishkin, J. S., and Luskin, R. C. "Does Deliberation Increase Public-Spiritedness?" *Social Science Quarterly* 2020; 101: 2163–2182.

Washington, G. Farewell Address. 1796.

Wojcieszak, M. "Deliberation and Attitude Polarization." *Journal of Communication* 2011; 61: 596–617.

Wood, N. "Bulgaria Invites Guests for a Day of Intense Democracy." *The New York Times*. https://www.nytimes.com/2007/05/07/world/europe/07bulgaria.html. Published May 7, 2007. Accessed February 14, 2024.

Young, I. M. *Intersecting Voices: Dilemmas of Gender, Political Philosophy, and Policy*. Princeton: Princeton University Press, 1997.

Young, I. M. *Inclusion and Democracy*. Oxford; New York: Oxford University Press, 2000.

Index

For the benefit of digital users, indexed terms that span two pages (e.g., 52–53) may, on occasion, appear on only one of those pages.

Achen, Christopher H. 17 *See also* Larry M. Bartels
Ackerman, Bruce A.
  "constitutional moments" 12–13, 24, 125, 144 n.47
    American Founding 12–13
    Civil Rights Movement 12–13, 24
    "Constitutional moments" 24
    New Deal 24
    Reconstruction 24
  "normal politics" 12
  We the People, vol. 1 12–13, 144 n.46, n.47
  We the People, vol. 2 12, 144 n.46
  We the People, vol. 3 12, 144 n.46
Aldrich, John H. 79, 154 n.3
"America in One Room" 81, 84, 89–91, 93, 98, 101, 115, 130–131
American Founders 5, 30, 39, 135
ancient Athens 4–5
  institutions
    Assembly 4–5
    Council of 500 4–5, 143 n.17
    graphe paranomon 4–5
    nomothetai 4–5, 143 n.18
    ostracism 15
  practices of 4–5
  random selection 4–5, 15
  rotation method (as described by Aristotle) 112–113
  trial of Socrates 6
Anderson, Benedict 1, 142 n.3
Apathy (among voters) 32–33
Aristotle 5, 15, 143 n.21, n.22, 145 n.51
Articles of Confederation 5, 125, 143 n.22, 161 n.38
"audience democracy" 3, 27–28

Bartels, Larry M. 17 *See also* Achen, Christopher H.
Benecke, Cord 142 n.1

"benign autocracy" 3, 79–80
"benign autocrat" *See* Mill, John Stuart
Bentham, Jeremy 10–11 *See also* utilitarianism and cost-benefit analysis
Berelson, Bernard 32–33
Bishop, George 8
Bolotnyy, Valentin 35, 73, 93, 148 n.66, 156 n.46, n.47, 157 n.50, n.51, n.53
Bradburn, Norman 77, 153 n.59
Brady, Henry E. 78
briefing materials (for Deliberative Polls) 53, 55, 64, 73, 81–82, 85, 87–88, 104, 107, 116–118, 120, 122–123

California 35, 76, 117–118, 159 n.17
Cammack, Daniela 143 n.19
campaign advertising 9, 35–36, 55, 89, 118
Canevaro, Mirko 143 n.18
  controversy re: *nomothetai*
Capitalism, Socialism, and Democracy *See* Schumpeter, Joseph A.
Center for Deliberative Democracy (now Deliberative Democracy Lab, Stanford University) 93, 157 n.55
Chambers, Simone 114, 159 n.9
citizens' assembly model 51, 107, 109, 131–134
Citizens' Convention for Climate, France (CCC) 107–108, 158 n.64
Citizens' Initiative Review (CIR) 77, 119, 160 n.24
Citizens' Jury 35
climate change 63, 93–94, 96–97, 128
colonial period (U.S.) 5
  Party competition during 30
  public voting 146 n.22
"competitive authoritarianism" 2
  rigged elections 2
  uncompetitive elections 2
competitive elections 6–7

174 Index

Constitution of Athens 5 *See* Aristotle
Constitutional Convention (US) 5–6, 18–19, 125
Considerations on Representative Government See Mill, John Stuart
Converse, Philip E. 8, 22, 52
cost-benefit analysis 10–11, 40, 131
"creedal passions" *See* Huntington, Samuel
Council of 500 4–5

Dahl, Robert A. 1–2
  A Preface to Democratic Theory 37, 44–45
  Democracy and Its Critics 3–4, 9–10, 41
  "minorities rule" 16
Deliberation Day 72–74, 111, 114, 124–126, 134–135
Deliberative Distortions/"Deliberative Distortions" 70–71, 73, 153 n.48, n.49 *See also* Robert Luskin, et al.
Deliberative Distortions/"Deliberative Distortions" 67–74 (as topic)
  domination by advantaged participants 67–71
  Polarization *See* polarization, threats to democracy
dualist theory 12
"deliberation within" 48 *See* Goodin, Robert
deliberative cues 74, 77–78
deliberative democracy *See also* Deliberative Polling
  and society
    before ballot propositions 50–51, 117–121
    by corporations 119–121
    expansive use of deliberative minipublics (rotation method) 15, 74, 111, 112–113, 114–116, 118, 121–122, 125–126, 133–134
    organized process of mass deliberation ("Deliberation Day") 72–74, 77, 110–111, 114, 124–125, 134–135
    in schools 123, 125
    use of technology 93, 110–111, 124–125
deliberative microcosms 18, 63, 104–107, 110 *See* minipublics
Deliberative Polling *See also* Fishkin, James S.; deliberative democracy
  advantages
    applicable to major governmental decisions 57, 65–67

    facilitates considered judgments of the public 7–8, 54–56, 65, 78, 87, 90–91, 96–97, 110–111, 114–115, 132
    helps reform electoral democracy 62–63, 64, 65, 67, 122–123, 125
    provides key policy inputs on contested issues 57, 64, 74–75, 106, 133–134
    can help develop a more deliberative society. 109–112, 121, 123, 125
    can help reform primary system 115
    can strengthen guardrails of electoral democracy 2, 79–80, 97–98, 101, 104, 113–114, 122–123
  institutionalization and quasi-institutionalization 64, 121–122, 125
  locations (partial list)
    Australia 70, 74, 77, 89, 113, 119, 127
    Bulgaria 89, 127
    China 70
    Denmark 74, 77, 119
    EU 70
    Japan 36, 56–60, 61–62, 77, 116–117, 122, 128, 133
    South Korea 47, 116–117, 128, 133
    US
      See America in One Room 81–85, 89, 90–91, 93–104, 106, 115, 130–131, 141
      California 76, 117–118
      Texas utilities 51–54, 120
  findings
    avoids "deliberative distortions" *See* deliberative distortions
    depolarization 75 *See* polarization
    reduces affective polarization via the contact hypothesis 89–90
    uses accuracy-based motivated reasoning 87–90
deliberative referendums 125–126
democracy
  classic forms 1–2
    Athenian 1–2, 4–6, 14–15, 34, 46–49, 60, 112–113, 133
    Madisonian *See* Madison, James
  participatory
    initiative 35, 68, 76–77, 117–119, 121
    referendum 16, 31–32, 35–36, 63, 74, 109, 118–119, 125–126

Index   175

town meeting 33–35
criticisms of
  competence of the electorate 17, 20
  tyranny of the majority *See* tyranny of the majority and tyranny of the minority
  partisan polarization 22–23, 31, 36, 50, 79, 84, 85–87, 88–90, 98
threats to 2
  deadlock 2, 10, 63–64, 79, 85–86
  manipulation 8–10, 16, 50, 79
  polarization 71–74, 79, 81, 83–84, 85–90, 93–94, 98, 100–101, 108
types of 3–4
  competitive democracy 26–27, 30, 32, 42–43
  deliberative-competitive 79
  direct 1–2, 5, 31–32, 35, 49, 54, 76, 113
  Liberal 9–10, 27, 32
  Participatory 15, 63, 125
  Polyarchy 3–4, 9–10, 27, 28–30, 44–45
democratic recession 2
Diamond, Larry 2, 81–82, 142 n.4, 154 n.10
Downs, Anthony 3
  "rational ignorance" 3–4

Electoral College. 5–6, 13, 18, 28, 44
"everyday talk" *See* Mansbridge, Jane

Farrar, Cynthia 142 n.2
Federalist Papers 29–30, 37–39, 112–113, 135
  Federalist No. 10 29–30 *See* Madison, James
  Federalist No 71 30–31 *See* Hamilton, Alexander
Fishkin, James S. *See* Deliberative Polling; deliberative democracy
focus groups 52, 54
"folk theory of democracy" 9, 17

Gallup, George 7
Gastil, John 34–35, 76, 80, 119, 148 n.65, 153 n.58, 154 n.6, 157 n.52, n.53, 160 n.23
Grönlund, Kimmo 124, 161 n.37
Goodin, Robert 8, 142 n.2
graphe paranomon See ancient Athens
Green, Donald P. 142 n.2
Gumz, Antje 142 n.1

Habermas, Jurgen 67–68
  "unforced force of the better argument" 67–68
  public opinion *versus* public will formation 151 n.15
Hamilton, Alexander
  Federalist No. 71 5–6
Hansen, Mogens Herman 143 n.18, n.20
  controversy re: *nomothetai* 4–5, 143 n.18
heuristics 7, 50–51, 75–76, 121
Hofstadter, Richard 30, 147 n.42, n.45
Hotelling, Harold 21–22
Hume, David 1, 6
Huntington, Samuel 32–33
"Idea of a perfect commonwealth" *See* Hume, David 6

Immigration. 8–9, 81, 82*f*, 116, 127–128
Inequality 68
issue ownership 8–9
  abortion rights 8–9
  crime 8–9
  immigration 8–9
  social security 8–9
issue publics 75–76

Kunda, Ziva 87

Lafont, Cristina
  "blind deference" 55–56, 62, 78
Landemore, Hélène 49–50, 80, 107, 131–133
Lee, Frances E. 142 n.7
Lenz, Gabriel S. 25
Lerner, Joshua 35, 93, 148 n.66, 156 n.46, n.47, 157 n.50, n.51, n.53
Levitsky, Steven 142 n.4, n.5, n.8
Lodge, Milton 86
Lotteries 101
Lupia, Arthur 68, 76
Luskin, Robert et al. 70–71, 73, 136*t*, 138*t*, 139*t*, 152 n.41, 153 n.48, n.49 *see also* "Deliberative Distortions"/Deliberative Distortions

Madison, James
  Federalist No. 10 5–6

Madison, James (*Continued*)
　theory of "refined" public opinion 5–6, 30–31;81, 84, 98
Manin, Bernard 3, 14–15, 27–28, 143 n.13, 147 n.36
Mansbridge, Jane 12, 112–113, 144 n.44, 148 n.63, n.64
　"everyday talk" 12, 144 n.44
Marx, Christopher 1, 142 n.1
Mill, John Stuart 2–3
　"benign autocrat" 6
　Considerations on Representative Government 34
　"good despot" 2–3
　plural voting 18
minipublics
　deliberative minipublics 26, 30, 50–51, 69, 75, 85–86, 110, 114–122
　types of
　　citizens' assemblies 51, 109, 113, 133–134
　　citizens' juries 51, 133–134
　　consensus conferences 51
　　Deliberative Polls *See* Deliberative Polling
"minorities rule" *See* Dahl, Robert A. 1–2
misinformation 86, 118
mob rule 6
Muller, Jan-Werner 142 n.5

nationalism 142 n.3
nomothetai See ancient Athens
Norton, Anne 68

Page, Ben 24
Pateman, Carole 34–35
"perfect commonwealth" 6 *See* Hume, David
"phantom opinions" 8–10, 52, 55
"plural voting" 18 *See* Mill, John Stuart
policy elites 3
　mandarins 3
　"China model" 3, 6–7
policy experts 3
political parties 37, 44, 46–47, 65, 78
popular control 1, 3, 13, 16–18, 19–21, 22–23, 25–32, 34, 36, 46–47, 48–49, 63, 75, 77, 78–79, 80–81, 125–126, 133–135

populism 2
　threats posed by 2
　rouses public anger 2
　may reject unfavorable election results 2
public voting *See* colonial period (U.S.)
public will *See* "will of the people"

random sampling 1
"rational ignorance" *See* Downs, Anthony
Rawls, John 128
Referendums 16, 29, 35–36, 63, 74, 109, 118–119, 125–126
rotation method *See* ancient Athens; deliberative democracy
"rule and be ruled in turn" 15

Sandefur, Justin 142 n.2, 144 n.34, n.43
scaling deliberation 111
Schumpeter, Joseph A. 1–2, 9–10, 17, 26–27, 32, 39–42
Shapiro, Robert 24
Shays's rebellion 6
Singapore 3, 10–11
Sintomer, Yves 15, 145 n.51, 151 n.13, n.14
Siu, Alice 64, 81–82, 120, 152 n.30, n.39, n.40, 154 n.10, 160 n.26
Sniderman, Paul M. 78
Socrates
　trial of 6
"spirit of party" 29–30 *See* Washington, George
Stanford AI-Assisted Online Deliberation Platform 93–97
Sunstein, Cass R. 71–73, 86–87, 108
"synthetic" public opinion 9 *See* Schumpeter, Joseph A.

Taber, Charles 86
"talking cure" 1, 142 n.1, n.2
"tyranny of the majority" 1, 32, 36–37, 38–39, 40–44, 59–61, 113
"tyranny of the minority" 1

utilitarianism 10–11, 144 n. 42

Washington, George. 13, 29–30, 36, 113
"will of the people" 1, 23–24, 49–60, 79–80

Ziblatt, Daniel 142 n.4, n.5, n.8